T0312035

INTELLIGENT AUTOMATION

Welcome to the World of HYPERAUTOMATION

INTELLIGENT AUTOMATION

Welcome to the World of HYPERAUTOMATION

Learn How to Harness Artificial Intelligence to
Boost Business & Make Our World More Human

PASCAL BORNET
IAN BARKIN – JOCHEN WIRTZ

 **World Scientific**

NEW JERSEY · LONDON · SINGAPORE · BEIJING · SHANGHAI · HONG KONG · TAIPEI · CHENNAI · TOKYO

INTELLIGENT AUTOMATION

Taking the robot out of the people, making our world more human[1]

1   The quote "take the robot out of the human" comes from Professor Leslie Willcocks, London School of Economics, in "The next acronym you need to know about: RPA", 2016, published by McKinsey. https://www.mckinsey.com/business-functions/mckinsey-digital/our-insights/the-next-acronym-you-need-to-know-about-rpa

Welcome to the world of
HYPERAUTOMATION

A pragmatic and action-oriented guide to transforming
organizations with Hyperautomation

A reflection on the impact of automation and artificial
intelligence on work, society and our world

Pascal Bornet — Ian Barkin — Jochen Wirtz

Published by

World Scientific Publishing Co. Pte. Ltd.

5 Toh Tuck Link, Singapore 596224

USA office: 27 Warren Street, Suite 401-402, Hackensack, NJ 07601

UK office: 57 Shelton Street, Covent Garden, London WC2H 9HE

British Library Cataloguing-in-Publication Data
A catalogue record for this book is available from the British Library.

INTELLIGENT AUTOMATION: WELCOME TO THE WORLD OF HYPERAUTOMATION
Learn How to Harness Artificial Intelligence to Boost Business & Make Our World More Human

ISBN 978-981-123-548-1 (hardcover)
ISBN 978-981-123-559-7 (paperback)
ISBN 978-981-123-584-9 (ebook for institutions)

For any available supplementary material, please visit
https://www.worldscientific.com/worldscibooks/10.1142/12239#t=suppl

Desk Editor: Ong Shi Min Nicole

Printed in Singapore

We dedicate this book to our children and
to all the children in the world.

We owe them the best future.

Testimonials
(in alphabetical order)

"The most pressing question we face today – *Is this time different?* – results from the rise of Intelligent Automation. Read this book for a careful but refreshing, grounded but provocative, and cautionary yet hopeful perspective, not just on the future of work, but on the future of humankind."

Ajay Agrawal, professor at the University of Toronto, founder of the Creative Destruction Lab, and author of *Prediction Machines: The Simple Economics of Artificial Intelligence*

"The book presents a compelling case for Intelligent Automation (IA), supported by data and historical examples of change. If you needed convincing about IA, this is absolutely the book to read."

Sarah Burnett, Executive Vice President, distinguished analyst, AI & Business Transformation, at Everest Group

"Intelligent Automation is here, it is real, and it is about to change everything. This book is a must-read for all who care about both business and societal impact. It has been written by some of the top digital thought leaders on the planet. Thank you, Pascal Bornet, Jochen Wirtz, and Ian Barkin!"

Frank Casale, Founder of the Institute for Robotic Process Automation and Artificial Intelligence (IRPAAI)

"This book on Intelligent Automation is a must-read today for any organization executive – for profit or not. It describes in detail the advantages of human-and-robot interaction, emphasizing corporate, personal, and societal benefits. If you have not started to implement automation yet, this book can help be a catalyst for action. If you have already started your journey, effectively scaling automation programs will be the critical difference in winning in the Automation First era."

Daniel Dines, Co-Founder and CEO at UiPath

"AI may be the buzzword today, but how will we use this new technology to build, reshape and direct our society, businesses and organizations? In "Intelligent Automation" an answer is given. The book makes a compelling argument that we need to be smart about using AI and in doing so we need to understand the key role that humans will play more than ever. A great and thought-provoking read!"

Professor David De Cremer, Provost Chair in Management and Director of the Centre on AI Technology for Humankind at NUS Business School, National University of Singapore, and author of *Leadership by Algorithm: Who Leads and Who Follows in the AI Era?*

"Pascal Bornet, Ian Barkin and Jochen Wirtz's new book easily tops my favorites this year. While we've all read the headlines, IA still seems a mystery in terms of its impact on our job, business, enterprise, and world. What I particularly liked is that they don't just repeat the reassuring waffle of 'new jobs emerging to replace old jobs that are now automated.' Instead, they embrace the truth: Work, as we know it, will probably disappear. And yet, this book asks the questions that really count: What is our purpose in life? Is it work? Might not an automation-centric future enable us to get back to our real true purpose – to be more human? Could the end of work lead to a golden age of well-being? I'll be buying the first copies for my children so that they understand the future they are helping to shape."

Barbara Hodge, Principal Analyst and Global Digital Editor at The Shared Services and Outsourcing Network

"Automation is going to bring profound changes to our society. Intelligent Automation is the roadmap for the best version of a more human future. A future in which technology is used to augment our humanity and strengthen our connection to each other and to ourselves. This book is essential reading for anybody who cares about the future of work."

Arianna Huffington, Founder & CEO at Thrive Global

"AI is not a magic wand. Through their hands-on experience of numerous implementations across industries, the authors provide a practical guide to what technologies can achieve in businesses today. I am glad to see that this book shows that there is no such thing as Artificial Intelligence but that it's all about us, humans, understanding and learning how to use these new, powerful, tools in order to get the best out of them."

Dr. Luc Julia, CTO and SVP Innovation at Samsung, co-creator of Apple Siri, and author of *There is no such thing as Artificial Intelligence*

"A thoughtful, clear, and well-researched book! Intelligent automation is one of the most significant disruptions of the white-collar labor market since the PC. Still, it is unclear to many practitioners what technologies make up that term. The authors lay out a bright and articulate description of the technology that comprises IA and the business environment that consumes it."

Cliff Justice, Partner, US and Global Lead, Intelligent Automation at KPMG

"A global ex-McKinsey consultant, a high-flying tech entrepreneur, and one of the world's leading academics at the frontier of business knowledge. These three authors came together as one team to write a powerful, insightful, and immediately useful book on the future of work, life, and society. This new book shines a light into the future we will all be sharing."

Ron Kaufman, New York Times bestselling author of *Uplifting Service*

"Bornet, Barkin, and Wirtz have earned their automation "street credentials" through years of helping clients gain benefits from intelligent automation. Therefore, they know of what they write. The authors meaningfully distinguish between artificial intelligence (AI) and Intelligent Automation (IA). While AI is ensconced with Hollywood-levels of fear and hype, IA is a realistic Wall Street-to-Main Street business strategy supported by a collection of tools to redesign knowledge work. The authors describe what IA technology actually does today. Most refreshingly, the authors recognize that the implications of IA are emergent and therefore avoid naïve predictions. I think this book will be a welcome read in any graduate business course on contemporary strategy, automation, ethics, or information technology."

Professor Mary Lacity, Director of the Blockchain Center of Excellence, at the University of Arkansas

"An absolute must-read not only if you are interested in deepening your knowledge of Artificial Intelligence and Automation Technologies but also if you care about forming your own opinion on how these tidal forces of change, at the core of the Fourth Industrial Revolution, will reshape our societies and forever change the way we live."

Frederic Laluyaux, President and CEO at Aera Technology

"This book needed to be written. Intelligent Automation is taking hold. An excellent summary and guide on how to make it work."

Craig Le Clair, Forrester Research, author of *Invisible Robots In The Quiet Of The Night*

"This book is an insightful exploration of Intelligent Automation and the future of work. It is helping us understand the challenges and opportunities that automation, RPA, deep learning, and artificial intelligence represent."

Dr. Kai-Fu Lee, Chairman and CEO of Sinovation Ventures, President of Sinovation Ventures Artificial Intelligence Institute, and New York Times bestselling author of *AI Superpowers*

"This well-articulated book provides excellent insights into Intelligent Automation technologies, their early and potential applications, and their impact on work, business, and people. I especially enjoyed the sizing and opportunity sections. The world is at the cusp of unprecedented transformation."

Alex Lyashok, Co-founder and CEO at Workfusion

"This is an excellent book to understand how AI is enabling the era of Intelligent Automation and how it is transforming the future of work. Bornet, Barkin, and Wirtz have done an excellent job of capturing this moment of a major technological change and its impact on our society. A must-read for anyone involved in the digital transformation of today's enterprises."

Shariq Mansoor, Founder and Chief Technology Officer at Aera Technology

"One of the most important books of our times! A must-read for everyone that wants to understand how Intelligent Automation is transforming our world and why this means that we have to completely rethink the nature of business and the concept of work as we know it today."

Bernard Marr, Internationally best-selling author and strategic business & technology advisor, author of *The Intelligent Company*

"In this thoughtful book, the authors make the indisputable point that the upside of IA on the future of work outweighs any downside. The book provides a great perspective for any organization looking to understand better how AI will augment, not replace, the human experience."

Asheesh Mehra, Co-founder and CEO at AntWorks

"Humans are generally creatures of habit. But we are not made for repetition. The world of Intelligent Automation (IA) is giving us the opportunity to refocus on our creativity; it is opening us up to an infinite realm of possibilities."

Sylvia Saw McKaige, Founder and CEO at Salween Group

"Bornet, Barkin and Wirtz weave together a masterful and optimistic collection of insights that give us a genuine vision of what our automated world will look like. In today's business environment, nothing is more valuable than human insight, empathy, creativity and energy. The authors tell the story of how IA gives us the time and confidence to hone these qualities as routine, low value and repetitive work is digitized. This book is also more relevant than ever, with the current Pandemic Economy and our huge reliance on digital technologies to keep businesses, school and governments functioning."

Phil Fersht, Founder and CEO, HFS Research

"This book brilliantly demonstrates the full potential of IA to impact our society, save millions of lives, and conserve trillions of dollars. Anyone interested in these topics simply cannot afford to pass this book up!"

Leonard A. Schlesinger, Baker Foundation Professor, Harvard Business School, President Emeritus, Babson College

"Bornet, Barkin, and Wirtz have been able to brilliantly describe and provide guidelines to maximize the impact and benefits of Intelligent Automation. They present this analysis at employee, customer, company, global economy levels, and even from a society point of view. It is rare to read a book about technology which includes such diverse levels of analysis and reading. As an outcome, this creates a rich book useful and accessible to a wide variety of audiences. This guidebook is instrumental for success in the Fourth Industrial Revolution."

Klaus Schwab, Founder and Executive Chairman at the World Economic Forum

"Leaders of core technologies, 'back-office operations,' and revenue/customer-facing business functions alike can all benefit from the authors' articulation of how Intelligent Automation can – and will – in so many ways transform the global human condition."

Prag (Pragnesh) Shah, Global Head Experience & Innovation at Princess Cruise Lines, Ltd.

"This book is right on the spot; the future impact of IA depends on humans understanding its values and capabilities to build the entire ecosystem that will change the world. The impact of AI and automation is the black swan of our generation. The book helps leaders and curious people to understand the situation better and redefine their approach to ensure the brightest future."

Harel Tayeb, CEO at Kryon

"Can you imagine an organization where everything that can and should be automated is? That's the philosophy of Hyperautomation. This field guide is essential reading as you prioritize your exploration and exploitation of the 'art of the practical' to help you automate activities optimally at speed."

Cathy Tornbohm, VP Distinguished Analyst at Gartner

"A must-read book that not only enables a deep understanding of Intelligent Automation but also presents its incredible potential to achieve a higher societal purpose."

Tiger Tyagarajan, President and CEO at Genpact, and Board Member at Catalyst

"A powerful assessment of the promises and practicalities, *Intelligent Automation* is a timely guide replete with examples and advice culminating in a detailed, sane mapping of where all this could lead."

Leslie Willcocks, Professor at London School of Economics, co-author of *Robotic and Cognitive Automation: The Next Phase*

Table of contents

INTRODUCTION: UNDERSTANDING IA . . . 23

PART ONE: THE PROMISE OF IA FOR A BETTER WORLD 53

PART TWO: IA TECHNOLOGIES EXPLAINED

PART THREE: HOW ORGANIZATIONS SUCCEED IN IMPLEMENTING IA

About the authors

Pascal Bornet is a recognized global expert and pioneer in the field of intelligent automation. He is passionate about the capacity of artificial intelligence and automation to make our society more human. Bornet is a senior executive with 20+ years of experience leading digital business transformations and creations. Over the last ten years, he has founded and led the "Intelligent Automation" practices, first for EY (Ernst & Young) and then for McKinsey & Company. These lines of business delivered high-impact results to corporate clients across industries through innovation, research, strategic investments, and cutting-edge technology developments. In these contexts, he successfully led hundreds of intelligent automation transformations at scale across industries and functions. He has also created and managed a proven track record of distinctive, innovative solutions, technologies, and IP portfolios.

Bornet is a recognized author, thought leader, lecturer, and speaker on artificial intelligence, automation, and the future of work. He is also an influencer on the same topics, elected Top Voice in Technology 2019; he has more than 300,000 followers on LinkedIn and Twitter. Bornet holds an MBA from the University of California Los Angeles, an MBA from the National University of Singapore, a Master of Science in Management from EM-Lyon/Saint-Etienne, as well as several certifications in Data Science and Finance (US CPA).

 linkedin.com/in/pascalbornet/

 twitter.com/pascal_bornet

Ian Barkin is Chief Strategy & Marketing Officer at SYKES. He is a globally recognized thought leader and veteran in the Intelligent Automation space. Barkin co-founded Symphony Ventures, a pure-play Intelligent Automation consulting company. Built in 2014, the company had more than 225 employees in 2019, providing cutting-edge advisory services in Intelligent Automation to companies across all sectors. Symphony Ventures was acquired for US$69 million in 2018 by SYKES, a NASDAQ-listed global leader in Customer Engagement Services.

Barkin is a seasoned leader and innovator in Digital Operations, Robotic Process Automation (RPA), Intelligent Automation, Business Process Outsourcing (BPO), and the Future of Work. He is the author of popular LinkedIn Learning courses on RPA and the leadership best practices in the age of Intelligent Automation. He has a proven track record of digital transformation solution development and sales of complex global engagements. Barkin holds an MBA from MIT Sloan School of Management, and a BA in Economics and Psychology from Middlebury College.

  linkedin.com/in/ianbarkin

twitter.com/ibarkin

Jochen Wirtz is Vice-Dean MBA Programmes and Professor of Marketing at the NUS Business School, National University of Singapore (NUS). He is also a research affiliate with the NUS Centre on AI Technology for Humankind, an international fellow of the Service Research Center at Karlstad University, Sweden, an Academic Scholar at the Cornell Institute for Healthy Futures (CIHF) at Cornell University, US, and a Global Faculty of the Center for Services Leadership (CSL) at Arizona State University, US. Previously, Dr. Wirtz was the founding director of the UCLA – NUS Executive MBA Program, ranked #6 globally in the Financial Times 2016 EMBA rankings (from 2002 to 2017) and an Associate Fellow at the Saïd Business School, University of Oxford (from 2008 to 2013). Dr. Wirtz is a leading authority on services marketing and management. His research has been published in over 100 academic journal articles, including six features in *Harvard Business Review*. He has received over 40 awards in recognition of his excellence in research and teaching. His more than 20 books include *Services Marketing – People, Technology, Strategy* (World Scientific, 9th edition, 2021), and *Essentials of Services Marketing* (Pearson Education, 4th edition, 2021). With combined sales of over 800,000 copies, they have become globally leading services marketing textbooks.

Dr. Wirtz has worked with international consulting firms, including Accenture, Arthur D. Little and KPMG, and major service firms around the world. He has been an angel investor in a number of start-ups, including Accellion (www.accellion.com, exit in 2020), TranscribeMe (www.TranscribeMe.com) and Uplifting Service (www.UpliftingService.com). Dr. Wirtz received his Ph.D. from the London Business School. He holds a professional certification in banking. Originally from Germany, Professor Wirtz spent seven years in London before moving to Asia. Today, he shuttles between Asia, the US, and Europe.

 linkedin.com/in/jochenwirtz

 twitter.com/JochenWirtz

Key contributors to the book

We would like to thank the following people, without whom we would never have been able to present such a thoughtful and informed perspective on the impacts of Intelligent Automation on the worlds of work, life, health, education, culture, and more (in alphabetical order):

Ralph Aboujaoude Diaz

Key contribution: key success factors, RPA, IA

David Ashton

Key contribution: reinventing society with IA

Sebastien Bourguignon

Key contribution: blockchain

Francis Carden

Key contribution: low-code, no-code, artificial intelligence

Lee Coulter

Key contribution: overall structure of the book, key insights

Samiran Ghosh

Key contribution: artificial intelligence, machine learning

Bernard Golstein

Key contribution: reinventing education with and for IA

Mohsin Khan

Key contribution: machine learning, IA use cases

Mahesh Panbude

Key contribution: RPA, IA use cases

Mael Plougastel

Key contribution: overall structure of the book, key insights

Gaurav Sharma

Key contribution: RPA, IA use cases

Thomas Zakrzewski

Key contribution: blockchain, Internet of Things

Preface: Why this book?

While Intelligent Automation (IA) has already started to become a pivotal lever to enhance customers' experience and boost business productivity, very little has been written on it. The first sources were a blog[2] written by Bornet in early 2017, an article by McKinsey,[3] followed by a standard by IEEE,[4] all referenced later in this book. In 2018, a reference book[5] by Lacity and Willcocks covered some aspects of IA, together with other themes. Since then, most of the literature available today has come from technology vendors in the form of articles, white papers, or implementation use cases. But, while we have seen many books in the fields of artificial intelligence, machine learning, or robotics, a **comprehensive reference guidebook** had never yet been written on the topic of IA. Hence, it seemed critical to us, the authors, to objectively document and build the latest insights on this field in a first reference document.

This also explains why working on this book has been challenging, building the content almost from scratch; it took us more than a year to write this book. We have tried to **concentrate** the **wealth of experience** not only from ourselves but also from a large and growing

---

2   Bornet et al., 2017. "Intelligent automation is about creating synergies between RPA, cognitive, chatbots and AI". https://www.linkedin.com/pulse/from-robotic-process-automation-rpa-artificial-ai-journey-bornet/

3   McKinsey, 2017. "Intelligent process automation: The engine at the core of the next-generation operating model". https://www.mckinsey.com/business-functions/mckinsey-digital/our-insights/intelligent-process-automation-the-engine-at-the-core-of-the-next-generation-operating-model

4   IEEE Std. 2755-2017, IEEE Guide for Terms and Concepts in Intelligent Process Automation.

5   Mary C. Lacity and Leslie P. Willcocks, 2018. "Robotic Process and Cognitive Automation - The Next Phase".

community of IA leaders from diverse organizations, geographies, and industries.

The primary purpose of this book is **to share our passion** for this new concept called IA that we strongly believe can improve our world significantly. We would like to **inform, inspire, and educate** more people on the power of IA. As we will demonstrate in the book, it is critical that we expand the uses of IA to help solve the most pressing issues of our world and create an opportunity to build a new, more human society.

On top of this, it seemed essential to us **to establish IA as a field**, with its own frameworks, use cases, methods, and critical success factors. We have tried to document our knowledge, drawing from years of failures and successes in designing and implementing IA. Nevertheless, this work is not meant to carve these frameworks in stone. This is just a sketch, a beginning; it provides a foundation for further and broader evolutions of our field. A field has its practitioners. We dedicate this book to them and to those who are joining this growing community every day. A mere five years ago, our roles as Intelligent Automation practitioners did not exist. In July 2020, searching for "Intelligent Automation" on LinkedIn, we could find more than 145,000 profiles mentioning it in titles, roles, or job descriptions. It is impressive how quickly the worlds of consulting, services, and work have changed.

In this book, we also wanted **to clarify the purpose of IA**. We have often heard IA professionals being referred to as "job killers": people who are automating the work of other people, causing them to be laid off, just for the sake of generating productivity gains. With this book, we want to clarify that not only does IA not displace roles, but it creates more, and the new ones are more exciting than the legacy ones. We demonstrate how it helps workers to find fulfillment in their work and augment their capabilities, and could help bring a renaissance to the future of work.

Several technology vendors pretend that IA is a universal solution that is cheap, easy to implement, and delivers a high return on investment. This is not true. In this book, we have been careful in painting a more **neutral picture** of IA, not only depicting its benefits but also presenting its limits and challenges. We have built upon these points to offer recommendations for fair and successful uses of IA.

Over the last several years, we have witnessed that **technological innovation is rapidly accelerating**. Thanks to advances in the fields of process automation and machine learning, the boundaries of what can be identified, interpreted, and automated are continually being pushed. For example, it used to take months to design and write automation scripts able to perform work. With the help of deep learning, we can now achieve this in hours. This enables automation programs to learn patterns and behaviors by themselves, without the need for a developer to write code. With that, we grow ever closer to IA being generated by technology (explained in Part Three of the book) involving incredible scalability.

These advancements will have **a significant and disruptive impact on the world of work**. With such powerful technologies, an increasing amount of the work performed by millions of people across the globe in captive and outsourced back-office functions (e.g., finance & accounting, supply chain & logistics) might soon be automated. Furthermore, can you imagine the impact of such a technology on the three million U.S. call center professionals[6] and the many millions more across the world? What else could have such an impact on the 3.5 million truck drivers in the US and across Europe where self-driving truck pilots are already underway?

It seemed crucial to us to document and share the imperatives that need to be in place to **prevent the negative impacts of IA at scale** on our societies. It is not a matter of "if" it will happen; it is a question of "when." We leveraged this book to convey a warning message to companies and governments. In order to capture the full potential of IA at scale, there are imperatives to anticipate potential issues and get prepared.

Finally, we believe **it is timely**, as our world is slowly recovering from the COVID-19 crisis. This book aims at guiding leaders in improving the resilience of their organizations and building the capacity to anticipate and overcome future similar downturns.

We hope you will enjoy this read and that it will shift your thinking and action!

---

6   King White, 2015, "How Big is the U.S. Call Center Industry Compared to India and The Philippines?". https://info.siteselectiongroup.com/blog/how-big-is-the-us-call-center-industry-compared-to-india-and-philippines

Additional book assets available online

We have also built an extension of this book in the form of **a dedicated website**. It not only introduces the book, but also allows our readers to ask questions and keep connected with the latest insights through a blog and regular newsletters.

Website: www.hyperautomationbook.com or www.intelligentautomationbook.com

On the same website, for people who are reading this book on paper, we provide **digital access to the footnotes via this link:**

https://intelligentautomationbook.com/footnote/

The purpose is to create a unique and interactive reading experience. With the book in their hands, readers are able to open the footnote links on their smartphone or tablet in just one click, **taking advantage of the videos and other articles in real time**. We recommend this to fully enjoy watching the demos and reading the additional digital content that we share throughout the book.

Additional information about the book and disclaimers:

- The profits from this book will be donated to a charity that supports education about new technologies for people in need.

- The ideas reflected in this book are solely the views of the authors. They do not necessarily reflect the views of any company or organization.

- The funding and writing of this book have not been associated with any organization. This is a warranty of the neutrality of the views provided by the authors.

- The authors have chosen to keep the book short, easy to read, and accessible to a broad audience. Hence, they have deliberately decided to highlight key concepts and themes across the wide spectrum of IA, rather than enter into the detail of each of the topics covered. They have done their best to provide information sources so that interested readers can explore further.

Awful pictures that Intelligent Automation (IA) can help change

The following pictures show some realities of our current world that IA aims at changing or at least influencing. We expect these thought-provoking photos to trigger your interest in knowing more about the topic.

Awful picture 1: The finance department of a leading multinational company, Oct 2019
Source: Photo taken by the authors

Awful picture 2: Long queue of clients at a bank branch, Aug 2020
Source: Photo taken by the authors

Awful picture 3: Long queue of clients at a train station in China, Dec 2019
Source: Photo taken by the authors

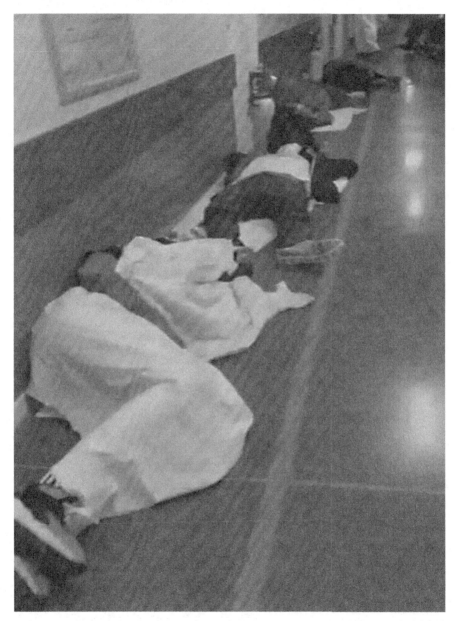

Awful picture 4: Sick people lying on the ground in an overcrowded hospital in Madrid, April 2020
Source: Newsflash

Awful picture 5: According to publications, physician burnout has been a growing problem over the years 2018–2020
Source: collage made by the authors

Weekly initial claims for unemployment insurance

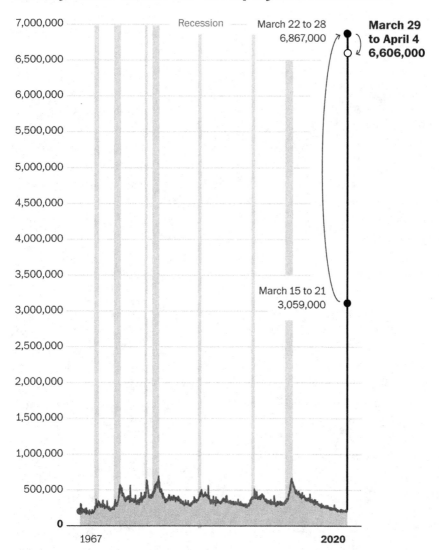

Note: Seasonally adjusted
Sources: Labor Department via FRED

THE WASHINGTON POST

Awful picture 6: Massive historical level of unemployment due to the COVID-19 pandemic in the USA where 6 million people lost their jobs (3 million in a week); April 2020

Source: The Washington Post

Awful picture 7: Polluted beach in India, Dec 2019
Source: Photo taken by the authors

Awful picture 8: Poor child in Vietnam, April 2019
Source: Photo taken by the authors

INTRODUCTION:
UNDERSTANDING IA

- Do you know how Netflix is able to generate $1 billion in additional revenue yearly?
- How has Unilever significantly increased by 25% the diversity of new talent hired? How did ANZ Bank reduce operational costs by more than 40%?
- How can our world potentially save 10+ million lives per year?
- How can we triple our global budget for education, help restore our planet from pollution, or eliminate hunger forever?
- How can we increase the resilience of our health and economic systems to safeguard people's lives and livelihoods even during pandemics or crises?
- How can governments address the needs of our aging populations, improve services to citizens, reduce debt, and increase economic growth?
- And how can we provide a new renaissance for our society, making it more human and reinventing what we call "work"?

We believe the best answer to all these questions is:

INTELLIGENT AUTOMATION

(also known as Hyperautomation)

This book is the first one to focus specifically on the new and game-changing concept of **Intelligent Automation** (IA). IA, or "Intelligent Process Automation", is a new notion, officially coined in 2017 by IEEE[7]. More recently, IA has been given different names, including **Hyperautomation** (by Gartner), Integrated Automation Platform (by Horses For Sources), and Cognitive Automation (by several sources).

Through our experience, research, and discussions with the leaders of global organizations, we believe that IA is one of **the most important drivers of enterprise efficiency and competitive relevance in the future**. We are also convinced that IA can **solve many of the most pressing issues in our world**, like improving education, caring for our planet, and saving lives. IA is becoming so ubiquitous and impactful that it has been listed as the number one technology trend for 2020 by Gartner.[8]

We, the authors, draw our perspectives from a decade of first-hand experience implementing IA for the world's leading companies and public institutions… and we appreciate the complexity of the craft. This is why we have set out to create a pragmatic and action-oriented guide for those looking to capitalize on the potential for IA.

By providing real-life use cases, we seek to raise awareness and explain the benefits and critical success factors of implementing IA for customers, employees, companies, and even society as a whole.

---

7   Institute of Electrical and Electronics Engineers (in charge of setting the standards in the computer science industry), 2017. "IEEE Std. 2755-2017, IEEE Guide for Terms and Concepts in Intelligent Process Automation".

8   Gartner, 2019. "Top 10 Strategic Technology Trends for 2020". https://www.gartner.com/smarterwithgartner/gartner-top-10-strategic-technology-trends-for-2020/

We also seek to offer, through the lens of IA, a unique analysis and view of the future of business, customer experience, work, and society. We've set out to create a resource that is easy to read and accessible to a broad audience.

Understanding the power of IA through an example

In the near future, IA undoubtedly has the capacity to deliver the highest technological impact on organizations. As an illustration, let us take two of the most popular and impactful technologies of our current times: artificial intelligence and robotics. We have seen compelling use cases using one of these two capabilities. **The power of IA is such that it can meet most of the needs artificial intelligence or robotics can't satisfy individually**. The explanation is that IA combines not only the capabilities of both but also other complementary ones like sensing the environment or structuring workflows of information. By connecting capabilities, IA increases the breadth and depth of the impact of each technology involved. Case Illustration 0.1 presents a real-life example of this concept.

Case illustration 0.1: Credit card fraud management use case

Credit card transaction fraud is a critical topic. It causes annual losses of some \$28 billion[9] and is a source of frustration for customers, retailers, and financial institutions. It is so prevalent that we believe it has happened at least once to most of our readers. As clients, we often blame our bank for not identifying these issues earlier and warning us. Also, even though losses tend to be insured, reimbursements take months. And before that, customers have to go through several administrative and inconvenient tasks, including filling in forms, providing evidence, and calling.

Banks proactively monitor transactions to flag potential fraud; a typical high-level process is shown in Figure 0.1.

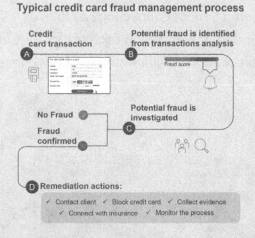

Figure 0.1: Typical fraud investigation process
Source: © Bornet, Barkin & Wirtz

---

9   The Nilson Report, 2019. "Payment Card Fraud Losses Reach \$27.85 Billion: Annual Fraud Statistics Released by The Nilson Report". https://www.prnewswire.com/news-releases/payment-card-fraud-losses-reach-27-85-billion-300963232.html

Context: In 2019, to improve customer experience and limit its losses due to card fraud, a leading bank decided to leverage the latest technologies. It **created a state-of-the-art machine learning-based program** to identify fraudulent transactions automatically. The impact of this application was beneficial for the bank, which increased the volume of fraud resolved by 30% in less than four months. Nevertheless, while it improved the speed and completeness of the fraud identification process, **the employees' and clients' experience worsened** (see stage 1 in Table 0.1).

Solution: To address this issue, the bank decided to **take a more holistic approach**. It requested support from a team in charge of IA at one of its subsidiaries. The first action from this team was to review and redesign not only the activity of fraud identification but also, more broadly, **the end-to-end process** with an emphasis on the customer and employee experience (see stage 2 in Table 0.1). While 20% of the process was automated with machine learning, the IA team succeeded in automating more than 80%.

Outcome: As a result, the **customer and employee experience drastically improved**. Most of the tedious tasks were now performed by technology (see stage 3 in Table 0.1). Overall, the bank increased the number of fraudulent transactions solved by 70% and generated more than $100 million in additional savings per year.

The advantage of using IA has been to provide the capabilities to solve the problem holistically. It illustrates how the concept of IA has the power to create end-to-end touchless processes, cutting across an organization and delivering a broad range of benefits. We have summarized the key aspects of this transformation in Table 0.1 below.

Table 0.1: A journey towards IA for a bank fraud system

Leveraging Intelligent Automation to enhance a bank fraud management system		
Stages in the transformation journey	① **Before transformation (manual)** ② **New system leveraging machine learning (only)**	③ **New system leveraging Intelligent Automation (incl. machine learning)**
Timeline	*Before Jun 2019*	*Jun to Dec 2019*	*Jan 2020 onwards*
Description of the key process activities	❶ Transactions were checked manually on a sample basis. ❷ Investigations, collection of evidence, and credit card blocking were performed manually by the team. ❸ Communication (with clients and insurance companies) was performed manually by the team.	❶ All transactions were checked (no more sampling). The system could identify potentially fraudulent transactions in just a few seconds by analyzing client transactions, as well as their behavioral and demographic data. ❷ Investigations, collection of evidence, and credit card blocking were still performed manually by the team. ❸ Communication (with clients and insurance companies) was still performed manually by the team.	❶ The same machine learning-based system was used. ❷ Investigations and collection of evidence were performed using an intelligent workflow. Credit card blocking actions were automated using robotic process automation. ❸ All event-triggered communications were automated. The system proactively provided clients with early warnings of potential fraud, enabling them to take prompt and easy actions. Clients and insurers had access to a 24/7 intelligent chatbot to answer their questions and update them on the status of the fraud resolution process.
Morale of the bank's fraud investigation team	Medium • The process was very manual, and repetitive.	Low • The team faced difficulties in coping with the workload, which increased drastically as the system was identifying more potentially fraudulent transactions. • In addition, the bank employees complained about their work becoming more tedious, repetitive, and less fulfilling. While the fraud team used to leverage its intuition, strategy, and analysis to identify and investigate fraud, this role was now taken by the system. The team's new role was primarily to focus on collecting, indexing, and archiving the fraud evidence.	High • The team's workload decreased, and the work became more fulfilling as most of the repetitive and tedious activities were performed by technology. • As an outcome, the team could focus on more value-adding activities, like building relationships with clients, managing the exceptions (e.g., investigating the most complex cases) and monitoring the overall process to anticipate any issues. • The team was also able to focus on constantly improving the new system, increasing its accuracy levels, and extending its scope to manage additional payment means like cheques and bank transfers.
Client satisfaction (rated on a scale from 1 to 5, 5 being very satisfied)	3/5	2/5 Rationale: the high workload decreased the team's responsiveness in answering clients' questions and the time it could dedicate to client relationships.	4/5 Rationale: early communication on potential fraud identification, 24/7 support, reduction by half of the end-to-end process time (from the identification of the fraud to the reimbursement by the insurance).

Who should read this book, and why?

The book offers several levels of reading. Therefore, it can fit a broad range of expectations across a large audience. The target readers are company leaders, regulators, academics, thought leaders, project managers, experts, consultants, employees, students, or anyone interested in the future of work. The book will fulfill different expectations, depending on the level of experience and exposure of each reader.

For **readers who know IA well,** this book provides, in one place, all the key content you would need in one resource: guidelines, toolkits, references, and success stories and failures. It also includes a comprehensive list of critical success factors and a use case library by function and by industry. These tools will help you to champion IA in your own organization. This work is also a medium for change management and education. You should consider sharing it with your management, colleagues, and clients in order to prepare them for the transformation. Finally, through this book, we aspire to bring a heightened level of purpose to our profession. Beyond augmenting people by refocusing them on more exciting, value-added activities, IA also brings the potential for a renaissance of our society, making it more human. In this book, we set out to demonstrate how.

For **readers who are starting their IA journey**, this is an opportunity to understand the pre-requisites of IA, anticipate and mitigate the pitfalls, and support building a roadmap for the coming years. You will fully benefit from every part of this book. It is your toolkit for transformational success.

And, for **readers who are just discovering IA** and who are interested in the future of work and its impact on our society: we hope we can provide an eye-opener on cutting-edge concepts that will change our world forever and at a rapid pace.

Finally, **no matter your level of exposure** to IA, we set out to de-dramatize the narrative around job loss due to AI, robotics, and automation. Instead, we provide our perspective on the vast opportunities for our institutions, our communities, and our societies to reinvent themselves by focusing on fundamental human values.

What will you learn from this book?

The Industrial Revolutions started over 200 years ago, automating "blue-collar" work in the agricultural and manufacturing industries. They provided massive and structural benefits to our society, such as the reduction of famine and an increase in standards of living, and they relieved people from laborious manual work.

IA, also called Hyperautomation, is one of the most recent trends in the broad field of artificial intelligence. It is a cutting-edge combination of methods and technologies, involving people, organizations, machine learning, low-code platforms, robotic process automation (RPA), and more.

IA ushers in a new revolution: that of office work, automating "white-collar" work. Today, office work accounts for more than 80% of the job roles in our global economy, such as lawyers, financial controllers, or call center operators. Like the previous automation revolutions, we believe IA will have a significant impact not only on employment but more broadly on our society.

PART ONE of this book covers the promise of IA for a better world. Even though IA has only been coined recently, its applications have spread incredibly quickly, validating its promise. It has already been adopted by more than 50% of the world's largest companies, including ADP, JP Morgan, Lloyds Banking Group, Netflix, and Unilever. The expected impact on business efficiency is in the range of 20 to 60%. It involves the significant improvement of the customer and employee experience and the vast enhancement of process compliance. These benefits are available to all organizations, across industries, and regardless of function. This book provides a comprehensive **library of more than 500 IA use cases** to illustrate our point (provided at the end of the book). In addition to being a key improvement lever, we also demonstrate that adopting IA has now become a condition for business survival.

We also demonstrate how IA has the potential to save over 10 million lives every year and realize $10 trillion of cost savings. Such a vast amount of money would allow us to triple our global budget for education, help restore our planet from pollution, or even eliminate hunger! On top of that, IA has the potential to bring the next renaissance to our society by changing the way we work, making our world more human.

PART TWO explains the technologies leveraged by IA. IA automates knowledge work by mimicking four main capabilities of workers: execution, language, vision, and thinking & learning (see Figure 0.2). IA combines various technologies, including machine learning, sentiment analysis, data management platforms, speech analytics, data visualization, image and video analysis, biometrics, intelligent chatbots, smart workflows, low-code platforms, robotic process automation (RPA), and several more. In this book, we explain these components of IA and provide examples of how they are used. When these capabilities are combined in solving complex end-to-end business issues, synergies are created, allowing greater benefits to be delivered. We also explain how these technologies integrate within the current IT landscape of an organization and how to build an IA implementation roadmap.

The roadmap to a successful Intelligent Automation transformation

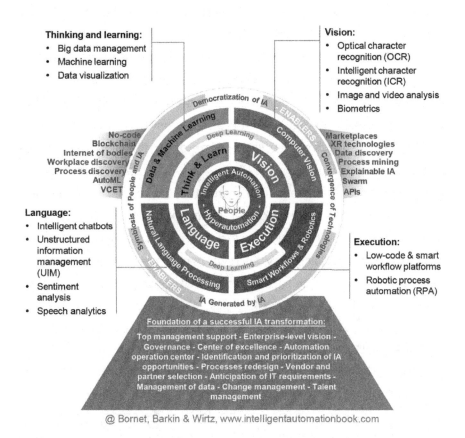

Thinking and learning:
- Big data management
- Machine learning
- Data visualization

Vision:
- Optical character recognition (OCR)
- Intelligent character recognition (ICR)
- Image and video analysis
- Biometrics

Language:
- Intelligent chatbots
- Unstructured information management (UIM)
- Sentiment analysis
- Speech analytics

Execution:
- Low-code & smart workflow platforms
- Robotic process automation (RPA)

@ Bornet, Barkin & Wirtz, www.intelligentautomationbook.com

Figure 0.2: A roadmap of the key notions covered in the book, including the capabilities (Part Two), the foundation of a successful transformation (Part Three), and the enablers (Part Three)

Source: © Bornet, Barkin & Wirtz[10]

PART THREE explains how to succeed in implementing IA. While impactful, implementing IA is certainly not a silver bullet. While it is easy to succeed in implementing a pilot on a limited scope, many organizations have been struggling to scale their transformations. Based on our experience of hundreds of IA initiatives, we have listed in detail the most important factors to enable organizational leaders to succeed in their transformations. In addition to these leading practices, the book describes four new trends that have started to help businesses scale IA. They are also levers that any organization can use to increase the speed and scope of its IA projects. Examples include the democratization of IA, the convergence of technologies, the symbiosis of people and IA, and the use of IA to implement IA (see Figure 0.2). In the longer term, expected innovations will leverage new concepts, such as the internet of bodies, blockchain, augmented and virtual reality, and swarm robotics. The book explains what these cutting-edge technologies and concepts will bring to the automation of knowledge work.

PART FOUR is about reinventing society and work with IA. Entering into the fourth industrial revolution with IA is not without risks. In our view, to prepare our world to effectively translate the key benefits of IA, our societies' roadmap should include some imperatives. New skills are required for workers to stay relevant while working with IA. How are we going to make sure people's skills stay relevant and evolve together with IA capabilities? In addition, according to economists, the use of digital technologies over the last decades has resulted in increasing wealth inequalities. Which mechanisms could we leverage to remediate this issue? On top of this, IA might have a strong impact on the level of employment of workers. A few possible scenarios are outlined. One involves more job roles created, while another foresees the displacement of a massive amount of the workforce. What are the actions we should implement today to get our world prepared for both scenarios?

What if we see a scenario where a large amount of human workload reduction happens? Considering this scenario in addition to the fact that, currently, 85 percent of employees worldwide don't feel engaged with their work[11], the book explains how IA could help redefine work. IA could offer our society the opportunity for a real renaissance by freeing us from many of today's tedious, repetitive, and unfulfilling work activities. The book describes how we could use our time for more meaningful activities for society, for our families, and ourselves. To get to this attractive future renaissance, we need strong support from institutions, governments, and companies.

Besides calling upon our own experience, we have further informed our definition and perspective on IA by conducting an **extensive industry survey** (the largest to date). Throughout the book, we will refer to this research, providing the insights from over **200 IA experts** around the globe. They have been generous in sharing their experience with us. We list their names in the last part of the book: "List of IA experts who joined the survey." This effort is dedicated, in part, to them and their passion for evolving and transforming IA.

---

11   Refer to Part Four of the book for detailed references.

What is IA?

IA, also called Hyperautomation, is a concept leveraging a new generation of software-based automation. It combines methods and technologies to execute business processes automatically on behalf of knowledge workers. This automation is achieved by mimicking the capabilities that knowledge workers use in performing their work activities (e.g., language, vision, execution, and thinking & learning). The goal of using IA is to achieve a business outcome, through a redesigned automated process, with no or minimal human intervention. As a result, IA increases process speed, reduces costs, enhances compliance and quality, increases process resilience, and optimizes decision outcomes. Ultimately, it improves customer and employee satisfaction and boosts revenues.[12]

IA focuses on automating the work done by knowledge workers, whose principal capital is knowledge. Examples include programmers, physicians, pharmacists, architects, engineers, scientists, designers, public accountants, lawyers, and any other workers whose line of work requires them to "think for a living."[13] As opposed to manual labor, which is material-based (common in manufacturing industries), **knowledge work** is information-based and commonly found in service industries. Simply put, IA is the "white-collar" version of the "blue-collar" industrial automation, which started in the 19th century.

---

12 This definition has been written by the authors, inspired by IEEE Std. 2755-2017. "IEEE Guide for Terms and Concepts in Intelligent Process Automation"

13 Davenport, Thomas H., 2005. "Thinking For A Living: How to Get Better Performance and Results From Knowledge Workers".

For example, IA is used to support and augment the tasks performed by lawyers, financial controllers, or call center agents.

An easy way to explain how IA works is to draw parallels with human capabilities. Through IA, we aim at creating "digital workers" (automation programs), which mimic the actions performed by human knowledge workers. To deliver a work outcome, we, as humans, carry out business processes (a succession of tasks), using our human capabilities. We make use of our capabilities to see, hear, speak, read, understand, act, react, and learn. IA is composed of a combination of technologies that reproduce these human capabilities to deliver business processes on behalf of human workers.

IA effectively creates a software-based digital workforce that enables synergies by working hand-in-hand with the human workforce. On the simpler end of the task spectrum, IA helps perform the repetitive, low value-add and tedious work activities such as reconciling data or digitizing and processing paper invoices. On the other end, IA augments workers by providing them with superhuman capabilities. For example, it provides the ability to analyze millions of data points (e.g., collected from the web) in a few minutes and generate insights from them (e.g., identifying customer behaviors with a direct impact on revenue).

By using IA, companies, and workers aim at building touchless business processes (i.e., those requiring minimal human interaction or intervention). Touchless processes, also called "straight-through", represent the highest level of process efficiency (e.g., productivity, rapidity, and cost control) and effectiveness (e.g., quality and compliance).

Unique characteristics of IA

IA has the following characteristics that explain its rapid expansion and its expected drastic impact on our world:

- It is **recent**. The term IA was coined only in 2017 by IEEE. It combines relatively new technologies; most of them have been developed in the past ten years.

- It is **universal**. Most functionalities can be applied across industries (e.g., banking, retail) and business functions (e.g., sales, operations, finance).

- It is **scalable**. After the first program is developed, scaling can be done instantaneously and indefinitely with virtually zero incremental cost. Increasing the capacity of a digital workforce is as simple as copying and pasting resources.

- It is **available 24/7**. IA capabilities deliver services on demand at any time and any day, ensuring the continuity and sustainability of automated processes.

- It is **reliable**. IA systems will always produce the same outcome, based on the same input. Assuming no change in the environment, their level of performance remains unchanged and accurate. When implemented using leading practices, IA systems are highly resilient.

- It is **economically attractive**. Most IA-related technologies are available at a reasonable cost and typically generate payback in less than a year.

- It is **accessible**. IA technologies tend to have intuitive and accessible user interfaces. The skills required to use most of these applications are limited or easy to acquire.

Differentiating IA from AI

Differentiating between artificial intelligence (AI), robotics, and other business process management (BPM) systems, including cloud and workflow platforms, can be complicated. Indeed, boundaries between these concepts are blurred, as they are emerging, continually evolving, and often converging (refer to Part Three, "The convergence of technologies"). However, to bring clarity to our discussion, we draw a few essential anchor points. We have based our analysis on our survey of over 200 IA experts and our own experience. From this, a summary of the current understanding of the key concepts that come together is shown in Figure 0.3.

The main points explaining this framework are:

- **AI**: The applications of AI that are related to IA are the ones associated with the automation of knowledge work. Hence, IA includes all uses of AI across industries, except, for example, gaming, arts, or fundamental research, which are excluded.

- **Robotics**: IA includes software-based robotics. Physical robots used in manufacturing are not considered part of IA.

- **Cloud, workflow, and business process management (BPM):** Platforms that demonstrate some form of intelligence are included in the scope of IA. Excluded are systems with limited ability to support end-to-end processes, and which provide little insights on the work activities performed.

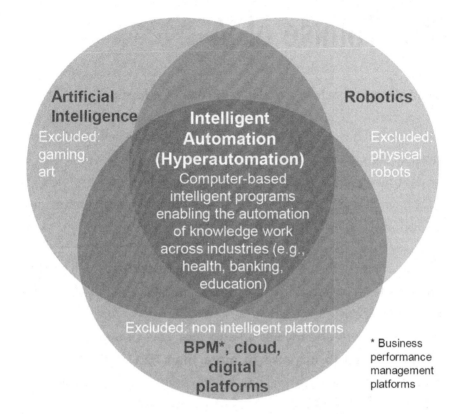

Figure 0.3: Positioning IA with other recent technology concepts
Source: © Bornet, Barkin & Wirtz

The promise of IA

IA has already reached a significant rate of adoption

86% of global business leaders recently surveyed believe that to stay ahead in their given domains, their organizations must deploy IA in the next five years.[14] Another survey by Gartner found that 42% of CEOs have already begun the process of digital transformation, and 56% reported gains after implementing IA.[15]

Because of its unique characteristics, we estimate that IA will be able to reach a level of adoption and sophistication in the next five years which took industrial automation over 200 years. According to a Deloitte survey, **IA already has an adoption rate of over 50%**.[16] This rate is **expected to increase to more than 70% in the next two years**. If this continues, IA will have achieved near-universal adoption within the next five years.

Even though IA is still a new field, **its capabilities are progressing exceptionally quickly**. Some of these technologies are very recent, like deep learning or robotic process automation (RPA). In fact, UiPath, a 40-person RPA start-up just five years ago, has ridden the explosive growth curve of this automation technology to become the

---

14 Avanade, 2017. "Global Research on Intelligent Automation". https://www.avanade.com/en-us/media-center/press-releases/intelligent-automation

15 Amy Ann Forni and Rob van der Meulen, 2017. "Gartner Survey Shows 42 Percent of CEOs Have Begun Digital Business Transformation". Gartner. https://www.gartner.com/newsroom/id/3689017

16 Harvard Business Review, 2019. " How Companies Are Using Intelligent Automation to Be More Innovative ". https://hbr.org/sponsored/2019/12/how-companies-are-using-intelligent-automation-to-be-more-innovative

highest valued AI company in the world by 2019 with a valuation of USD 7 billion.[17]

Other technologies have been with us longer, but have recently witnessed significant advances. For example, machine learning, which dates back to the early 1950s, is now playing a pivotal role in enabling efficient object detection and neural machine translation thanks to deep learning.

Estimating the **size and growth of the IA market** is not an easy exercise because of the multitude of studies and the differences in their methods and scopes. Here is our selection of the most recent and established ones:

- AI, which is closely connected to IA, has been gathering momentum for nearly two decades now. Forbes data shows that the number of AI start-ups has increased 14 times since 2000, and investments in AI start-ups have increased six times over the same period.[18]

- According to Gartner, the number of companies implementing AI technologies has grown by 270% in the past four years.[19]

---

17 Mike Wheatley, 2019. "UiPath becomes world's most valuable AI startup". https://siliconangle.com/2019/04/30/uipath-becomes-worlds-valuable-ai-startup-cool-7-billion/

18 Louis Columbus, 2018. "10 Charts That Will Change Your Perspective On Artificial Intelligence's Growth". https://www.forbes.com/sites/louiscolumbus/2018/01/12/10-charts-that-will-change-your-perspective-on-artificial-intelligences-growth/#7eabdaeb4758

19 ZDNet, 2019, "Enterprise adoption of AI has grown 270 percent over the past four years". https://www.zdnet.com/article/enterprise-adoption-of-ai-has-grown-270-percent-over-the-past-four-years/

- The global intelligent process automation market size is expected to reach $15.8 billion by 2025, rising at a market growth of 12.5% CAGR from 2020 to 2025.[20]

- The global machine learning market size was valued at $6.9 billion in 2018 and is anticipated to register an annual growth of 43.8% from 2019 to 2025.[21]

- Worldwide RPA software revenue grew by more than 60% in 2019 to $1.3 billion, making it the fastest-growing segment of the global enterprise software market. Global software companies, such as IBM, Microsoft, and SAP, are completing their portfolios of technologies by acquiring RPA software providers.[22] This is expected to increase awareness and potential adoption of this technology within their large customer bases.[23]

The scope of IA's impact represents 84% of the workforce in the US

For most of us, when hearing about automation, the image of a physical manufacturing robot comes to mind. Nevertheless, while the impact of physical robots has been significant in the last two centuries, it only accounts for a small effect on the future of work. In the US, for example, industrial and farming automation only

---

20 PR Newswire, 2020. https://www.prnewswire.com/news-releases/the-global-intelligent-process-automation-market-size-is-expected-to-reach-15-8-billion-by-2025--rising-at-a-market-growth-of-12-5-cagr-during-the-forecast-period-301004589

21 Grand View Research, 2020. "Industry analysis". https://www.grandviewresearch.com/industry-analysis/machine-learning-market

22 As an illustration, here is an article on the recent acquisition of Softomotive by Microsoft: https://flow.microsoft.com/en-us/blog/microsoft-acquires-softomotive-to-expand-low-code-robotic-process-automation-capabilities-in-microsoft-power-automate/

23 Gartner, 2019. "Worldwide robotic process automation market". https://www.gartner.com/en/newsroom/press-releases/2019-06-24-gartner-says-worldwide-robotic-process-automation-sof

accounts for 17% of the potential impact of automation on workload. Intelligent automation (the "digital workers") accounts for most of the rest (highlighted under "Services" in Table 0.2). **Due to the large scope, the impact of IA in the coming years is expected to be significant for employment and society.**

The scope of Intelligent Automation

| The scope of IA's impact represents 84% of the workforce in the US

Thousands of people, as of May 2019, according to the U.S. Bureau of Labor Statistics

Farming	3,900	3%
Manufacturing	**21,077**	**14%**
Goods producing, including manufacturing, mining, construction, durable and non-durable goods	21,077	
Services:	**129,997**	**84%**
Trade (wholesale and retail)	21,710	
Transportation, warehousing and utilities	6,097	
Information (e.g., publishing, telecommunications)	2,815	
Financial activities (e.g., banking, insurance, real estate)	8,656	
Professional and business services (e.g., accounting, administrative, management, engineering services, IT, legal)	21,408	
Education and health services (e.g., physicians, teachers, nurses)	24,176	
Leisure and hospitality (e.g., recreation, food services, accommodation)	16,699	
Other services (e.g., repair, maintenance, associations)	5,924	
Government (at federal, state and local levels, including administration, postal services)	22,512	
Total	154,974	100%

Table 0.2: USA employment breakdown by industry sector
Sources: adapted from the United States Department of Labor[24]

---

24   United States Department of Labor, accessed May 2019. "Seasonally adjusted figures for May 2019". https://www.bls.gov/news.release/empsit.t17.htm

IA viewed in parallel with automation in agriculture

Historically, agriculture was the first industry to be automated. The process of automating agriculture took over a thousand years. The outcome today is a thriving and highly efficient agribusiness.

As we can see from Figure 0.4, the level of automation has continued to increase, even since the 1990s. This is represented by the decline in the percentage of the global workforce working in this industry, falling from 44% in 1990 to 28% in 2017. Automation in agriculture has mainly been through the use of tractors, combine harvesters, milking machines, and hay press machines.

In parallel, the share of undernourished people in the global population has also decreased from 19% to 11%. This evidences how automation was instrumental in reducing the proportion of the world population suffering from hunger. **Thanks to automation, the agriculture industry has been able to increase its productivity continually, solving one of the most pressing world issues.**

The impact of automation in agriculture

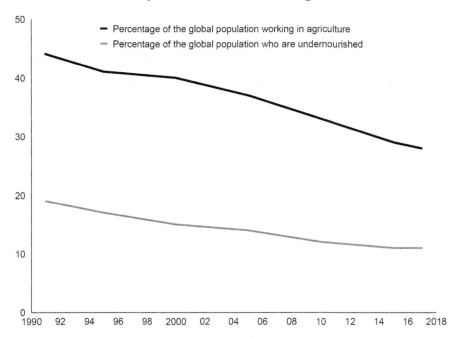

Figure 0.4: The impact of automation in agriculture
Source: adapted from the International Labour Organization, FAO SOFI, and World Bank[25]

We believe IA will have a similarly significant impact not only on employment but more broadly on our society. It will follow a similar trend of increasing the output produced while reducing the human workforce needed.

We expect IA's impact to have even higher velocity and magnitude. Algorithms are to white-collar workers what tractors were to farmers: a tool to dramatically increase the productivity of each worker, and

---

25 Number of people undernourished: FAO SOFI (2018) & World Bank (2017) https://ourworldindata.org/hunger-and-undernourishment; Global percentage of population working in agriculture: International Labour Organization, ILOSTAT database, 2018. https://data.worldbank.org/indicator/SL.AGR.EMPL.ZS?end=2018&start=1991&view=chart

thus shrink the total number of workers required to produce the same output. But unlike tractors, algorithms can be shipped instantly around the world at no additional cost. Once an algorithm has been sent out to millions of users, it can be continuously updated and improved with no need to create a new physical product.

Key definitions

Table 0.3 shows the definitions of key terms we used throughout the book. We have written these definitions leveraging our experience, as well as the information coming from the survey we conducted amongst IA experts.

Table 0.3: Key definitions

Artificial intelligence (AI): a combination of technologies able to reproduce human behavior and intelligence. It includes the capacity to sense the environment, analyze it, learn from it, and act on it. AI has applications in automating work (this is where it intersects with IA). However, unlike IA, AI also has applications in gaming, arts, education, and many other areas not connected to knowledge work. In addition, AI does not include the capability to execute actions or support workflows of tasks or data.

Automation: the action of a software program or machine which performs tasks usually performed by human workers. In the case of IA, which is about knowledge work automation, we will mainly refer to software-based automation.

Deep learning: a subfield of machine learning. It is a recent technology that enables machine learning to process complex data; for example, data that involves a large number of features and highly complex patterns, typically unstructured, such as pictures, movies, and language. This technology works on a similar basis to the structure and functions of a human brain. The deep learning model uses networks of neurons presented in superposed layers, with each layer performing a level of analysis of the input data (for example, to classify or recognize a pattern) and providing its output to the next layer.

Digital workforce: a digital version of the workforce, which is otherwise usually composed of human workers. When using digital robots and programs to automate processes, companies create a digital workforce. As IA automates more and more processes, the size of the digital workforce grows.

Machine learning: a subfield of artificial intelligence. It enables computers to learn and improve on their own, from experience, without being explicitly programmed. A machine learning algorithm can identify patterns in observed data (e.g., a growth trend in monthly sales revenue), build models that explain them (e.g., sales seem to be correlated to weather conditions), and predict future data (e.g., estimate future growth of sales considering the weather). Out of the different technologies used in the context of IA, machine learning has become the most used one.

Robot: This term is commonly used to describe an automation program, independently of the technology used. In the context of IA, we mainly refer to software robots (non-physical robots, also called "digital robots"). A robot is a program in charge of automating a specific work task or process. For example, a chatbot is a robot able to dialogue with users on their computers or smartphones.

PART ONE:

THE PROMISE OF IA FOR A BETTER WORLD

"The technology you use impresses no one.
The experience you create with it is everything."

Sean Gerety, user experience expert

P ew Research surveyed 4,000 American workers to understand their views on a future with artificial intelligence, automation, and robotics.[26] The first idea that came to these people's minds regarding these technologies was negative. Indeed, 72 percent reported that they were primarily worried about robots and computers being able to perform human jobs. The Pew survey demonstrates that our society does not seem to understand the full picture of the benefits it would get by using automation. **There is a need to educate**, and this is one of the purposes of this book.

Today, more people die from overwork and stress than from wars. More than 75 percent of people are dissatisfied with their jobs, which they view as too tedious and repetitive. Countries are facing growing debts, a constant fear of a coming recession, and later retirement ages. The cost of human error and fraud is almost equivalent to the total amount of money allocated globally to education.

Automation is a compelling class of technologies with the capability to address these major problems the world faces. In this section, we examine how this role cuts across domains like healthcare, education, and business. Finally, we answer the question: why does our world need more IA?

---

26   Aaron Smith and Monica Anderson, 2017. "Automation in Everyday Life". Pew Research Center. https://www.pewinternet.org/2017/10/04/automation-in-everyday-life/

IA is a business imperative

In this part, we present how the business environment is changing, making it more difficult for organizations to stay relevant and competitive, and to survive. We explain how business leaders can rethink and strengthen their business by leveraging IA. IA increases the efficiency of existing businesses and provides the opportunity to build new business strategies.

1. A new deal for businesses

How has the nature of businesses evolved in recent years?

To answer this point, we have started by selecting the largest companies out of the 2020 Fortune 500 list (i.e., companies with over 25,000 employees). The outcome was a list of 256 companies. We have then analyzed their profitability by **comparing their profit per employee**. Table 1.1 shows a ranking of companies with the highest profit per employee.

Ranking	Company name	Profit (million USD)	Number of employees	Profit per employee (USD)
1	Facebook	$18,485	44,942	$411,308
2	Apple	$55,256	137,000	$403,328
3	Alphabet (Google)	$34,343	118,899	$288,842
4	Microsoft	$39,240	144,000	$272,500
5	AbbVie	$7,882	30,000	$262,733

Table 1.1: A list of the largest Fortune 500 companies with the highest profit per employee
Source: adapted from Tipalti[27]

It is not surprising to find Facebook, Apple, Alphabet (Google), and Microsoft – companies at the top of the new digital economy – in this top-five ranking. The other company is in the health industry (AbbVie).

Let's now compare companies' profitability by date of creation. We collected the date when each of the 256 companies on our list was founded. From our research, we identified a strong correlation between the age of a company and its profitability per employee. The coefficient of correlation was -0.8. This demonstrates that, on average, **the older the company, the less profit per employee it generates**. As an illustration, Table 1.2 sorts by date of creation a sample of the most famous companies on our list.

---

27 Tipalti, 2020. "Profit per Employee". https://tipalti.com/profit-per-employee/

Year founded	Company name	Profit (million USD)	Number of employees	Profit per employee (USD)
1911	IBM	$9,431	383,800	$24,573
1940	McDonald's	$6,025	205,000	$29,392
1968	Intel	$21,048	110,800	$189,964
1975	Microsoft	$39,240	144,000	$272,500
1976	Apple	$55,256	137,000	$403,328
1998	Alphabet (Google)	$34,343	118,899	$288,842
2004	Facebook	$18,485	44,942	$411,308

Table 1.2: A list of global companies with the highest profit per employee
Source: research by the authors

What does that mean?

It signifies that the landscape of global companies is changing. **They require fewer and fewer employees; they are more and more automated, and they are less labor-intensive than their older peers**. It may also mean that adapting legacy organizations to new digital technologies is not an easy process. The older and the more established enterprises are, the more complex it is. In our experience, this is most likely due to the inertia created by legacy and by the complexity and cost of change. It means digital natives – the most recent companies to arrive in the marketplace – hold the advantage as the pace of innovation accelerates. Another illustration is WhatsApp's value. The company was acquired in 2014 for USD 19 billion (Facebook's largest investment to date). WhatsApp was then a five-year-old company with only 50 employees.

The 33-year average tenure of companies on the S&P 500 in 1965 narrowed to 20 years in 1990. And it is forecast to shrink to 14 years by 2026. About half of the S&P 500 will be replaced over the next ten years, according to Innosight.[28]

All businesses are going digital: the winners will be those who do so the quickest and to the greatest extent. It may be informed speculation to say the landscape of companies will change dramatically over the next few decades. Still, **one thing is sure: the winners – even the survivors – will be highly automated**, with the bare minimum of human involvement.

Two examples: Amazon currently employs 200,000 robots and 400,000 human employees, with the number of robots increasing at a much faster pace than the onboarding rate for humans.[29] Fifteen years ago, Goldman Sachs had 500 people trading stocks. Now only three people do this job. They are supported by a new team of nearly 200 technology specialists working for other departments as well.[30]

This environment of rapid change adds a new level of complexity for CEOs. Technological disruption and digital innovation have become critical factors of competitiveness on top of the more common ones, such as cost, talent, and geopolitics.

28 Scott D. Anthony, S. Patrick Viguerie, and Andrew Waldeck, 2016. "Corporate Longevity: Turbulence Ahead for Large Organizations". Innosight. https://www.innosight.com/wp-content/uploads/2016/08/Corporate-Longevity-2016-Final.pdf

29 The Game Of Brands, 2019. "Number of robots in Amazon's warehouses". Instagram. https://www.instagram.com/p/B05FbE9H2NI/?igshid=1wlp5z8fd5wa5

30 Sonali Basak and Christopher Palmeri, 2018. "A Goldman Trading Desk That Once Had 500 People Is Down to Three". Bloomberg. https://www.bloomberg.com/news/articles/2018-04-30/goldman-trading-desk-that-once-had-500-people-is-down-to-three

2. Increasing companies' efficiency

What can IA do for businesses?

When it comes to the **CEO agenda**, most sources (including Gartner[31], the World Economic Forum[32], and PWC[33]) are aligned on the **top three priorities**. And IA plays a crucial role in each of them:

1. New growth opportunities: new geographies, new business models, and using disruptive technologies within their markets.

2. Technology to help control costs and improve productivity.

3. The need to enhance digital skills for all executives, including the CEOs themselves.

Over the last 20 years, initiatives used by CEOs to improve the productivity of their businesses were focused on Enterprise Resource Planning (ERP) systems implementations, lean programs, or Shared Service Centers (SSC). Most of these programs were multi-year projects, requiring profound changes to the organization, people, and processes, and involving payback periods on the order of 2 to 5 years.

---

31 Katie Costello, 2019. "Gartner Survey Reveals That CEO Priorities Are Slowly Shifting to Meet Rising Growth Challenges". Gartner. https://www.gartner.com/en/newsroom/press-releases/2019-05-08-gartner-survey-reveals-that-ceo-priorities-are-slowly

32 Bill Thomas, 2019. "3 priorities for CEOs in 2019". WEF. https://www.weforum.org/agenda/2019/01/ceo-priorities-for-success-in-2019/

33 PWC, 2019. "22nd Annual Global CEO Survey". PWC. https://www.pwc.com/gx/en/ceo-agenda/ceosurvey/2019/gx.html

Unlike these initiatives, IA enables deployments in months, the technology can be scaled to infinity, and payback periods are usually less than a year.

According to the McKinsey Global Institute, the adoption speed of artificial intelligence is already a serious competitive differentiator. In essence, early adopters experience higher profit margins (+10–15% on average compared to laggards), and their free cash flows are expected to accelerate much faster.[34]

A Deloitte survey also shows that the benefits of adopting IA are significant. Participants reported that payback was less than 12 months, with an average of 20% of full-time equivalent (FTE) capacity provided by IA programs. **Automation met and even exceeded expectations** in many areas, including improved compliance (92%), quality and accuracy (90%), productivity (86%), and reduced costs (59%).[35]

According to a study by Statista, 84% of business organizations adopt AI because it gives them a competitive advantage over their rivals.[36]

3. Building new business strategies with IA

Two recent impactful business concepts are using IA as a foundation: new digital business building and ecosystems of data.

---

34 Jacques Bughin, Jeongmin Seong, James Manyika, Michael Chui, and Raoul Joshi, 2018. "Notes from the AI frontier: Modeling the impact of AI on the world economy". McKinsey Global Institute. https://www.mckinsey.com/featured-insights/artificial-intelligence/notes-from-the-ai-frontier-modeling-the-impact-of-ai-on-the-world-economy

35 Deloitte, 2018. "Deloitte Global RPA Survey". Deloitte, 2018. "Deloitte Global RPA Survey". Deloitte, 2018. "Deloitte Global RPA Survey". https://www2.deloitte.com/bg/en/pages/technology/articles/deloitte-global-rpa-survey-2018

36 Statista, 2019. "AI Statistics About Smarter Machines", https://techjury.net/stats-about/ai/

3.1. New digital business building

Insurance companies, banks, energy providers, and incumbent telecommunication companies need to digitalize their businesses to stay competitive against new pure digital entrants. In most cases, the fastest and most efficient way to achieve this is not to digitalize their existing business, but to create entirely new digital businesses that are highly automated. New digital businesses are centered around technology in the construction and delivery of the services or products. The experience for the customers is typically faster, cheaper, more seamless, and easier because it is accessible everywhere and user-friendly. Companies use their new digital business to gradually try, test, and incubate new technologies and concepts, and infuse them back to the legacy business. Sometimes, the new digital business even ends up becoming the new core business.

For example, while the toy market was shrinking, Lego launched new digital businesses embracing video games, social networks, blockbuster movies, and crowdsourced platforms.[37] With that, Lego increased its net profit by four times in 10 years, from 300 million euros in 2009 to 1.1 billion in 2019.[38]

---

37 Park R., 2018. HBS, "LEGOs: Still "The Apple of Toys"?" https://digital.hbs.edu/platform-digit/submission/legos-still-the-apple-of-toys/

38 Statista, accessed May 2020. "Net profit of the LEGO Group worldwide from 2009 to 2019" https://www.statista.com/statistics/292305/lego-group-net-profit/

Figure 1.1: Lego created LEGO Life, a social network community, where users are encouraged to share their physical play experiences. This move gives LEGO the power to play in the mobile and online space
Source: Lego[39]

Goldman Sachs launched the online personal loan platform Marcus in 2016 as the first step into building a consumer-facing franchise. In both cases, IA has become a critical enabler in creating new businesses from scratch. It serves two purposes: one is the survival of the legacy business; the other is the creation of a new, highly profitable business.

As McKinsey Senior Partner Ari Libarikian put it: "We believe that digital business-building is a requirement for long-term success. If you look at the Fortune 20 today versus the list 20 years ago, it's almost entirely different. Every company on the list today has regenerated itself through business-building or was a start-up a few years ago and has scaled massively."[40]

---

39   Access Lego Life on Google Play Store: https://play.google.com/store/apps/details?id=com.lego.common.legolife&hl=en

40   CXO Talk, 2019. "McKinsey: Leap Beyond Digital Transformation" https://www.cxotalk.com/video/mckinsey-leap-beyond-digital-transformation

3.2. Ecosystems of data

A data ecosystem is a set of actors working together in data and other shared resources. **It is an interconnected set of services enabling users to fulfill a variety of needs in one integrated experience**. Ecosystems act as gateways, offering customers a number of related services in a single interface. This avoids clients needing to switch between related services while lowering customer acquisition costs for the partners on the platform. In the banking industry, ecosystems can deliver customer-acquisition cost (CAC) savings of as much as 10 to 20 percent, according to McKinsey analysis.[41] Ecosystems integrate data, which helps companies to monetize it by creating value-added services and enhancing customer experiences. For instance, a bank might leverage its users' locations and spending trends to offer merchant-specific coupons or identify other opportunities for cross-selling products and services.

The Chinese **insurance group Ping An** has been a first mover and built a reference ecosystem. **It expanded beyond insurance into a broader set of ecosystems, such as banking, healthcare, smart cities, and housing**. As a result, in the past five years, Ping An accumulated nearly 500 million online users and created 11 new digital platforms across industries.[42] In addition, it increased its number of insurance agents to 1.4 million, all armed with the company's digital tools and apps. In the health area, in order to capture customers upstream as they start their insurance journey, Ping An launched Good

---

41   Sengupta S., 2019. "The ecosystem playbook: Winning in a world of ecosystems". https://www.mckinsey.com/~/media/mckinsey/industries/financial%20services/our%20insights/winning%20in%20a%20world%20of%20ecosystems/winning-in-a-world-of-ecosystems-vf.ashx

42   McKinsey Quarterly, 2018. "Building a tech-enabled ecosystem: An interview with Ping An's Jessica Tan". https://www.mckinsey.com/featured-insights/china/building-a-tech-enabled-ecosystem-an-interview-with-ping-ans-jessica-tan

Doctor. The app now fields more than 500,000 online consultations a day from customers who are looking for health-related advice.

DBS Bank, founded in 1968, embarked on its digital transformation journey (including ecosystems) inspired by platform players such as Alibaba or Tencent. Over the last five years, **DBS invested SG$1 billion annually** in its transformation, resulting in a substantial increase in digital customers from 33 percent in 2015 to 48 percent in 2018.[43]

"At DBS, we act less like a bank and more like a tech company."

DBS Bank CEO Piyush Gupta[44]

---

43   According to DBS CEO Piyush Gupta. https://www.dbs.com/livemore/q-dbs-ceo-piyush-gupta.html

44   https://www.dbs.com/innovation/dbs-innovates/at-dbs-we-act-less-like-a-bank-and-more-like-a-tech-company-with-dbs-bank-ceo-piyush-gupta.html

Improving the employee experience

In this part, we will demonstrate that the employee experience is critical to business success, describe the current status of this experience, and show how IA can help boost it. Finally, we will provide recommendations on how an organization can seize the opportunity to improve its employees' experience.

1. The importance of employees' experience

According to an article in Harvard Business Review, **enterprises that drive initiatives to enhance employee experience are four times more profitable** than those that do not.[45] In addition, the Mercer 2019 Global Talent Trends study demonstrates that effective and relevant day-to-day work experience is essential for retaining top talent. Mercer found that thriving employees are three times more likely to work for an organization that:

- Enables quick decision-making

- Provides tools and resources for them to do their job efficiently.[46]

---

45 Jacob Morgan, 2017. "Why the Millions We Spend on Employee Engagement Buy Us So Little". Harvard Business Review. https://hbr.org/2017/03/why-the-millions-we-spend-on-employee-engagement-buy-us-so-little

46 Stacy Bronstein, 2019. "Making Organizations "Future-Fit" Is Top of Mind, New Study Finds". Mercer. https://www.mercer.com/newsroom/with-more-business-disruption-expected-making-organizations-future-fit-is-top-of-mind-new-study-finds

We believe the recent COVID-19 crisis has reinforced this point. Organizations able to anticipate issues and support their people physically, mentally, and financially have become the new global references. Countries like Taiwan[47] or companies like Apple[48] have shown an exemplary response to the crisis. Both have focused their first efforts on anticipating the worst for their employees. They have then reacted by protecting the health and livelihood of their people.

We believe that, in the future, **the winners will be the organizations succeeding at managing their employees' safety and experience**. Attracting and retaining the best talents is critical for the customer experience and, ultimately, business success.

2. The current state of employees' experience

Work is a key element in our lives. One-third of our life is spent at work, and the average person will spend 90,000 hours at work over a lifetime.[49] Yet **85% of employees across the globe don't feel engaged with their work**. They often feel that it is too repetitive and not fulfilling. The number is higher in some countries than in others (70% in the USA versus 94% in Japan).[50]

Imagine spending the workday keying in invoices or reconciling data (perhaps you don't have to imagine it). That is what millions of

---

47   James Griffiths, 2020. "Taiwan's coronavirus response is among the best globally" https://edition.cnn.com/2020/04/04/asia/taiwan-coronavirus-response-who-intl-hnk/index.html

48   Luke Filipowicz, 2020. "Apple's response to the pandemic has been exemplary — I'm impressed". https://www.imore.com/apples-response-pandemic-has-been-exemplary-im-impressed

49   Gettysburg College, n.d. "One third of your life is spent at work". https://www.gettysburg.edu/news/stories?id=79db7b34-630c-4f49-ad32-4ab9ea48e72b&pageTitle=1%2F3+of+your+life+is+s pent+at+work

50   Jim Clifton, 2017. "The World's Broken Workplace". Gallup. https://news.gallup.com/opinion/chairman/212045/world-broken-workplace.aspx

people across the globe do 8 to 10 hours per day – every workday. In 2018, there were 1.5 million bookkeeping, accounting, and auditing clerks – just in the United States. It gives a glimpse into how many people around the world, particularly in lower-cost countries (e.g., India, Philippines), focus their attention on these kinds of rule-based and repetitive tasks.[51] IA offers to liberate employees from these tedious tasks by automating them, allowing people to refocus on more nuanced and value-adding activities.

In order to understand the state of the current employee experience better, we have researched across different sources to estimate the typical breakdown of an employee's daily work activities: Table 1.3 shows the outcome of this work.

51 E. Mazareanu, 2019. "Accounting industry in the U.S. – Statistics & Facts". Statista. https://www.statista.com/topics/2121/accounting-industry-in-the-us/

Average percentage of time spent by employees	% Time Current
Individual thinking, research, admin time	**42%**
Administrative tasks	16% ▮
Productive thinking time	10%
Productive time doing work– non-routine	8%
Productive time doing work– routine	8% ▮
Collaboration – internal & external	**49%**
Unproductive messages – reading / writing	14% ▮
Unproductive meetings	12% ▮
Productive collaboration (e.g. meetings, workshops)	9%
Productive emails	9%
Socializing	5%
Others / non-work / social media / interruptions	**9%**
Total	**100%**

▮ Work activities considered tedious

Table 1.3: Average percentage of time spent by employees on daily tasks
Source: Research by the authors combining different sources[52]

We can see the **high proportion of time spent on unproductive, routine, and administrative activities** (highlighted above). Research shows that for more than 50% of employees, wasteful meetings and excessive emails are reported to be the main obstacle in their work.[53]

---

52   Some of the sources used during the authors' research include: Workfront, 2018. "2017–2018 State of Enterprise Work Report"; Deloitte Access Economics, 2014. "Stancombe Research and Planning"; HBR, Julian Birkinshaw and Jordan Cohen, 2019. "Make Time for the Work That Matters".

53   Workfront, 2019. "State of Enterprise work report 2019". https://www.workfront.com/blog/state-of-work-2019

Also, only a third of employees currently have access to effective collaboration tools or AI applications.[54]

3. What do employees expect as an experience?

69% of employees expect that automation will give them more time to do their primary job duties, and 86% of employees think the use of automation in the workplace will let them think of work in new and innovative ways.[55]

The question is then, besides removing tedious tasks, what would make people happier and more engaged at work? Studies have found that **people like to have opportunities to solve problems in their work**. Also, **variety** among tasks at work leads to increased happiness and higher productivity.[56] Based on these findings, the promise of IA to change how people work seems a welcome development.

Based on our research, the employee experience would be improved by switching to the "ideal" daily division of activities, as shown in Table 1.4.

54 McKinsey, 2019. "Global AI Survey: AI proves its worth, but few scale impact".
    https://www.mckinsey.com/featured-insights/artificial-intelligence/global-ai-survey-ai-proves-its-worth-but-few-scale-impact

55 Workfront, 2019. "State of Enterprise work report 2019".
    https://www.workfront.com/blog/state-of-work-2019

56 Jordan Etkin and Cassie Mogilner, 2016. "Does Variety Among Activities Increase Happiness?"
    Journal of Consumer Research. https://doi.org/10.1093/jcr/ucw021

Average percentage of time spent by employees	% Time Current	% Time Ideal
Individual thinking, research, admin time	**42%**	**45%**
Administrative tasks	16%	
Productive thinking time	10%	25%
Productive time doing work– non-routine	8%	20%
Productive time doing work– routine	8%	
Collaboration – internal & external	**49%**	**55%**
Unproductive messages – reading / writing	14%	
Unproductive meetings	12%	
Productive collaboration (e.g. meetings, workshops)	9%	25%
Productive emails	9%	20%
Socializing	5%	10%
Others / non-work / social media / interruptions	**9%**	
Total	**100%**	**100%**

Table 1.4: Ideal average percentage of time employees could spend on daily tasks
Source: © Bornet, Barkin & Wirtz

Note that this ideal time division would also fit well with the imperative of a profitable company, as employees would focus on the work activities which generate the most value for companies (i.e., productive tasks).

4. The potential levers to improve employees' experience

We have identified three levers to enable the transition from the current breakdown of employee activities to the ideal division of activities. They are:

- **Automate**: companies should identify and automate routine activities, such as generating a PowerPoint presentation for a weekly meeting or recording invoices in accounting software.

- **Augment**: organizations should seize the opportunity to increase the value of work activities delivered by employees. IA is used as a crucial component here, with, for example, the generation of insights through advanced analytics to help decision making.

- **Abandon**: some work activities do not fit with leading practices for efficient work, and represent an obstacle to the employee's experience. These activities should be reduced or eliminated. For example, restricting the volume of meetings and email traffic is essential.

We call these levers **the "Triple-A artifact"**. It has proven to be a handy framework to help organizations build their action plans to boost their employee experience. Table 1.5 shows how the three levers can move the employee experience towards its ideal state, with IA being a key enabler of all of them.

Table 1.5 shows that, according to our research, out of all the work activities performed by employees (row "Total"), 42% could be automated using IA, 32% could be augmented, and 26% could be eliminated. The table also presents the details for each work activity.

Average percentage of time spent by employees	% Time Current	Opportunity for transformation		
		Automate	Augment	Abandon
Individual thinking, research, admin time	**42%**	**22%**	**15%**	**5%**
Administrative tasks	16%	11%		5%
Productive thinking time	10%	3%	7%	
Productive time doing work – non-routine	8%		8%	
Productive time doing work – routine	8%	8%		
Collaboration – internal & external	**49%**	**17%**	**17%**	**15%**
Unproductive messages – reading / writing	14%	6%		8%
Unproductive meetings	12%	5%		7%
Productive collaboration (e.g. meetings, workshops)	9%	2%	7%	
Productive emails	9%	3%	6%	
Socializing	5%	1%	4%	
Others / non-work / social media / interruptions	**9%**	**3%**		**6%**
Total	**100%**	**42%**	**32%**	**26%**

Table 1.5: Potential levers to help transition employees to an ideal division of time among their daily tasks
Source: © Bornet, Barkin & Wirtz

In order to work towards reaching the ideal work distribution through our Triple-A approach, we have seen successful organizations implement the following three types of actions.

1. Provide employees with a **personalized dashboard to monitor their work-life balance and healthy work habits**. Platforms collect employees' activity data (e.g., calendar and email activity) and analyze it to create the insight necessary to give directions and improve work behavior over time. Different types of platforms are readily available on the market, including:

   • **Workplace collaboration analytics**. These applications help with the collection of data from users' collaboration activities (e.g., emails, meetings) to understand collaboration patterns and identify opportunities to improve work behavior. For example, they coach users in organizing efficient meetings with no more than four people, or in having at least one weekly talk with each of the team members.[57]

   • **Stress and mental health trackers**. These tools monitor stress levels and mental health using sentiment analysis based on employees' actions, interactions, and communications (e.g., emails, calls, instant messages). Some of these tools can also connect with smartwatches to collect additional data, such as heartbeats and activity levels. Some of these solutions also include an analysis of users' facial expressions using computer vision.[58]

---

57 Examples of such platforms include Microsoft Workplace Analytics https://www.microsoft.com/ microsoft-365/partners/workplaceanalytics and Work Insights (Google) https://gsuite.google. com/products/workinsights/

58 Examples of such platforms include Woebot https://woebot.io/ and Moodkit https://apps.apple. com/us/app/moodkit/id427064987

- **Time tracking**. These applications track the time spent by an employee on each application and work task. They take screenshots, manage the timestamps for teams, and help to visualize where employees are most effective and where they potentially need help.[59]

- **Organizational network analysis**. This tool collects and analyzes employee interaction data to identify influencers, leaders, nodes, and change agents. These applications are useful for analyzing and improving collaboration patterns between employees.[60]

2. Give employees **access to value-add AI-based applications** to improve their work experience and to reduce the time allocated to tedious tasks. Such applications include email management support (e.g., triage by categories and importance to the reader, filtering), expense management, time optimizers, AI-based personal assistants, meeting optimizers (e.g., transcription, time coaching, schedulers), information and document management tools, project management support, apps to promote relaxation, and many others. We particularly recommend the following:

- **Workplace tool data search**. This type of application acts as a Google search for the workplace environment. It allows users to launch a single search across all personal

---

59 Examples of such platforms include Time Doctor and Track.ly.

60 Examples of such platforms include Polinode and OrgMapper.

and shared files, emails, and applications. It helps to dramatically accelerate the search for information.[61]

- **Meeting schedulers**. These applications help to schedule meetings without the all-too-common back-and-forth emails, connecting to colleagues' calendars and providing the time slots available.[62]

- **Email triage and filtering**. These applications automate the triage, classification, and prioritization of emails based on user behavior observed over time.[63]

3. **Coach employees in real time, leveraging an AI-based virtual assistant.** This can guide employees towards healthier working practices, manage their stress in real-time, and encourage them to comply with best practices in workplace collaboration. Solutions are available, but they are still developing.[64] We believe there is an opportunity to create more compelling platforms that bring more benefits to the employee. Here is an example of the interactions a virtual assistant could help to manage for employees:

---

61 Examples of such platforms include Workona, GestStation and Veamly.

62 An example of such a platform is Calendly.

63 Examples of such platforms include Activeinbox and Sanebox.

64 Here is one of these solutions: https://products.office.com/en-in/business/myanalytics-personal-analytics

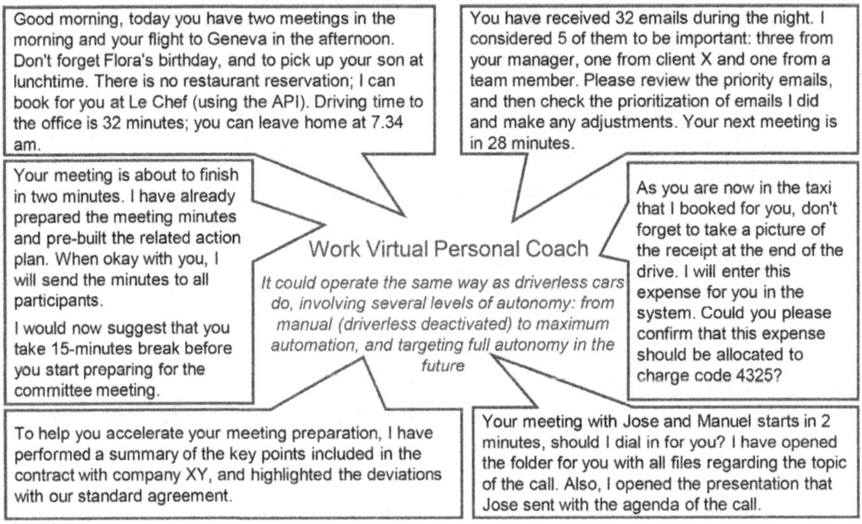

Good morning, today you have two meetings in the morning and your flight to Geneva in the afternoon. Don't forget Flora's birthday, and to pick up your son at lunchtime. There is no restaurant reservation; I can book for you at Le Chef (using the API). Driving time to the office is 32 minutes; you can leave home at 7.34 am.

You have received 32 emails during the night. I considered 5 of them to be important: three from your manager, one from client X and one from a team member. Please review the priority emails, and then check the prioritization of emails I did and make any adjustments. Your next meeting is in 28 minutes.

Your meeting is about to finish in two minutes. I have already prepared the meeting minutes and pre-built the related action plan. When okay with you, I will send the minutes to all participants.

I would now suggest that you take 15-minutes break before you start preparing for the committee meeting.

As you are now in the taxi that I booked for you, don't forget to take a picture of the receipt at the end of the drive. I will enter this expense for you in the system. Could you please confirm that this expense should be allocated to charge code 4325?

Work Virtual Personal Coach

It could operate the same way as driverless cars do, involving several levels of autonomy: from manual (driverless deactivated) to maximum automation, and targeting full autonomy in the future

To help you accelerate your meeting preparation, I have performed a summary of the key points included in the contract with company XY, and highlighted the deviations with our standard agreement.

Your meeting with Jose and Manuel starts in 2 minutes, should I dial in for you? I have opened the folder for you with all files regarding the topic of the call. Also, I opened the presentation that Jose sent with the agenda of the call.

Figure 1.2: How an AI-based personal coach could support employees in their day-to-day work

Source: © Bornet, Barkin & Wirtz

Boosting the customer experience

Companies often lose clients because they don't understand their clients' needs, so they don't deliver satisfaction and value. Others do not know how to retain customers at risk of switching. Competitors who are able to reduce prices or increase service levels drastically are often the winners.

In today's business environment, faster services – whether opening a new bank account, subscribing to a mobile phone service, or approving a new mortgage – becomes a competitive advantage with a direct impact on top and bottom lines.

What are clients looking for today, and how can IA help?

To answer this question, let us look at **best-in-class companies and their Net Promoter Scores**[65] **(NPS)** – a key indicator of customer satisfaction.

The NPS is calculated based on the answer to a simple question: "How likely is it that you would recommend [this brand or service] to a friend or colleague?"

The NPS is obtained by subtracting the percentage of Detractors (people unhappy with your brand/service) from the percentage of Promoters (loyal enthusiasts who will keep buying and refer others).

---

65   Net Promoter, n.d. "What is Net Promoter?" https://www.netpromoter.com/know/

As a result, NPS can range from a low of -100 (if every customer is a Detractor) to a high of 100 (if every customer is a Promoter).

The companies with the highest NPSs in 2019 were Starbucks (77), Airbnb (74), Netflix (68), Apple (63), Amazon (62), and Vodafone (60). What do these brands have in common, and what can we learn from these commonalities about IA? According to our analysis, they share three characteristics:

1. A responsive and omnichannel focus on customer service

1.1. Omnichannel

Almost 90% of global customers think brands should provide an omnichannel experience. They should be able to switch between channels (e.g., phone, email, chat) and agents (different customer service staff) without losing context. Accomplishing this requires excellence in collecting all relevant information from customer complaints, support requests, and comments – then sharing them across all customer-facing touchpoints. For example, once Amazon customers report an issue, they do not have to repeat that information in other interactions. Amazon's centralized database makes issue-related information readily available to other service representatives. IA can play a crucial role here in regularly updating these records and sharing them consistently across systems.

1.2. Responsiveness

According to global customer satisfaction surveys, customers expect almost immediate answers to their questions.[66] Poor service can cause up to 66% of global consumers to stop doing business with one brand and switch to another.[67] Leading brands use chatbots or cognitive agents to provide first-level resolution 24 hours a day, seven days a week. Based on our experience, they can typically deal with 30–50% of live client interactions (e.g., calls, chats) relating to common or standard questions. In addition, they log queries or direct customers to the appropriate customer service representative for more information. Another growing trend leveraging IA is the use of self-service platforms, where users can solve their issues by themselves or with the help of other users. According to research, an increasing proportion of customers prefers them.[68] And based on our experience, 50% of customers' requests can be solved with these platforms, reducing the workload of customer service teams. Either way, smart and automated communication solutions enable customers to get the answers they need when they need them.

2. Customized offers and innovative products

2.1. Customized offers

Collecting and analyzing behavioral and demographic data from prospective buyers helps companies understand customers' needs

---

66 Engage Customer, n.d. "Customer satisfaction on the rise globally".
    https://engagecustomer.com/customer-satisfaction-on-the-rise-globally/

67 TrendWatching, 2014. "The Future of Customer Service".
    https://trendwatching.com/trends/future-customer-service/

68 Steven Van Belleghem, 2013. "The Self-Service Economy".
    http://www.slideshare.net/stevenvanbelleghem/the-self-serving-economy

in order to create customized offerings. This is a faster and more efficient approach than mass marketing campaigns or using sales representatives. The findings of a study showed that 78% of online consumers said that personally relevant content increases their purchase intent. Personalization can also reduce customer acquisition costs by as much as 50%.[69]

This use of data analytics is another critical application of IA, and it is not only about past behavior but also anticipated future actions. These algorithms predicting the products that specific clients may buy next can be used to optimize cross-selling and up-selling. For example, Netflix achieved impressive results from the algorithm it uses to personalize recommendations to its 100 million subscribers worldwide. Netflix estimated these customized search results saved it $1 billion in annual revenues that would otherwise be lost to canceled subscriptions.[70]

2.2. Innovative products

Game-changing products (and services) come from creating a culture of innovation and a company attuned to listening. Every client commendation, comment, and complaint is an opportunity to fine-tune an existing product or to create a new one. It is critical to collect client feedback and be able to generate insight from it.

IA is at the heart of this, with analytics and machine learning playing a crucial role. IA's self-service platforms and cognitive agents address and, at the same time, harvest common customer questions and

---

69   Ellie Behling, 2017. RRD. "10 Personalization Statistics You Need to Know: Why Personalized Marketing is the Way to Go". https://blog.rrdonnelley.com/personalization-statistics/

70   McKinsey Global Institute, 2017. "Artificial intelligence: The next digital frontier?"

issues. In the meantime, IA also gives employees the time to then translate these findings into innovative solutions and products. For example, Netflix encourages employees to develop ideas about how to improve customer service.[71] Google is another example, as they ask engineers to spend 20% of their workweek on creative projects of their choice.[72]

3. Exceptional customer experience

3.1. Agent enablement and augmentation

Service representative performance is cited as a common pain point, with 60% of global customers[73] ranking it as a top frustration – at times, making companies vulnerable to media repercussions. Improved training is a conventional solution. But more proactive, innovative approaches include leveraging IA sentiment analysis to monitor agent interactions and reducing call fatigue by using chatbots and RPA as collaborative robots.

Hotel chain Wyndham uses 13,000 robots to guide employees through the customer-facing processes across thousands of locations (e.g., check-ins, check-outs, or updates of client information in the system). Using an attended robotic process automation solution, the company implemented a "just in time" process guidance and

71 Dorothy Pomerantz, 2014. "How A Culture Of Innovation Could Win Netflix Some Emmys". Forbes. https://www.forbes.com/sites/dorothypomerantz/2014/08/20/how-a-culture-of-innovation-could-win-netflix-some-emmys/#3e24ecae19cd

72 Laura He, 2013. "Google's Secrets Of Innovation: Empowering Its Employees". Forbes. https://www.forbes.com/sites/laurahe/2013/03/29/googles-secrets-of-innovation-empowering-its-employees/#76d6d52957e7

73 Tricia Morris, 2013, "2013 Customer Service Expectations & Frustrations". Business 2 Community (originally published on Parature). https://www.business2community.com/customer-experience/2013-customer-service-expectations-frustrations-infographic-0681531

automation solution. Real-time instructions were popped up on the screen of their customer-facing agents to guide them in their discussions with clients. Other programs helped to prefill information coming from other systems (e.g., pasting client data from the loyalty system to the booking system).

3.2. Speed, quality, and tone of customer service

A SuperOffice global customer service benchmark report provides a wealth of insights into what makes an exceptional customer experience and how IA can support it. This study is based on a fundamental assumption: how companies answer customer emails can be used to assess how they manage customer support. Researchers sent 1,000 companies an email with two questions: "Do you have a phone number I can call?" and "Where can I find pricing information on your website?" Responses were measured on speed, quality, and tone across five customer experience categories. Results showed that the majority of companies failed to meet even minimal customer experience expectations. Specifically, 62% did not even respond to the customers' email. Of those companies that did respond, only 20% answered questions in full on the first reply.[74]

One use case that demonstrated the power of IA in customer service is Vodafone. Before implementing IA, Vodafone's customer service processes were cumbersome and time-consuming, dissatisfying agents and customers alike. After IA implementation, the average call time was reduced from 10–20 minutes to 4–8 minutes. Call wrap-up (logging of the topic discussed and scheduling follow-ups) went

---

74 SuperOffice, n.d. "Customer Service Benchmark Report".
    http://www.superoffice.com/resources/guides/customer-service-benchmark-report/

from 5–10 minutes to zero because this post-call processing stage was completely automated.[75]

Based on our experience, **80% of a customer journey can become digitally touchless and fully omnichannel.**[76] **As an impact, we have seen companies increase customer satisfaction as measured by the NPS by more than 15 percentage points, reduce the contact center workload by over 50%, and quintuple the "service to sales" ratio** (number of up- and cross-sales during a service interaction).

---

75   Jacada, n.d. "Vodafone "SAVES" Customers with Jacada". Featured Customers. https://media. featuredcustomers.com/CustomerCaseStudy.document/jacada_vodafone_86215.pdf

76   For an academic perspective on the future role of service robots see Jochen Wirtz (2020), "Organizational Ambidexterity: Cost-Effective Service Excellence, Service Robots, and Artificial Intelligence", Organizational Dynamics, Vol. 49, No. 3; and Jochen Wirtz, Paul Patterson, Werner Kunz, Thorsten Gruber, Vinh Nhat Lu, Stefanie Paluch, and Antje Martins (2018), "Brave New World: Service Robots in the Frontline", Journal of Service Management, Vol. 29, No. 5, 907-931, https://doi.org/10.1108/JOSM-04-2018-0119

Avoiding $10 trillion of losses due to fraud, errors, and accidents per year

IA has the potential to help reduce significant financial losses due to fraud, errors, and accidents (and work-related illnesses). This section estimates the potential savings IA could bring in these areas. These savings are critical for our society, as these sums of money could be reallocated to meaningful uses such as health or education. We have identified three sources of losses: fraud, errors, and work-related accidents and diseases.

1. Losses due to fraud

In 2018, **USD 5 trillion** (6% of global GDP) **was lost due to fraud globally**, according to research from Crowe and the University of Portsmouth's Centre for Counter Fraud Studies (CCFS).[77] The amount of money lost to fraud has more than doubled in the last ten years. The main reasons mentioned by the authors are: (1) greater individualism (less commitment to collective moral and ethical norms), (2) increasingly complex and remote systems and processes (making them more difficult to oversee and easier to hack), and (3) controls that struggle to keep up with an increasing pace of change in business.

---

77 Jim Gee and Professor Mark Button, 2019. "The Financial Cost of Fraud 2019". Crowe. https://www.crowe.com/uk/croweuk/-/media/Crowe/Firms/Europe/uk/CroweUK/PDF-publications/The-Financial-Cost-of-Fraud-2019.pdf

Across industries and geographies, IA, using robotics and machine learning, has demonstrated the ability to solve some of these problems. For example, IA not only makes transaction processes more efficient, but it also generates log files for every action, creating transparency and ease of compliance. Machine learning leverages the digital information created by these programs to recognize predictive patterns and project trends. Also, blockchain could be used to identify the origin of funds used in transactions, identifying owners and any related parties. These safeguards leveraging IA already exist; it just depends on us to expand their use to wider scopes and applications.

2. Losses due to errors

The cost of errors is enormous:

- **Medical errors in the US incur an estimated economic value of almost USD 1 trillion**[78] – and 86% of those mistakes are administrative.[79]

- 80% of US medical billings contain at least minor mistakes – creating unnecessary annual healthcare spending of $68 billion.[80]

- The above estimates are for the US only; we could not find a global evaluation. A conservative estimate at a worldwide level could be twice to three times this amount.

---

78   Luke Slawomirski, Ane Auraaen and Niek Klazinga, 2017. "The economics of patient safety". OECD. https://www.oecd.org/els/health-systems/The-economics-of-patient-safety-March-2017.pdf

79   ReferralMD, n.d. "30 Healthcare Statistics That Keep Hospital Executives Up At Night". https://getreferralmd.com/2016/08/30-healthcare-statistics-keep-hospital-executives-night/

80   Nick Tate, 2017. "4 in 5 Medical Bills Contain Errors: Here's What You Can Do". Newsmax. https://www.newsmax.com/Health/Headline/medical-bill-error-mistake/2017/08/04/id/805882/

3. Work-related accidents and diseases

The International Labour Organization (ILO) estimates that **the annual cost** to the global economy **from accidents and work-related diseases due to stress alone is a staggering $3 trillion**.[81] IA can play a significant role in monitoring the level of stress, reducing the workload, performing the more laborious, riskier tasks, and leaving the most exciting activities to the human workers. We explain how to achieve this objective in Part One: "Improving the employee experience".

In conclusion, the analysis in this section shows that **IA has the potential to deliver total savings of approximately $10 trillion per year**. This amount is the rough equivalent of the combined annual global expenditure for education and health. Of course, a benefit of this magnitude won't take place over just 5 to 10 years. It will likely require 10–20 years. Now let us imagine we can reach 50% of these savings in the coming ten years and that they can be redeployed through regulation, taxation, or other mechanisms. The $5 trillion losses saved by IA could mean that, in practical terms, thanks to higher adoption of IA:

---

81   International Labour Organization, 2019. "Safety and Health at the Heart of the Future of Work". ILO. https://www.ilo.org/wcmsp5/groups/public/---dgreports/---dcomm/documents/publication/wcms_686645.pdf

- Global budgets allocated to education could be more than doubled.[82]

- Or, global healthcare budgets could be increased by more than 70%.[83]

- Or, environmental investments could be multiplied almost twentyfold.[84]

- Or, hunger and malnutrition could be ended. [85]

- **...What are we waiting for?** [86]

---

82 Global Education Monitoring Report Team, 2018. "Global education monitoring report, 2019: Migration, displacement and education: building bridges, not walls". UNESCO. https://unesdoc.unesco.org/ark:/48223/pf0000265866

83 Emergo by UL, n.d. "Worldwide Spending on Healthcare". https://www.emergobyul.com/resources/worldwide-health-expenditures

84 United States Environmental Protection Agency, n.d. "EPA's Budget and Spending". https://www.epa.gov/planandbudget/budget

85 Multiple approaches exist to end hunger and reduce undernutrition through different investment packages, specific targets, measures, and policy pathways, leading to a wide range of costs. Estimates range from $7 billion to $265 billion per year.

   Shenggen Fan, 2018. "The multibillion dollar question: How much will it cost to end hunger and undernutrition?" ReliefWeb. https://reliefweb.int/report/world/multibillion-dollar-question-how-much-will-it-cost-end-hunger-and-undernutrition

86 Here is a useful summary of how IA can help governments: McKinsey, 2019. "How governments can harness the power of automation at scale". https://www.mckinsey.com/industries/public-sector/our-insights/how-governments-can-harness-the-power-of-automation-at-scale

Saving 10+ million lives per year

IA can do more than achieve tremendous efficiency gains and quality improvements. It also has the power to save lives, avoiding early deaths, and extending life expectancy. This is what we will demonstrate in this part of the book.

In 2017, around **56 million people died in the world**. The figure is roughly the same every year. An analysis of the top ten causes of death provides insights into how IA has the potential to reduce early deaths.[87]

---

87 World Health Organization, n.d. "WHO Mortality Database". https://www.who.int/healthinfo/mortality_data/en/

Share of deaths by cause in the world

Data refers to the specific cause of death, which is distinguished from risk factors for death, such as air pollution, diet and other lifestyle factors. This is shown by cause of death as the percentage of total deaths.

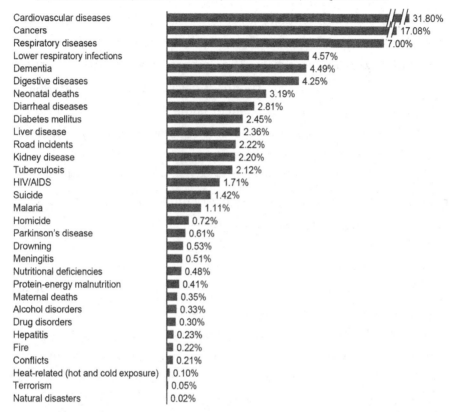

Cause	Percentage
Cardiovascular diseases	31.80%
Cancers	17.08%
Respiratory diseases	7.00%
Lower respiratory infections	4.57%
Dementia	4.49%
Digestive diseases	4.25%
Neonatal deaths	3.19%
Diarrheal diseases	2.81%
Diabetes mellitus	2.45%
Liver disease	2.36%
Road incidents	2.22%
Kidney disease	2.20%
Tuberculosis	2.12%
HIV/AIDS	1.71%
Suicide	1.42%
Malaria	1.11%
Homicide	0.72%
Parkinson's disease	0.61%
Drowning	0.53%
Meningitis	0.51%
Nutritional deficiencies	0.48%
Protein-energy malnutrition	0.41%
Maternal deaths	0.35%
Alcohol disorders	0.33%
Drug disorders	0.30%
Hepatitis	0.23%
Fire	0.22%
Conflicts	0.21%
Heat-related (hot and cold exposure)	0.10%
Terrorism	0.05%
Natural disasters	0.02%

Figure 1.3: Share of deaths by cause in the world in 2017
Source: figure built using the data from IHME, Global Burden of Disease[88]

---

88   IHME, Global Burden of Disease, accessed and extracted on October 2019.
     http://ghdx.healthdata.org/gbd-results-tool

1. Preventing deaths from non-communicable diseases through research

Non-communicable, chronic, long-term diseases cause more than 70% of deaths. These diseases are not passed from person to person and typically progress slowly. The largest killer in this category, responsible for one-third of all deaths, is cardiovascular disease, which affects the heart and arteries. Cancer is the second largest cause of death. It is followed by diabetes and several respiratory diseases. Beyond the non-communicable factor, a common denominator to these diseases is the essential resource needed to find a cure: **research**. IA's ability to assist with documentation and checks of research means it can play a crucial role in clinical trials.

Another characteristic of non-communicable diseases is that the recovery rate is higher when they are detected early. **Disease diagnosis** is an area where IA's machine learning can play a crucial role and make valuable contributions. For example, machine learning has shown the ability to analyze thousands of lung or breast scans and identify cancer with a success rate exceeding 80% – higher accuracy than achieved by doctors. Machine learning also has the advantage of speed. In essence, it performs scan diagnosis work in minutes (even seconds), whereas even experienced doctors require hours.

For example, **acute kidney injury (AKI) is responsible for an estimated two million deaths per year globally,** according to the University of Pittsburgh.[89] AKI is challenging to diagnose because it exhibits a number of various symptoms, including abnormal blood

---

89   Peerapornratana S., 2019. "Acute kidney injury from sepsis: current concepts, epidemiology, pathophysiology, prevention and treatment". https://www.kidney-international.org/article/S0085-2538(19)30601-5/pdf

pressure or blood volume. As a result, AKI is typically spotted only when it has reached a late stage. At that time, irreversible damage has occurred and the condition is either fatal or requires long-term dialysis.

The current method for detecting AKI includes a daily assessment of laboratory test results over several weeks. Using IA, DeepMind's **new approach uses a deep learning algorithm** trained on the anonymized data of 700,000 patients (e.g., demographics, health records, test data). This program can identify AKI two days earlier than the standard approach, using an app called STREAMS. It sends easy-to-read results and graphs directly to clinicians.[90] These capabilities provide the patient and their doctor with more time for critical treatment interventions.

2. Avoiding deaths due to medical errors

According to a recent study by Johns Hopkins, more than 250,000 people in the United States die every year because of medical errors, making it the third leading cause of death after heart disease and cancer.[91]

The tragic story of Emily Jerry vividly illustrates the impact of medical errors on the victims and their families.[92] Emily was two years old when she lost her life after a pharmacy technician filled her intravenous bag with more than 20 times the recommended dose of sodium chloride.

---

90   Nenad Tomašev et al., 2019. "A clinically applicable approach to continuous prediction of future acute kidney injury". Nature. https://www.nature.com/articles/s41586-019-1390-1

91   Ray Sipherd, 2018. "The third-leading cause of death in US most doctors don't want you to know about". CNBC. https://www.cnbc.com/2018/02/22/medical-errors-third-leading-cause-of-death-in-america.html

92   Emily Jerry Foundation. https://emilyjerryfoundation.org/emilys-story/

"Medical-care workers are dedicated, caring people, but they are human. And human beings make mistakes," said Emily's father. Precisely because it is not human, IA can check prescriptions and catch lapses in compliance with physician instructions and standard medical protocols (24/7, and with no tiredness).

Other medical applications of IA include the **remote monitoring of patients' health** in their hospital rooms in real time. Such systems collect patients visual information, body movement data, and vital data (such as heart rate or blood pressure) 24/7. They alert nurses in real time in case of emergency. Based on the data collected, the system can detect patterns and trends in each patient's health. For example, it predicts heart attacks, strokes, sepsis, and other serious complications. As a result, this type of IA-based system helps to free up the time of physicians from data collection while customizing the number of required nurse visits.

3. Reducing deaths from preventable causes in the Third World

One of the most shocking consequences of the disparity in resources between First World and Third World environments is the number of deaths in developing countries from avoidable causes. For example, about **1.6 million people died from diseases related to diarrhea in 2017**, putting it in the top 10 causes of death. In some Third World countries, diarrhea is one of the largest killers.

A major contributing factor in these deaths is a **shortage of physicians**. Caused by demand outstripping supply, this shortage is a growing concern in many countries around the world. The World Health Organization (WHO) estimates that there is a global shortage of 4.3 million physicians, nurses, and other health professionals.[93] The nations with critical shortages of physicians and other health care workers are shown in Figure 1.4.

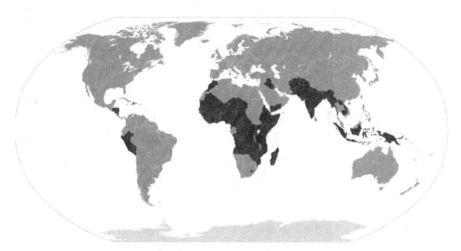

Figure 1.4: Nations identified with critical shortages of physicians and other health care workers
Source: Wikiwand[94]

Technology powered by IA can help to address the shortage of health professionals in various ways. For example, **IA provides global access to physicians and caregivers** through applications like Babylon.[95] Another application called Tissue Analytics instantly diagnoses chronic wounds, burns, or skin conditions just by taking a photo from a smartphone.[96] The technology, launched in 2015 and publicly available on Android/iOS, has been so successful that over 150 facilities were already using it in early 2020. These programs

---

93 Yolanda Smith, n.d. "Physician Shortage". News Medical. https://www.news-medical.net/health/Physician-Shortage.aspx

94 Wikiwand, accessed May 2020. https://www.wikiwand.com/en/Physician_supply

95 Babylon website: https://www.gpathand.nhs.uk/

96 Tissue Analytics website: https://www.tissue-analytics.com/

make it possible for anyone to access free online diagnosis and care support, from anywhere, at any time.

Because of the lack of quality roads and infrastructure, **accessing remote locations is another challenge**. In order to address this issue, intelligent drone delivery helps to deliver vaccines and other medical treatments to the right place at the right time. In 2017, for the first time, a newborn's life was saved thanks to a vaccine delivered by drone. Zipline International uses intelligent drones to deliver blood, platelets, fresh plasma, and other vital medical supplies to remote locations. By 2019, Zipline International was operating in Rwanda, Ghana, and Tanzania. It had already made 13,000 blood deliveries and flown more than 1,000,000 km. In Rwanda, more than 65% of blood deliveries use Zipline drones. The drones weigh approximately 10 kg and can deliver medical supplies up to 80 km in 45 minutes.

You can refer to the **"IA use case library"** presented at the end of the book for more examples of applications of IA in the health sector.

4. Reducing traffic fatalities with IA-assisted and driverless applications

Road accidents incur a high death toll in developed and emerging countries alike, claiming 1.2 million lives in 2017. Researchers estimate that self-driving cars could reduce these traffic fatalities by up to 94 percent by eliminating human error as the main cause of those accidents.[97]

---

97   US Department of Transportation, n.d. NHTSA. https://www.nhtsa.gov/sites/nhtsa.dot.gov/files/documents/13069a-ads2.0_090617_v9a_tag.pdf

IA benefits in reducing traffic fatalities can be realized even before the widespread adoption of autonomous driving by using IA to assist and monitor human drivers. For example, IA technology can be used to detect and alert about drowsiness or dangerous driver behavior using an internal camera.[98] Already, adaptable kits exist that can change virtually any car into an autonomous vehicle.[99]

We believe that the combination of IA technologies has the potential to reduce early deaths and extend healthy life expectancy conservatively by 10–30%. That is, using an average of 20% of the **annual fatality rate of 56 million people, 14 million early deaths could be avoided every year**. This is the equivalent of the populations of Switzerland and Singapore put together.

---

98 Pascal Bornet, 2019. "Vehicle Action Prediction, using Artificial Intelligence".
    LinkedIn. https://www.linkedin.com/posts/pascalbornet_artificialintelligence-datascience-technology-activity-6515121577095458816-Mtmo

99 Pascal Bornet, 2019. "The first universal self-driving add-on kit".
    LinkedIn. https://www.linkedin.com/posts/pascalbornet_artificialintelligence-innovation-technology-activity-6517034557676584960-TpJ8

Building a society more resilient to crises

"COVID-19 (has) achieved in six to eight weeks what the evangelists of automation have not managed... for more than five years."

Ilan Oshri, Professor at the University of Auckland's Graduate School of Management

Improving the resilience of our world to pandemics and crises has become crucial. Let us take the example of the coronavirus crisis, also called the COVID-19 crisis. In our view, this crisis evidenced **the need for more resilient systems to support our society**. Our health and economic systems, mainly managed by a human workforce, have been put under extreme stress. Hospitals were desperately in need, while economies were falling into downturns.

In order to avoid overburdening the capacities of hospitals with too many infected people, and to stop the spread of the virus, most countries decided to lock down their populations at home. Four billion people around the world were encouraged or forced to work from home. This resulted in many organizations and schools operating remotely. Companies that were more digitalized and automated have overcome or at least coped better with this crisis. Still, most organizations faced problems of broken processes, resulting in issues like:

1. Missing cash

During the crisis, **many businesses and customers faced cash flow issues**; cash flow management became more vital than ever. If a business was unable to collect its accounts receivable on time, its cash flow was significantly impacted. For many companies, the collection and application of cash was a manual task, and the lack of digitization and automation of cash processes caused the failure of millions of companies around the world.

Only organizations that automated key parts of their accounts receivable processes were able to lessen the impact. For example, based on our own experience, automating the cash allocation process allowed a major manufacturing company based in Korea to survive. It decreased the number of outstanding invoices by more than 50% (a few hundreds of millions of dollars) in less than three weeks.

2. Discontinued operations

Service operations and corporate functions (e.g., logistics, human resources, customer services) were also strongly impacted. Providing access and connectivity to systems and hardware, and managing their performance remotely, has been challenging for many organizations. A famous hospital in Italy faced pressing issues due to the lack of automation of its physicians' work scheduling process. This had an impact on its capacity to accept new patients and save more lives. The crisis was a catalyst to **provide access to systems to most employees and customers remotely and securely**. Winning organizations have been the ones that digitalized end-to-end journeys at the onset and converted paper-based data into digital information at the source.

3. Missed revenues and dissatisfied customers

Several organizations, especially in retail, have been **forced to discontinue some lines of business** or close storefronts. Many were not digitalized and not accessible to clients online. When physical branches and stores closed, millions of customers around the world were confronted with the absence of service availability and the inability to connect with their usual providers. This was equally applicable to organizations in the business-to-business space where order intake and order management was often handled manually. At the same time, their digitally enabled competitors were able to leverage this opportunity. They sustained or even increased their revenue while they grew their market share.

For example, organizations that were leveraging intelligent chatbots for customer service were able to mitigate the lack of available human call center agents. They **routed the traffic towards their digital workforce**, available 24/7 and consistently across communication channels. The most successful organizations brought their customer services to the next level by leveraging self-service mechanisms, social media-based service, and sentiment analysis.

4. Demotivated employees

Working from home became a challenge: isolation, lack of support, constant distractions, limited ability to unplug from work, and anxiety due to the crisis. This impacted employees' motivation, efficiency, and work-life balance, created stress, and sometimes even affected their physical and mental health. Leading companies were able to provide their employees with safety, connectivity, and remote work tools. They **leveraged analytics to support process transparency and remote**

monitoring of the work executed. They also utilized downtime to initiate re-skilling and training on key topics, including future skills such as robotic process automation and analytics. Organizations that invested in reskilling employees to manage automated processes were typically able to recover more quickly.

IA is able to operate our systems reliably. In addition, it has the power to deliver business processes with limited human intervention. Our experience of the COVID-19 crisis suggests that to make our society more resilient for future crises, we should increase the use of IA.

We have discussed the great potential IA has for our society in many ways. The purpose of this section is not to provide accurate estimates. Rather, it is **to stimulate creativity and impart a sense of urgency in applying greater degrees of IA** to the landscape of work, health, and global citizenry.

IA has so much potential to improve our world... what are we waiting for?

Key takeaways of Part One

- Even though IA emerged less than ten years ago, its potential has already been proven in global companies like JP Morgan, Unilever, and Netflix. IA has the potential to **increase an organization's efficiency** by 20–60%. IA's impact is compelling, targeting both top (e.g., through enhanced customer experience) and bottom lines (e.g., by enabling higher efficiencies).

- We demonstrate that IA has become **a business imperative**. Adapting legacy organizations to new digital technologies is difficult for older, more established enterprises. This is most likely due to the cost of change and to the complexity of managing change. For this reason, about half of the S&P 500 is likely to be replaced over the next ten years. To help our readers rethink their businesses, we present two recent impactful transformation concepts leveraging IA: new digital business building and data ecosystem platforms. In addition, the first companies to adopt IA can generate benefits before their competitors. It provides them with a competitive advantage, resulting in higher market share and in the capacity to save money that can be reinvested in further IA transformations and service innovation. These compelling benefits are available to all organizations across industries and functions. The reader is provided with **a compelling library of IA use cases** to support this assertion and enable further study (refer to "Asset: IA use cases library" at the end of the book).

- We present how IA can improve the **employee experience**. IA helps to take away the most mundane work activities, and it helps to augment employee capabilities. As a result, IA improves employee engagement and creates a healthier workplace and work-life balance while boosting employee performance. To support this objective, companies can leverage IA to analyze the work activities performed by their employees and use three levers to improve them. They can either augment (increase the value of work activities delivered by employees), automate or abandon work activities (e.g., inefficient work practices such as abundant emails). We call this approach the "Triple-A artifact", and we explain how IA powers it. The tools used to implement this approach include value-add AI-based applications, personalized dashboards to monitor healthy work habits, and AI-based coaching assistants.

- **Customers** are the primary beneficiaries of IA as they get better services and products at lower prices. Currently, the most representative use cases relate to innovative and customized products and services, and to highly responsive and omnichannel customer services available 24/7. Levers such as self-service platforms, customer data analysis, cognitive agents, and task automation significantly improve the customer experience. Based on our experience, 80% of a customer journey can become digitally touchless and fully omnichannel. As a result, we have seen companies increase customer satisfaction by over 15 percentage points as measured by NPS while reducing the contact center workload by over 50%.

- IA has substantial benefits to bring to **our society at large**, especially in healthcare and education. We demonstrate that IA has the potential to save 10+ million lives by avoiding early deaths. It supports clinical trials and disease diagnosis, avoids medical errors, and reduces deaths from preventable causes, especially in developing countries. In addition, IA can avoid $10 trillion of losses every year (e.g., by reducing fraud, errors, and work-related diseases and accidents). These savings could be used to triple global budgets for education, finance the protection of our planet, or eliminate world hunger. IA also helps to dramatically increase the resilience of our financial and health systems to future crises and pandemics.

- At the end of the book (refer to "Asset: IA use cases library"), we offer an extensive **library of IA use cases** organized by business function and industry. This is the largest library of use cases publicly available (more than 500 IA use cases).

PART TWO:
IA TECHNOLOGIES EXPLAINED

A framework for explaining the power of IA

IA automates knowledge workers' activities by mimicking **four main capabilities**:

- **Vision** (e.g., viewing the environment, recognizing objects and signs),

- **Execution** (e.g., typing, clicking, filling in forms, and authenticating),

- **Language** (e.g., using language to read, speak, write, and interact), and

- **Thinking and learning** (e.g., analyzing, creating insight, predicting, making decisions, and adjusting).

As shown in Figure 2.1, each of the four main capabilities is enabled by technology. Some technologies might be able to perform only a single capability (e.g., robotics can only execute). In contrast, some others, like machine learning, might cut across several (language, vision, and thinking & learning). As technologies constantly advance, this framework is ever-evolving.

Note that the human capabilities related to the senses of touch,[100] taste, and smell[101] are applied only in rare use cases by IA and are therefore not covered in this book.

Figure 2.1: the four IA capabilities
Source: © Bornet, Barkin & Wirtz

---

100 Watch this video of the first world's first haptic telerobotic system. It transmits realistic touch feedback to the user located anywhere in the world. https://youtu.be/ZJh6T5TADsc

101 One of the rare examples where machine learning is used to support smelling and tasting senses: Esat Dedezade, 2019. "Meet the world's first AI-created whisky". https://news.microsoft.com/europe/features/meet-the-worlds-first-ai-created-whisky/

As we will explain in Part Three, IA transformations are, above all, business transformations, where people and business goals are at the center. Technology comes as an enabler.

In the following sections, we will present each of the IA capabilities, the key technologies they are using, their characteristics, examples of use cases, and evolutionary trends. We pay particular attention to **equipping you with the information you would need while choosing amongst these technologies or going through a vendor selection process**. Finally, we will explain how these technologies can be brought together successfully into a comprehensive IA implementation roadmap and how they will fit into an organization's existing IT landscape.

Capability 1: Vision

"The eyes of the digital workforce."

Figure 2.2: The vision capability within the IA framework

Description and applications

This capability allows computers to perceive, interpret, and understand elements of the visual world, like environments, objects, signs, or letters. In the context of IA, it mainly enables the processing of documents, images, videos, and biometric information. For example, it helps to automate the processing of invoices or to identify anomalies, such as signs of diseases on medical images.

Key technologies

The overarching technology is called computer vision (CV). While it used to be coded as a set of rules, computer vision is nowadays mainly enabled by deep learning techniques. In the context of IA, the four key technologies presently using computer vision are optical character recognition (OCR), intelligent character recognition (ICR), image and video analysis, and biometrics. We show how they bring value in document capture and processing, generating insights from images and videos, and identifying identities.

1. Optical character recognition (OCR)

1.1. Character recognition

This technology is used to identify and digitize alphabetical or numerical characters presented in images (e.g., a scanned copy of a contract). It avoids this data needing to be typed manually by a human operator on a computer. These digitalized characters can then be used by other digital technologies leveraging, for example, smart workflow platforms, natural language processing, or machine learning.

1.2. OCR

OCR has been used for the last two decades for this purpose. The limits of using OCR as a standalone technology to capture and process documents is its inability to manage unstructured documents. This means documents that are not presented using exactly the same standards and layout (e.g., invoices that are different from one vendor to another) won't be processed accurately by OCR. ICR, as discussed in the next bullet, is needed in that case. This explains why most OCR solutions on the market have now been repackaged into ICR solutions, broadening their capabilities and improving the accuracy of the outcome.

2. Intelligent character recognition (ICR)[102]

Also called intelligent data capture or intelligent document processing, ICR combines the use of OCR to digitize documents, natural language processing to extract and interpret information (refer to "Capability 3: Language"), and machine learning for pattern recognition (refer to "Capability 4: Thinking & learning"). **This technology unlocks the capacity for IA to manage and process scanned images or documents** (e.g., invoices, people's IDs, contracts, financial information, receipts). Such a platform allows the processing of about 80% of documents to be automated. Exceptions (e.g., documents in a different language, with low image quality or presenting a higher level of complexity) are handled manually. The system can be trained in a few months, using a supervised learning technique. This approach involves feeding the system with a set of data comprising the scanned documents and their expected output (digitalized characters).

---

102 Popular technology vendors are Abbyy, Taiger, Workfusion and Antwork.

Case illustration 2.1: Use case of intelligent character recognition (ICR)

ICR helped to automate the processing of 400,000 invoices annually

Context: A manufacturing company used to receive over 400,000 invoices per annum from more than 500 suppliers. It used to have 29 people keying in these invoices all day – a highly mundane task.

This invoice data capture is a complex process to automate because invoices are unstructured data. All invoices contain largely the same information, but depending on the vendor, the layout is different. For example, all invoices present a price, a date, and a vendor name. But this information is rarely displayed the same way. For example, the vendor's name might be displayed at the top or bottom of the page, while the dates might use different formats. Hence, there is a need for a more intelligent technology than a standard OCR application.

Solution: Intelligent Character Recognition (ICR) technology is a solution that uses Optical Character Recognition (OCR) to recognize the characters on a scanned document or image, natural language processing (NLP) to understand the words and their meaning, and machine learning to identify patterns and learn over time. This technology has been on the market for five years and is continuously improving.

Outcome: Using this solution, this company was able to reduce the invoice capture workload by more than 70% in about four months. As a result, the 29-person team was redeployed. Specifically, six people were upskilled to manage the redesigned process. However, their role changed completely from repetitively keying in invoices to training the IA system, performing quality checks, and handling exceptions. Twenty-one people were retrained to assume roles in other departments and worked on more interesting and value-add tasks such as business performance commentaries, insights, and analysis. Finally, two employees were retrained to work in the transformation team in charge of deploying similar transformations to other processes.

3. Image and video analysis

Image and video analysis is the extraction of meaningful information from digital images. It is used to generate insights that can be leveraged in triggering automated actions (e.g., decisions, alarms, actions). It includes both static images and videos. Key benefits include processing speed and accuracy, providing the capacity to process an enormous amount of images and videos in a short time. The range of applications is broad, across several industries, including medical image diagnosis, retail store automation, business processes documentation, and autonomous vehicles.

3.1. Medical image diagnosis[103]

The technology mainly helps with the **detection of the presence or absence of medical conditions that are visible in images** like CAT scans, X-rays, MRIs, and other clinical images. For example, image analysis is used for breast cancer diagnosis. Current methods for assessing breast cancer risk are based on markers such as age, family history of breast and ovarian cancer, hormonal and reproductive factors, breast density, and visual examination of mammograms. However, these markers are only weakly correlated with breast cancer. To solve this issue, a team from MIT (CSAIL) and Massachusetts General Hospital (MGH) created a new deep learning model based on image analysis. It can predict from a mammogram (X-ray radiography) if a patient is likely to develop breast cancer in the coming five years. Instead of having physicians spending valuable time scrutinizing X-ray images, the new program helps in delivering faster and more

---

103 The main technology vendors on the market are Philips, Siemens and IBM Watson. New entrants with innovative solutions are Arterys, Gauss Surgical, and Zebra Medical Vision.

accurate outcomes. Trained on mammograms and known outcomes from over 60,000 patients, the model learned the subtle patterns in breast tissue that are precursors to malignant tumors.

Another example is Chester, the first AI radiology assistant. This mobile application, which is free and available to all users on Android/iOS, can diagnose 14 diseases from chest X-ray pictures. The system has been designed to be used as a reference to confirm or aid in diagnosis. Accuracy is estimated to be 80%.[104]

3.2. Retail store automation

When applied in the retail industry, image and video analysis are used to support **understanding of customer behavior, automate assessment of the level of product inventories, automate check-out, and analyze surveillance videos**. In 2018, Amazon created the first automated supermarket, called Amazon Go. In this store, cameras are placed in the ceiling above the aisles and on shelves. Supported by computer vision, these cameras can determine when an object is taken from a shelf and who has taken it; it then gets added to the customer's virtual basket. If an item is returned to the shelf, the system is also able to remove that item from the basket. The network of cameras allows the platform to track people in the store at all times, counting them, and providing traffic analytics. Some detectors can also connect to people's phones to propose customized promotions based on demographic or behavioral data. Cameras and detectors also ensure that the right items are billed

---

104 Pascal Bornet, 2019. "Chester, the first AI Radiologist Assistant".
    LinkedIn. https://www.linkedin.com/posts/pascalbornet_artificialintelligence-technology-
    innovation-activity-6521401764753829888-GuSo

to the right shopper when clients walk out. The technology used in Amazon Go is very advanced (and expensive).

Even though they are not as complete, **some affordable technology solutions are already available on the market to support stores**. In 2017, startup Alpoly launched a similar application that can be deployed by all retail businesses, simply leveraging existing surveillance cameras in stores.[105] The solution automates the store check-out and re-stocking. In addition, a mobile app leverages clients' purchase history to guide them in any store to find their favorite items (using preloaded store maps).

Another existing solution, called V-Count, leverages surveillance cameras to provide customer traffic analytics and generate real-time promotions based on customers' behavioral data.[106]

---

105 Fast Company, 2017, "This AI Startup Wants To Automate Every Store Like Amazon Go". https://www.fastcompany.com/40493622/this-ai-startup-wants-to-automate-every-store-like-amazon-go

106 Pascal Bornet, 2019. "V-Count". https://www.linkedin.com/posts/pascalbornet_innovation-iot-technology-activity-6492994239268524032-6N4P

Figure 2.3: Computer vision supporting shop automation by simply using surveillance cameras
Source: Courtesy of Alpoly[107]

3.3. Business processes documentation[108]

Existing process documentation is a key requirement before improving or automating a process. Typically achieved through observation and process walkthroughs, manual process documentation is very time- and resource-consuming. **The technology leverages computer**

---

107 Pascal Bornet, 2019. "Intelligent Shopping now available for all shops". https://youtu.be/adPMISvy8Qo

108 Technology vendors on this market are Epiplex or Legito.

vision to detect the applications and objects used by computer users. The user just presses a button at the start and at the end of performing a process. The output is an automatically generated flowchart, including screenshots of each step of the process. Such solutions started to come onto the market 15 years ago.

3.4. Autonomous vehicles

The technology enables **self-driving cars** to understand their environment using cameras, lidar, radar, and ultrasonic sensors. It helps detect objects, lane markings, signs, and traffic signals. As an outcome, image analysis helps autonomous cars to navigate safely, anticipating and avoiding obstacles.[109]

4. Biometrics

Biometrics refers to the measurement and statistical analysis of people's unique physical and behavioral characteristics. Most of the current applications of biometrics are based on computer vision.

Compared to a systematic physical check of people, biometrics recognition offers advantages of ease of use, convenience, and rapidity. In addition, it offers a high level of reliability, as biometrics are non-transferable (they can't be stolen like a password) and change little over a user's life.

The technology is mainly used for identification and access control, or for identifying individuals who are under surveillance. Techniques used in biometrics recognition include facial recognition, fingerprints,

---

109 In this video, you can watch what a Tesla's full autopilot (IA-based) sees: https://youtu.be/U1EyUGI7A48

finger geometry (the size and position of fingers), iris recognition[110], vein recognition, retina scanning, and DNA matching.

Biometrics is helping to deliver tremendous benefits, not only by automating the authentication of employees to their workplace and workstations but also by transforming immigration and customs checks.

For example, from 2022, most Singapore residents will be able to go through immigration checkpoints without taking out their passports. With an Automated Border Control system, they will be identified on the go by biometric markers that include irises and facial features. This new solution is expected to reduce the immigration processing time by about 40 percent.[111] Building such a system is an achievement and will be a world first. Massive amounts of data need to be retrieved and processed in real time to decide whether or not to grant entry. Ts transformation will also change how the 6,000 border control officers across different job functions work.

An exciting example of facial recognition technology application is PimEyes. This technology helps people find their pictures on the Internet to defend themselves from scammers, identity thieves, or other illegal use of people's images.[112]

---

110 Watch the first iris tracking technology and read how it opens the door to amazing applications: https://youtu.be/vE-T6DUaZ1w

111 Vanessa Gu, 2019. "Singapore's vision for hands-free immigration clearance". GovInsider. https://govinsider.asia/innovation/singapores-ica-hands-free-immigration/

112 Dave Gershgorn, 2020. "This Simple Facial Recognition Search Engine Can Track You Down Across the Internet". https://onezero.medium.com/this-simple-facial-recognition-search-engine-can-track-you-down-across-the-internet-518c7129e454

Capability 2: Execution

"The hands and legs of the digital workforce."

Figure 2.4: The execution capability within the IA framework
Source: © Bornet, Barkin & Wirtz

Description and applications

Execution (or action) is about "doing", actually accomplishing step-by-step process tasks in digital environments (e.g., on computers or servers). Such activities include typing text, clicking on buttons, routing information, filling in forms, and authenticating users. Typical automated processes involve logging in and out of systems, compiling data and preparing reports, reconciling data, sending emails, enabling interfaces between systems, and performing spreadsheet analyses.

This capability is a foundation for end-to-end automated business process delivery. It acts as a glue, connecting the technologies across capabilities. For example, it can support the collection of data through vision or language capabilities (e.g., a historical report on swimsuit sales). It can then convey this data to the "think & learn" capability, to create insight (e.g., analyze the correlation between sales and weekly weather forecast). This insight can then be used as a basis for decision making (e.g., design specific promotion campaigns during the rainy weeks). It can then help execute a resulting action (e.g., automatically schedule these promotions in the systems).

Key technologies

The three key technologies supporting this capability include smart workflow, low-code platforms, and robotic process automation (RPA). Each of these technologies is described in the following subsections. Because these technologies can be used alternatively, we also explain when to use RPA versus smart workflow platforms.

1. Smart workflow[113]

A smart workflow platform is a prepackaged solution that is configured to support business processes by driving specific data and action flows. A smart workflow platform helps to automate predefined standard processes (e.g., client onboarding for an energy company, or patient billing for hospitals). It **includes data entry and data routing** according to a predefined flow. It **involves rules, automated steps, manual steps, and decision points**. As an illustration, Figure 2.5 presents a smart workflow platform to support a recruitment process.[114]

Figure 2.5: A smart workflow platform to manage a recruitment process
Source: Courtesy of Pega Systems

---

113 Popular vendors on the market include Pega, Appian and Mendix.

114 Pega Systems, n.d. "Award-winning case management and BPM for continuous operational excellence". https://www.pega.com/products/pega-platform/case-management

2. Low-code platforms

Low-code platforms offer the capacity for business users (also called "citizen developers") to **develop their own programs using a user-friendly visual development environment** (e.g., drag-and-drop). Low-code platforms allow anyone in a company to create applications without specific coding skills. For example, they enable any user to create interfaces between systems and workflows, such as forms to collect data, reports, and approval processes.[115]

Most platforms on the market include now both the smart workflow and low-code technologies components. Most vendors propose prepackaged solutions specific by industry and function. Let us take, for example, the claims process for an insurance company. For this process, the platform allows the insurance company's client to record their claims online. The claims are then routed, through the platform, for approval to the program in charge of checking their eligibility. Based on the outcome, the claim may be automatically settled. If it is not, an email is automatically sent by the platform to the client to explain the reason for the rejection. If there is any issue in the process, another email is sent to an employee to resolve it. Finally, these platforms include some analytics functionalities. They allow analysis of the performance of the process and the time taken by each step, and the identification of areas of improvement.

---

115   Here is an example in action of a low-code platform: Mendix, 2018. "Developing in Mendix Low-code Platform". YouTube. https://youtu.be/rXR6IFxVOXE

3. Robotic process automation (RPA)[116]

This involves a configurable software tool (also called a "software robot") that uses business rules and sequences of actions. It interacts with the computer the same way a human does and automatically completes processes in any number of different applications. **Effectively, any action that a person can do on a computer using a mouse or keyboard can be accomplished by such a "robot".** It is typically used to automate routine tasks such as copying, pasting, opening applications, sending emails, and more. Simply think of it like a super-robust Excel macro that can work on any application (not only Excel), which is resilient and infinitely scalable (unlike Excel macros).

We usually apply RPA to perform transactional, repetitive, rule-based actions in a digitalized environment. RPA cannot think, see, nor understand. These robots are sometimes referred to as "dumb robots", only able to reproduce what they have been developed for. However, rather than "dumb", we like to think of these robots as "well behaved". Indeed, they enable rapid, highly accurate processing. Figure 2.6 shows an RPA configuration supporting a loan application process where the robot applies a rule resulting in three different actions depending on the amount of loan requested.

---

116 Popular vendors on the market include UiPath, Automation Anywhere and Blue Prism.

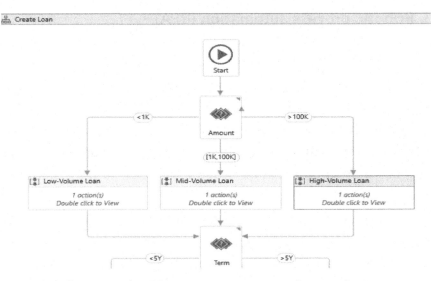

Figure 2.6: Illustration of an RPA program automating a loan application process
Source: Courtesy of UiPath[117]

RPA helps to produce two types of automation: assisted (also called attended) and unassisted (or unattended) automation. **Assisted automation** (also referred to as "robotic desktop automation", or RDA) runs on people's desktops and executes actions hand-in-hand with the employee. For example, from our experience, any call center agent needs to open 5 to 8 different applications when serving a client during a call. Opening these applications and looking for the name of the client in each of them takes 10 to 20% of the total time of a call. RDA helps to pre-open these applications at the right screen. When the call is finished, another time-consuming activity for the agent is to document the actions taken during the call for traceability purposes. Similarly, for this task, RDA is able to note down each action taken by the agent during the call to serve the customer.

---

117 UiPath, 2020. "UiPath 2020.4 Monthly Update: A Studio Edition for Everyone".
   https://www.uipath.com/blog/april-2020-uipath-monthly-update

In contrast, **unassisted automation** works in the background and does not typically involve interactions with employees. For example, it is used to manage the client information collected from webforms to feed a workflow system while onboarding clients in a bank. Unassisted robots can work autonomously 24/7, usually through queues of cases, only alerting an employee when something goes wrong.

Configuring RPA programs is quite user-friendly. It usually requires a few weeks of training for a business user to master most of the functionalities. In addition, most tools will involve a process task recorder to increase the speed of development. After the user presses a button, the program records the tasks performed by the user on the computer, and it uses this recording to precode the robot. This will help to generate about 10 to 40% of the code automatically. The cost of an RPA license is quite low (from free to $8,000 per year). For these reasons, RPA was heavily hyped in the years from 2015 to 2019. Attracted by the promise of low-hanging fruit, companies rushed to implement these programs. Unfortunately, likening RPA to Excel macros, most organizations have done it without proper governance and program management (refer to Part Three of the book on implementation success factors). As a result, many RPA projects failed, negatively impacting the reputation of business automation.

For the next five years, due to the large volume of RPA-suitable tasks in organizations, its ease of implementation, and its low cost, we expect this technology will remain a key focus for organizations. For further detail, we invite you to look at Barkin's LinkedIn Learning course titled "Introducing Robotic Process Automation",[118] in which he dives further into the details, capabilities, and applications of RPA.

4. When to use RPA versus smart workflow platforms?

These technologies can be used interchangeably. The leading practice is to use smart workflow and low-code platforms as a foundation of the overall automation platform. RPA is used when IA needs to be integrated with legacy systems or automation of bespoke processes. Here is the explanation:

For a well-defined, standard, and stable process involving hand-offs between people and systems, it is preferable to use a **smart workflow platform**. Such platforms offer pre-developed modules. These are ready-to-use automation programs customized by industry and by business function (e.g., onboarding of clients in retail banking). In addition, they are modular. For example, a module might include a form for client data collection, and another module might support an approval workflow. In addition, these modules can be linked to external systems and databases using connectors, such as application programming interfaces (APIs), which enable resilient data connectivity. Hence, with smart workflows, there is no need to develop bespoke internal and external data bridges. This integration creates a system with high resiliency and integrity. In addition, the standardization by industry and function of these platforms, combined with the low-code functionality, helps to accelerate the implementation.

---

118 I. Barkin, 2019. LinkedIn Learning, "Introducing Robotic Process Automation".
  https://www.linkedin.com/learning/introducing-robotic-process-automation/

There are no ready-to-use modules with **RPA**. Most of the development is bespoke, and all process flows need to be built almost from scratch. The connections also need to be constructed. This results in a more flexible design and implementation of the programs developed, which can fit with more specific business requirements. The key advantage of RPA is that it allows the creation of automation programs that can involve legacy systems (e.g., those which can't use APIs) or address non-standard requirements (e.g., onboarding of clients for a broker insurance company under Singapore regulations). However, with RPA, the lack of native integration amongst the components has weaknesses. For example, it involves less robustness, weaker data integrity, and lower resilience to process changes. If one part of an RPA program fails, the whole end-to-end process is stopped.

As an outcome, based on our experience, the leading practice is to use low-code and smart workflow platforms as a foundation of the overall automation platform. In contrast, RPA is used for any integration of the overall platform with legacy systems or for automation of bespoke processes.

Capability 3: Language

"The ears and mouth of the digital workforce."

Figure 2.7: The language capability within the IA framework
© Bornet, Barkin & Wirtz

Description and applications

This capability gives machines the ability to read, speak, write, interact, interpret, and derive meaning from human language. In the context of IA, it mainly concerns language interactions with employees, clients, suppliers, and partners through diverse channels, including phone, messaging, and interactions with smart devices. Key functionalities include text translation, information extraction, information summary, information categorization (e.g., spam filters), sentiment analysis, speech-to-text, text-to-speech, predictive text typing, or voice understanding. For example, machine translation helps to overcome barriers due to foreign languages. Google Translate is used by 500 million people every day to understand more than 100 world languages.

Key technologies

The overarching technology is called natural language processing (NLP). While NLP is theoretically focused on the processing of language when received (i.e., read or interpreted), natural language generation (NLG) is the expression of a language in the form text or speech. To simplify our presentation, and as commonly accepted in the IA community, we will use NLP, by default, to describe the concept of both processing and generation of language.

While NLP used to be coded as a set of rules, it is nowadays mainly enabled by deep learning techniques. Large amounts of labeled data help the system identify relevant correlations between words and sentences. Language is broken down into shorter elemental pieces to teach the machine to understand their relationships. By doing this, the computer can ascertain the meaning behind a sentence.

In the context of IA, the key four technologies presently using NLP are intelligent chatbots, unstructured information management, sentiment analysis, and speech analytics.

1. Intelligent chatbots[119]

Chatbots have been around since 1966. But over the last decade, machine learning and especially deep learning technology have propelled their capabilities to an entirely new level. By 2023, the number of chatbots is anticipated to surpass the number of humans in the world.[120] As proof of the speed of technological progress, chatbot technology has, in a very few years, become so capable that it can be easily confused with humans. The more advanced chat technology can seamlessly use several communication channels such as messaging (e.g., Slack, Facebook), SMS, text, and voice (e.g., voice-based assistants such as Siri, Alexa).

There are two key types of chatbots: one powered by a set of rules (basic chatbots), and the other powered by deep learning (called intelligent chatbots or cognitive agents). The use of chatbots covers a wide range of fields. These include front-office processes such as sales, services, and support, and back-office functions such as human resources and IT helpdesks. Chatbots can answer questions, converse, collect information, schedule appointments, and much more.

The most advanced type of chatbot is called a "**cognitive agent**". On top of the standard chatbot capabilities described above, cognitive agents include the ability to learn from conversations between people, execute actions (like processing changes in systems), and improve themselves over time. In addition, they can observe people's reactions using a webcam, recognize sentiments, and adjust their

---

119 Popular technology vendors include Nuance, IPSoft, and Kore.ai.

120 Sarah Perez, 2019. "Voice assistants in use to triple to 8 billion by 2023". TechCrunch. https://techcrunch.com/2019/02/12/report-voice-assistants-in-use-to-triple-to-8-billion-by-2023/

behavior accordingly. Each conversation can be captured, analyzed, and aggregated to deliver real-time insights.

A **typical interaction between a human and a cognitive agent** using natural language processing is sequenced as follows:

1. A human talks to the cognitive agent;

2. A sensor (e.g., microphone) captures the audio;

3. The speech is converted into text using speech-to-text transcription;

4. The text is processed as data to create an outcome (e.g., build a reply, insight, or prediction);

5. The outcome is generated in the form of text;

6. The text is converted into speech using a text-to-speech transcription, enabling the machine to respond to the human in spoken language.

Figure 2.8: A digital healthcare assistant delivering care to more patients at lower costs
Source: courtesy of Soul Machines[121]

Examples of uses of cognitive agents include Jamie, designed by ANZ Bank in New Zealand. It is able to help onboard new clients and guide them through the bank's main services. It answers their questions and acts for them (for example, it can order a new credit card).[122] Another example, presented in Figure 2.8, is the project "Digital Healthcare for Tomorrow". Dr. Lance O'Sullivan, a public health advocate and founder of iMoko, developed a solution for delivering more care to more patients at lower costs, in the form of a digital healthcare assistant. We recommend you watch the video provided in the footnotes section.[123] Another well-known case is from the Swedish appliance company SEB. It uses a cognitive agent for both its IT help desk (supporting 15,000 employees) and its customer service department (supporting 1 million

---

121 Soul Machines, 2018. "Digital Healthcare for Tomorrow". https://youtu.be/D2cRUAZm2mc

122 Soul Machines, 2018. "Jamie's first 100 days". YouTube. https://youtu.be/eyoBgNY1KA0

123 Soul Machines, 2018. "Digital Healthcare for Tomorrow".
   YouTube. https://youtu.be/D2cRUAZm2mc

customers). Case illustration 2.1 shows an example of cognitive agent implementation at a hotel chain.

Google Duplex is a recent and highly publicized example of the most cutting-edge use case of this technology (we recommend you watch the video provided in the footnote). Released in 2018, this program is able to conduct a phone call transaction in the same way a human would. The example shown was of Google Duplex booking appointments in a hair salon and a restaurant. People receiving the calls were unaware that they were speaking to a chatbot.[124]

Case illustration 2.2: A cognitive agent implementation

A cognitive agent helped to improve client satisfaction while reducing employee turnover significantly

Context. A hotel chain needed to manage more than 20,000 client interactions per day through emails, calls, messages, and social media. This workload used to be managed by a team of 240 customer care agents servicing clients 24/7, mainly supporting sales, room reservations, inquiries, and after-sales. This team was facing low employee morale and high employee attrition, with an annual turnover of 40%. The low morale was mainly due to high and uneven workload, work pressure, and long shifts. These problems resulted in low service quality, rated less than 5 out of 10 by the chain's customers. In order to solve this situation, the hotel chain decided to launch a digital transformation effort, including the implementation of a cognitive agent.

---

124 Google, 2018, "Google Duplex: A.I. Assistant Calls Local Businesses To Make Appointments". https://youtu.be/D5VN56jQMWM

Solution. The company built a cognitive agent able to dialogue consistently across channels (e.g., emails, messaging, voice, and social media). This technology was also able to learn from observing conversations between people and to improve itself over time (using machine learning). It could execute actions (like processing changes in systems) and recognize users using their voice or face (using biometrics). It could also understand emotions by watching users through webcams. Its look and behavior were designed to be very similar to those of human agents. This increased acceptance of the cognitive agent by clients and improved their personal connection with it.

Outcomes. After a 3-month transformation project, the hotel chain was able to enjoy the following improvements:

- Client satisfaction score increased from 5/10 to 9/10, with improved reactivity and quality;

- Employee morale improved, with over 70% decrease in employee turnover;

- The cognitive agent mainly covered the night shifts;

- The cognitive agent had taken a large part of the team's workload. As a consequence, the team size was reduced. The remaining team members could then focus on the more complex and exciting interactions that require higher-level relationship skills. The team members who left were moved to mostly higher value-add roles in other units.

2. Unstructured information management (UIM) platforms

Most of the information produced in the world is unstructured. It is dispersed, in different formats, inconsistent, and not connected. It is resource-intensive and error-prone to perform traditional keyword research and manual scanning to try to find and analyze such information.

UIM platforms are used to extract the meaning from large amounts of data and create insights from them. In particular, they help to extract, categorize, and classify data. They transform unstructured data into structured information that is readable and searchable, and they leverage it to create meaningful insights. These platforms are usually specific by industry and by function. Here are a few examples:

- Organizations in **healthcare**, pharmaceuticals, and biotechnology struggle to make sense of the mass of textual data that they face daily. These include journal articles, patents, lab notebooks, clinical reports, internal documents, and health records; the list is endless. UIM platforms[125] help to create a central intelligence by digesting all these documents. As an outcome, they help to improve care delivery and disease diagnosis, and bring down costs. For example, Amazon Comprehend Medical, a UIM platform, is a service that extracts disease conditions, medications, and treatment outcomes from patient notes, clinical trial reports, and other electronic health records.

---

125 Popular technology vendors include Iodine, Optum and 3M.

- In the **human resources industry**, UIM systems[126] support the search and selection phases of talent recruitment. They allow the analysis of large quantities of resumes and job advertisements in different formats. The outcome is a match of demand and offer, identifying the skills of potential hires and spotting prospects even before they become active in the job market.

- In the **legal industry**, UIM platforms[127] help to digest acts, new laws, regulation amendments, contracts, documentation of evidence, litigation letters, and notes. They automate routine litigation tasks, help legal teams save time, drive down costs, and shift strategic focus. For example, JP Morgan developed a program that reviews commercial loan agreements. It does, in a few seconds, what used to require an estimated 360,000 hours of human lawyers' time, interpreting commercial-loan agreements.[128]

- UIM platforms are even applied to **aircraft maintenance**.[129] They help mechanics to synthesize information from large aircraft manuals. They also find meaning in the descriptions of problems reported verbally or handwritten by pilots and other humans.

- Released in June 2020 by OpenAI, **GPT-3** (Generative Pre-trained Transformer) **is the most powerful NLP model** at the time we are publishing the book. It is the third-generation

---

126 A popular platform is Sovren.

127 A popular platform is LexNLP.

128 Hugh Son, 2017. "JPMorgan Software Does in Seconds What Took Lawyers 360,000 Hours". Bloomberg. https://www.bloomberg.com/news/articles/2017-02-28/jpmorgan-marshals-an-army-of-developers-to-automate-high-finance

129 A popular platform is offered by CaseBank Technologies.

language model created by OpenAI, a for-profit San Francisco-based artificial intelligence research laboratory. The model leverages deep learning to produce human-like text. It has been trained with one trillion words of data coming from the web and uses 175 billion parameters, which is 100 times more than the previous generation model (GPT-2). Its high level of accuracy opens the door to many new applications. Here are some of them:

o For example, this model can understand complex inquiries and retrieve any information available on the web to answer it, such as the populations of states or people's Twitter usernames. It can also understand and match complex data patterns. We recommend watching the video provided in the footnotes.[130]

o It can also generate the code to build a new machine learning model, just by understanding a description of the required output.[131]

o The GPT-3 model is also able to answer complex medical questions without any specific training. An illustration is provided in the footnotes.[132]

---

130 P. Bornet, 2020. "Impressive new Excel function". YouTube. https://youtu.be/Fmsgby05_vU

131 P. Bornet, 2020. "When AI creates AI…". YouTube. https://youtu.be/v5CS9njzIcc

132 P. Bornet, 2020. "GPT-3 can also answer complex medical questions". LinkedIn. https://www.linkedin.com/feed/update/urn:li:ugcPost:6691715336192032768?commentUrn=urn%3Ali%3Acomment%3A%28ugcPost%3A6691715336192032768%2C6691716183357571072%29

- In the context of IA, UIM platforms are also **necessary for other IA capabilities**. The "execution" capability of IA can only work based on structured data. For example, an RPA robot always requires its input data to be consistent in format and structure. As for the "thinking & learning" capability, it requires a large amount of labeled and structured data to create insights and train machine learning models. For example, it is used to predict the price of a stock based on information automatically collected from the media and the web. Hence, in the context of IA, a key use of UIM platforms is to extract and categorize information and to transform unstructured data into structured information to make it actionable by other IA capabilities.

3. Sentiment analysis[133]

Sentiment analysis refers to **contextual text mining that identifies and extracts subjective information to understand social sentiment**. Sentiment analysis involves various models. Some simply focus on polarity (e.g., positive, negative, or neutral). Others detect feelings and emotions (e.g., angry, happy, proud, or sad), and some can even identify intentions (e.g., interested or not interested).

By automatically analyzing customer interactions and feedback (e.g., from call or social media interactions), brands can listen attentively to their customers and tailor products and services better to meet their needs. The key uses of sentiment analysis include the following:

- Brand reputation measure, assessment of communication campaign impact, and product launch.

---

133 Popular vendors include Hootsuite, Quick Search, and Critical Mention.

- Identification of negative mentions in social media (e.g., alerts) in order to be proactive in answering complaints and prevent a possible crisis. This can be for a product, a brand, or a company.

- Monitoring the brand's sentiment in social media to compare against the competition. See Figure 2.9, which compares the evolution of customers' sentiments for McDonald's and Burger King.

- Providing real-time information about customer choices and decision drivers; for example, identifying keywords or actions that can have an impact on customer sentiment and using them to improve satisfaction or trigger sales while interacting.

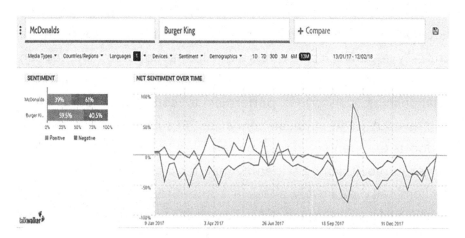

Figure 2.9: McDonald's versus Burger King - the battle of the sentiment
Source: courtesy of Talkwalker[134]

---

134 Talkwalker, 2019. Competitive benchmarking. https://www.talkwalker.com/blog/sentiment-analysis-guide

4. Speech analytics[135]

Also known as customer engagement analytics or interaction analytics, **speech analytics combines the capabilities of UIM platforms and sentiment analysis platforms**. It is often specifically designed for call centers. Speech analytics can capture conversations held via phone, email, text, webchat, and social media. The system transcribes all discussions using speech-to-text and turns them into searchable, structured data that machine learning can then use to gain insight into what customers feel or think. The data is analyzed in real time by a sentiment analysis algorithm. This insight can be put into action by providing direct feedback to supervisors and agents through visual cues, notifications, and reports. If the client sentiment proves to be critically negative, it also offers alerts to managers so that they can intervene promptly. It helps to improve the efficiency of customer relationships, call agent performance, compliance adherence, and revenue generation, and enhance the customer experience. It supports the identification of patterns leading to successful sales. For example, it can help identify that, for a certain product, when a client talks positively about a competitor, giving him a $100 voucher triggers a sale in 70% of cases.

The information collected during client communication can also be used in real time by an algorithm to identify opportunities to cross-sell or up-sell, based on customer behavior, past transactions, and demographics. For example, a bank's machine learning algorithm might detect, by analyzing credit card transactions, that a client usually buys travel insurance just after

---

135 Popular vendors include Nice, Verint, and CallMiner.

purchasing a flight ticket. The algorithm will then prompt the call agent to propose travel insurance while in conversation with that client. The video in the footnote provides an example in action of a program using speech analytics to enable cross-selling through client intent detection.[136]

---

136 Servion Global Solutions, 2017. "Virtual Assistant - powered by Artificial Intelligence" (start watching the demo at 0:57), YouTube, https://youtu.be/ThtetGx5ct0

Capability 4: Thinking & learning

"The brain of the digital workforce."

Figure 2.10: The "thinking & learning" capability within the IA framework
Source: © Bornet, Barkin & Wirtz

Description and applications

This capability is about creating insight from data through analysis and prediction to support decision-making. It allows employees to be augmented, providing them with insights from data to guide their actions and decisions. It can also trigger automated process activities. For example, the prediction that a client might be fraudulent could trigger a message to a customer representative to investigate the case.

Key technologies

Three main technologies support this capability: big data management, machine learning, and data visualization. Big data management allows the extraction and preparation of data. Data is then fed to algorithms to generate insights (using machine learning) required for actions or decisions made by computers (again using machine learning) or by humans (based on data visualization).

1. Big data management

Data is the fuel of any machine learning initiative. Data management is the process of acquiring, validating, integrating, storing, protecting, preparing, cleaning, and using data in an accessible, reliable, and meaningful way. Data quality is a crucial prerequisite to ensure the quality of predictions and other insights from data. The best machine learning algorithm can't produce valuable insight if it uses low-quality data.

Managing data effectively and efficiently helps to produce valuable insights and improves the quality of these outcomes over time. Nevertheless, data is difficult to find and often goes missing. In addition, very often, data sets are housed in insulated, disparate systems where access is restricted. Furthermore, data is often presented in inconsistent formats, including missing fields or duplicate entries.

In addition to data storage, key applications of big data management are:

- Data virtualization, which provides an overview of the data available in different sources, often presented in a graphical format. It helps to understand visually what data is available and where.

- Data integration, which orchestrates data consolidation from different sources.

- Data preparation, which helps with sourcing, shaping, cleansing, and sharing diverse data sets.

- Data quality, which conducts data assessment, cleansing, and enrichment on large data sets, using parallel operations on distributed data stores.

Data management activities can be performed using historical data. But other applications require data management activities to be performed in real time (called "streaming"), involving high resilience of the data management systems. One area of application of **data streaming** is fraud detection. For example, Amex aims to detect fraudulent transactions as early as possible to minimize losses. It uses a machine learning model that leverages data from a variety of sources, including card membership information, spending details, and merchant information. It detects suspicious events and makes a decision in milliseconds by comparing an event to a large dataset. This real-time approach has allowed the prevention of $2 billion worth of fraud cases.

2. Machine learning

This technology uses a set of algorithms that **parse data, learn from it, and then apply what has been learned to make informed decisions**. These systems automatically learn and improve from experience without being explicitly programmed. Machine learning can assist employees, business leaders, and even other systems in making optimal decisions based on past and present information.

Today, over 200 machine learning models exist.[137] Here we will discuss the most commonly used models, which are regressions, decision trees, and clustering,[138] followed by deep learning. While deep learning is not yet used as extensively as the other techniques, it is growing rapidly, and we view it as a key enabler of more exciting intelligent applications.

---

137 For more explanation on the different machine learning algorithms available, here is one of the most comprehensive sources of information: https://machinelearningmastery.com/a-tour-of-machine-learning-algorithms/

138 KDnuggets, 2019. "Which Data Science / Machine Learning methods and algorithms did you use in 2018/2019 for a real-world application?", https://www.kdnuggets.com/2019/04/top-data-science-machine-learning-methods-2018-2019.html

2.1. Regression analysis

This is a form of predictive modeling technique that investigates the relationship between a dependent variable (the target) and one or more independent variable(s) (the predictor). This technique is used for **forecasting, prediction, and time series modeling**, by finding and leveraging the causal effect relationship between the variables. It will continually adjust its forecast as new actual outcomes are injected into the model, making it learn continuously.

For example, regressions support workforce planning to ensure adequate staffing, or the identification of the talents that an organization should retain based on relevant traits, practices, and skills. Other applications include predicting the level of liquidity required for a finance department based on trends in disbursement.

2.2. Decision trees

These are graphical representations of a decision based on certain conditions. They are **useful in a decision-making process**, providing a simple representation of the flow of questions to be answered to get to a decision. They also provide an easy way to explain an ultimate decision. They are called decision trees because they start with a single box (or root), which then splits into several possible outcomes (leaves), according to conditions (branches). The leaves of the tree are the subsequent questions or the final outcomes. The branches are the possible routes from each decision, where the data is split amongst different options (e.g., yes or no).

Decision trees are not new; what machine learning brings here is **the capacity to identify the optimal split of the problem into relevant**

questions and connect them together in a logical way to achieve a final decision. Figure 2.11 shows how a decision tree is used to predict the diagnosis of a disease. Similar algorithms are used by platforms like Ada Health (a symptom checker app). According to this model, if someone has a runny nose, there is a 56% probability that it is caused by a cold (80%*70% = 56%). Note: this example has been only created for the sake of explaining the concept of a decision tree in machine learning.

If a patient has a runny nose, which disease might it be?

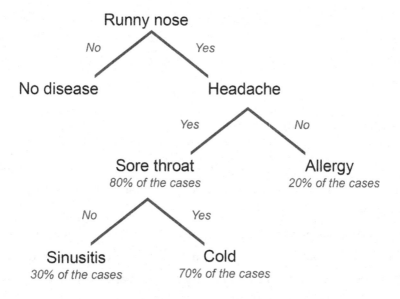

Figure 2.11: Example of a decision tree to diagnose a patient with a runny nose
Source: © Bornet, Barkin & Wirtz

2.3. Clustering

This can be defined as the task of identifying subgroups in the data such that data points in the same subgroup (cluster) are as similar as possible and are as different as possible to other clusters. In other words, **it is about finding homogeneous subgroups within the data**. Some uses of clustering algorithms include network traffic classification, document categorization, gene clustering, or product categorization.

For example, clustering is used in market segmentation, where we try to segment a client base into homogeneous groups to customize offers to them. The clustering algorithm helps to develop targeted, personalized campaigns by identifying homogeneous groups of clients using their demographics, products purchased, transactional behavior, and contact history.

2.4. Deep learning

Deep learning algorithms are inspired by how the human brain works. They are more powerful than other machine learning algorithms because they are made of numerous layers, each providing a different interpretation of the data analyzed. Deep learning techniques are **used when data features are numerous and there is a lack of domain understanding to identify and understand them**. This data is typically complex, such as images, videos, or voice recordings. For example, an image contains an indefinite amount of data features (e.g., points, edges, shapes, or objects), and some are relevant to the problem being solved, but others are not. Deep learning is used to solve problems such as image classification, natural language processing, and speech recognition.

For example, Morgan Stanley uses deep learning to test and fine-tune its analysts' investment strategies. By leveraging natural language processing, the program reads through millions of pieces of data per day. It scans annual reports, earnings reports, business news, and social media posts to estimate which companies' stocks are going to increase. Thanks to this algorithm, the bank has been able to outperform the market.[139]

2.5. The market for machine learning platforms

The market for machine learning platforms is **large and fragmented; therefore, it seemed essential to us to guide the reader into it**. This market is composed of three types of products: open-source, traditional, and cloud-only platforms. The latter two are also called commercial platforms.

Open-source platforms (e.g., Scikit Learn, Keras, PyTorch or R-Project) are freely available and may be redistributed and modified. Communities support the code. As these platforms are broadly used, it might be easier to hire talents with the required skills to use them. They are well-suited for smaller initiatives with lower requirements in terms of reliability and availability of the platform (where potential downtimes are less important).

In contrast, **commercial platforms** are developed and maintained by a single company. Commercial software includes two main categories: **traditional** platforms (e.g., SAS or Matlab) and **cloud-only** ones (e.g., AWS, Microsoft Azure, and Google Cloud). The providers of all these platforms offer dedicated customer support,

139 Thomas Franck, 2019. "Morgan Stanley used AI to study its own analysts and figured out how to beat the market". https://www.cnbc.com/2019/06/27/morgan-stanley-used-ai-to-study-its-analysts-and-beat-the-market.html

and the pricing is license-based (for the traditional ones) or pay-per-use (for cloud platforms). Cloud platforms provide the broadest range of connectivity with other technologies and a rich portfolio of tools. Furthermore, these platforms tend to become more and more user friendly, and the cloud feature enables scalability.

In conclusion, smaller companies with a limited budget might opt for open source platforms. Larger, more established, and more demanding companies would typically go with a commercial platform, enabling them to connect their different applications under the same roof. Companies with high growth objectives should leverage scalable cloud-based platforms.

3. Data visualization

Data visualization is the presentation of information and data in a pictorial or graphical format. It enables decision-makers to grasp difficult concepts and patterns more easily. By using visual elements such as charts, graphs, and maps, **data visualization provides an accessible way to see and understand trends, outliers, and patterns in data**. Data visualization helps to communicate complex statistical information intuitively and interactively.

New data visualization platforms help to combine multiple views of data to get rich insight. They use intuitive drag-and-drop functionalities and do not require programming. They can plug in almost any source of data and generate insight from real-time data.

For example, ICA is Sweden's largest grocery retailer, with over 8,000 employees. It has implemented a "self-service analytics" tool in the form of a data visualization platform to support the sharing of data insights with all levels in the organization. The platform's visual approach to analytics, combined with its ease of use, made it appealing to its users. Most employees were excited about using it and were able to start using this platform straight away. It provided employees with a quick and easy way to find answers to questions that would have previously required an entire analytics team to solve. **The new platform has helped drive a powerful new data culture throughout the company.**

As an illustration of such a data visualization, Figure 2.12 shows the dashboard of a loan officer supervisor in a bank. The trends in the different performance indicators of the function are presented graphically, enabling optimal decision making and communication.

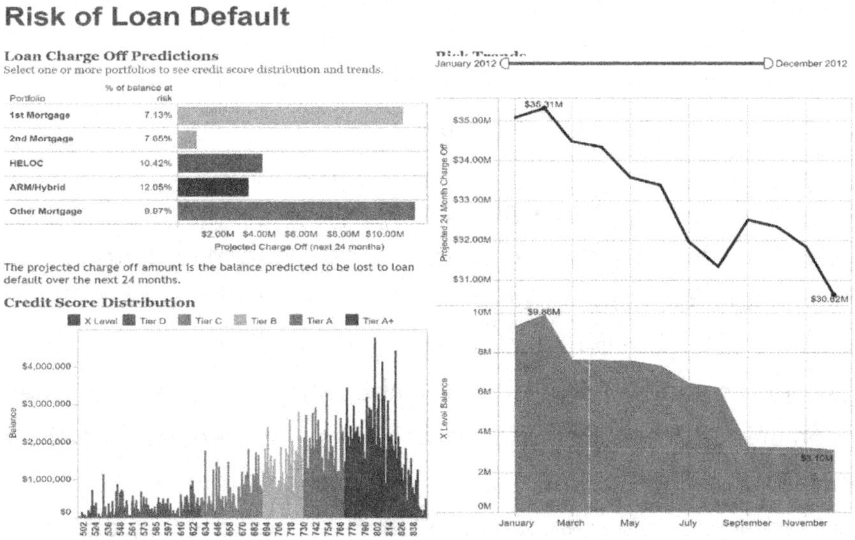

Risk of Loan Default

Figure 2.12: Data visualization presenting the "Risk of Loan Default" for a bank retail branch
Source: Courtesy of Tableau[140]

---

140 Tableau, 2018. Discovering the commercial benefits with data visualization.
https://datarootlabs.com/blog/complex-data-visualization-with-tableau-use-cases

Combining capabilities to create synergies

Each of the capabilities and technologies explained in this part of the book can deliver substantial advantages to organizations. Nevertheless, based on our experience, **the combination of these capabilities unlocks much broader and more impactful applications**. Appropriately combining these technologies helps to broaden the scope of automation, from piecemeal, isolated use cases to end-to-end automated processes. The combination of the value generated by each individual use case results in more than the sum of their values. Creating continuity in the automation of a process from its start to its end also helps to avoid bottlenecks and results in touchless, straight-through processes.

Examples of end-to-end processes include Purchase-to-Pay (i.e., the process from purchasing products or services through to paying the vendors for them), or Order-to-Cash (i.e., from the reception of the order from the client until reception of the cash). Case illustration 2.3 demonstrates how a bank onboarding process has been automated by combining IA capabilities. For recommendations on the implementation of such integrated solutions, see "Critical success factors in implementing IA" in Part Three of the book.

Case illustration 2.3: Example of a use case combining IA's capabilities

Combining IA capabilities to power a bank's client onboarding process

Context: The main objective of this banking process is to collect and assess future client data to provide better service and manage risk. In the past, this process was mostly manual, and hence, it was long and painful for clients and employees alike. It included the following process activities:

1. Manually collecting, checking, and keying in client ID documents, electricity bills, rental contracts, and other documents that prove the identity and address of a potential client.

2. Checking the future client's data against government databases and other references.

3. Assessing the risk of fraud and insolvency, mainly using static external sources.

4. Guiding the future client and answering questions during office hours.

Automating such an end-to-end process was not an easy task as it combines a wide range of capabilities, including executing, reading, dialoguing, understanding, analyzing, and learning. Unfortunately, there is no one single technology that is able to master all these capabilities. The only way to optimally automate this process was to integrate different technologies.

Description of the new solution: Chatbots helped to welcome prospective clients 24/7 and answer their questions. Application programming interfaces (APIs) allowed the sharing of data between the government regulator and the bank, and the collection of client information from other sources such as Google and Facebook. Analytics and machine learning estimated and continuously updated the risk levels and segmented the client pool to customize services. Computer vision and natural language processing helped to intelligently process unstructured documents such as bills, contracts, and identity documents. Robotic process automation supported the execution of the overall process, performing all rule-based activities such as reconciling data, checking data, and sending emails. An example of such a redesigned process is shown in Figure 2.13.

Outcome: This end-to-end process automation resulted in a reduction of process time by over 90%, a cost reduction of over 80%, enhanced compliance, and a significantly improved customer experience. At the overall bank level and after implementing 12 similar end-to-end processes over an 18-month period, the bank saw its total costs reduce by 15–20%, and its revenues increase by 10%.

A typical customer onboarding process leveraging IA

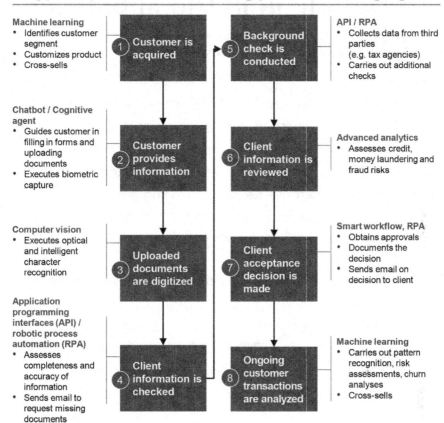

Figure 2.13: IA: a combination of technologies to deliver synergies

Source: © Bornet, Barkin & Wirtz

Positioning IA in the spectrum of existing technologies

When considering the use of IA technologies, we have often heard the following question from organizational leaders: "Are IA technologies designed to replace any of the traditional systems in a typical company's IT landscape? How does IA differ from foundational systems like our Enterprise Resource Planning systems (e.g., ERPs offered by SAP, Salesforce, and Oracle), mainframes, or other business process management systems (e.g., reporting systems)?"

The short answer is that IA acts on top of these foundational systems. The focus of IA applications is process activities that are currently performed by human workers who interact with and operate these foundational systems. These systems are tools. IA is not meant to replace them but use them as any human worker would. IA just helps to add intelligence and automation on top of foundational systems.

Foundational systems are the most appropriate to store and structure data, and to organize process flows. Indeed, they are stable, integrated, and maintained as part of the company's IT core infrastructure. For this reason, organizations should consider satisfying any new IT requirement and processes using these foundational systems as a priority. IA technologies should then only be used if the foundational systems don't have the required capabilities.

Building a compelling IA implementation roadmap

Company leaders often ask the question: "I have not yet implemented any of these solutions; which technology should I implement first? What is an optimal sequence for adopting these technologies?"

Our survey of over 200 IA leaders suggests that there is no standard answer to these questions and that **no capability is used more than others**. Table 2.1 shows the IA technologies most used by our respondents' organizations.

Answer choices	Percentage of total responses
Machine learning	87%
Natural language processing	82%
Robotic process automation	77%
Computer vision	75%
Chatbots and virtual agents	68%
Deep learning	61%

Table 2.1: Most popular IA technologies according to our survey amongst 200 IA experts
Source: © Bornet, Barkin & Wirtz

In the context of building an IA roadmap, there is no silver bullet. The choice of the technologies to be implemented first should be based on business needs and expected benefits. Refer to Part Three of the book to understand how to select, prioritize and implement these technologies.

Meanwhile, **to help you navigate how the various capabilities relate to each other**, here are the main differences and complementarities across technologies:

- The **Language** capability consists of technologies that are foundational to IA systems as they help to structure an organization's data. Without structured data, most of the other capabilities cannot produce their desired outcomes. Technologies under the language capability require medium to high skills (i.e., mainly data science and engineering) for implementation and maintenance. These technologies are still maturing, and their prices tend to be moderate to high.

- Technologies in the **Execution** capability tend to be used as a glue to connect the other capabilities. They are the key enablers to increase the breadth of the end-to-end automation program; for example, routing data from one capability to another and executing automated actions using data generated from other capabilities. These technologies tend to be user-friendly. They typically require only a few weeks of training for a user to be able to develop automation programs. The underlying technologies tend to be relatively simple, and hence prices are moderate.

- The **Vision** capability includes technologies that are used for more specific use cases, which tend to be industry or function-oriented. Depending on the technology, the prices and skills required might be high if they are specialized (e.g., computer vision in automotive or healthcare), or low if they are generic (e.g., optical character recognition).

- The technologies in the "**Thinking & learning**" capability are the intelligence dimension of an IA system. They are the key levers to increase the sophistication of an overall IA program and to enable strategic market differentiation. They can support the creation of customized client experiences or the unique operational intelligence of a supply chain model. These technologies can help to support the development or enhancement of the differentiating positioning of a business. The technologies in the thinking & learning capability are still maturing; hence, prices and level of required skills are moderate to high.

Key takeaways of Part Two

- IA enables the automation of knowledge work by mimicking human workers' capabilities. It includes **four main capabilities**: vision, execution, language, and thinking & learning. Each of these capabilities combines different technologies that can be used stand-alone or in combination to complement each other. Figure 2.14 summarizes the main technologies available for each capability.

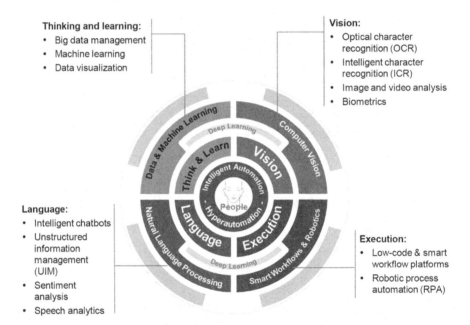

Thinking and learning:
- Big data management
- Machine learning
- Data visualization

Vision:
- Optical character recognition (OCR)
- Intelligent character recognition (ICR)
- Image and video analysis
- Biometrics

Language:
- Intelligent chatbots
- Unstructured information management (UIM)
- Sentiment analysis
- Speech analytics

Execution:
- Low-code & smart workflow platforms
- Robotic process automation (RPA)

Figure 2.14: the four IA capabilities and their related key technologies
Source: © Bornet, Barkin & Wirtz

- The **Vision** capability provides computers the ability to analyze images, recognize letters and objects, and view the environment. The overarching technology supporting this capability is computer vision, which is mainly enabled by deep learning techniques. The key technologies currently in use are optical character recognition (OCR), intelligent character recognition (ICR), image and video analysis, and biometrics.

- The **Execution** capability allows computer programs to accomplish actions in digital environments (e.g., typing, clicking, opening applications, and sending emails). The technologies supporting this capability include smart workflow and low-code platforms, and robotic process automation (RPA). This capability is a foundation for end-to-end automated business process delivery. It acts as a glue, connecting the technologies across capabilities.

- The **Language** capability gives machines the ability to speak, write, interact, interpret, and derive meaning from human language. The overarching technology is called natural language processing (NLP), which is nowadays mainly enabled by deep learning techniques. The key technologies that currently use NLP are intelligent chatbots, unstructured information management, sentiment analysis, and speech analytics. The Language capability presents technologies that are foundational to IA systems as they help to structure an organization's data. Without structured data, none of the other IA capabilities can produce their desired outcomes.

- The **Thinking & learning** capability gives computers the ability to analyze, create insights, predict, make decisions, and learn. The technologies supporting this capability are big data management, machine learning, and data visualization. They are the key levers to enable strategic market differentiation.

For example, they support the creation of customized client experiences or the unique operational intelligence of a supply chain model.

- The **combination of IA capabilities** helps to create synergies. It allows organizations to automate complex end-to-end processes.

- IA is not meant to replace the foundational systems already used by companies (e.g., ERPs, mainframes, and business performance management systems). Rather, **IA sits on top of an existing IT landscape**. The focus of IA applications is to automate activities that are currently performed by human workers, including how they interact with and operate these systems.

- In the context of building an **IA roadmap**, the choice of the technologies to be implemented first should be based on business needs and expected benefits. As to how the capabilities relate to each other: the language (to structure data necessary for other capabilities) and execution (to connect capabilities for end-to-end IA programs) capabilities are foundational to most IA systems. The thinking & learning capability is the intelligence dimension of an overall IA program, while the vision capability tends to be specific to some use cases or industries (e.g., health and automotive).

PART THREE:

HOW ORGANIZATIONS SUCCEED IN IMPLEMENTING IA

"The first rule of any technology used in a business is that automation applied to an efficient operation will magnify the efficiency. The second is that automation applied to an inefficient operation will magnify the inefficiency."

Bill Gates

Succeeding at an IA transformation is not easy, nor is it guaranteed. Despite the widespread global adoption of IA, there remain significant challenges to transforming initial efforts into large scale, enterprise-wide IA implementations.

What does "success" mean in the context of IA transformation?

Success is easy when implementing IA within limited scopes, through proofs-of-concept or pilots. However, scaling up the initiative across an organization introduces another level of complexity. The scaling-up phase is the most critical step to create momentum, generate the expected benefits, create economies of scale, and, most importantly, sustain the change. Examples of companies that have notably succeeded in their transformations at scale include Deutsche Bank, J.P. Morgan Chase, Pfizer, Procter & Gamble, Johnson & Johnson, Unilever, and Amazon.

In this part, we share the critical success factors for such initiatives based on our experience with over hundreds of transformations. We also present the latest developments in IA and the resultant new enablers and trends which will support scaling IA in the future.

What are the challenges of implementing IA?

In our experience, these challenges most often fall into one of a few specific categories: management vision and support, change management, data, technical limitations, costs and efficiency, talent, and overall complexity of the transformation.

1. Gaps in management vision and support

One critical challenge arises from companies' management failing to prioritize the right IA initiatives, extend the scope of the transformation, advocate for more interdisciplinarity, and set up the right governance.

We have seen many organizations facing the issue of starting their transformation by pursuing "weak" IA opportunities; that is, IA opportunities that are too small, limited in benefits, or not visible enough. It is critical to **prioritize the implementation of the IA initiatives which create a sufficient business impact to convince** management and employees of the power of IA. Failing to achieve this objective would result in the overall IA transformation being aborted or reduced in scope, due to being deprioritized in favor of alternative transformation levers. In order to ensure the IA transformation goes ahead, it is necessary to go through an exercise of comprehensive identification and assessment of the IA opportunities. This issue of starting an IA project with an inappropriate IA opportunity typically happens when companies rush the phase of identification and prioritization of IA opportunities. It also occurs when a few people in a company leverage IA to satisfy a need that impassions them, but which does not have a large enough impact to convince the rest of the company. The role of management in pushing for objective and compelling analysis of the portfolio of IA initiatives is vital.

The problem of lack of visible impact also arises from **the limitation in the scope of an IA transformation**, very often due to organizational silos. Management should actively advocate for having different parts of the organization work together. Failing to achieve this would result in limiting the scope and the potential benefits generated by the transformation. For example, after succeeding in a pilot IA implementation in the finance department of one of the divisions of a corporation, management should push to extend the scope of the transformation to the finance departments of the other divisions. This will increase the overall benefits generated by the IA transformation, creating the opportunity for larger investments while generating economies of scale.

Another common issue is **the lack of interdisciplinarity in the transformation**. In our experience, the highest impact is the result of multi-lever end-to-end process automation – not small, siloed implementations, focused on one single technology lever. To achieve this, management should advocate for getting the right talents from across the different parts of an organization to work together (e.g., data scientists, developers, business analysts). Interdisciplinarity is also about avoiding limiting the transformation to the implementation of one single technology lever (e.g., RPA), and about implementing IA on end-to-end processes instead of only a few process tasks. By combining talents and technology levers and targeting end-to-end processes, the organization will create synergies, build economies of scale, and remove potential bottlenecks. Organizations failing to achieve this are not able to scale their IA transformation.

The **absence of appropriate project governance** results in a lack of monitoring of the impact generated by the transformation, and confusion between the roles of the different actors on the project. Most often, this results in exceeded budgets, missed deadlines, and IA project failure. It is the role of management to set the IA transformation's objectives, clarify the roles and responsibilities, establish the appropriate committees to oversee the transformation, and follow the right indicators of progress. For example, if the IT department takes ownership of the project without involving business users appropriately, the outcome is usually a fantastic IA system, but one that does not deliver the expected business benefits.

2. Barriers due to change management

Resistance to change is part of human nature. And when the change involves something as crucial as potentially threatening people's current jobs, this **resistance can quickly turn into stiff opposition or even fear**. For IA implementations to succeed and scale, people must be educated about what it will mean to them in terms of benefits and opportunities. Management must make this education a reality (and this is one of the purposes of this book). An IA transformation can't be implemented without people, and it can't succeed without educating and convincing these people.

According to the Pew Research Center, 72% of Americans are very or somewhat worried about a future where robots and computers are capable of performing many human jobs.[141] This is particularly true for middle-class employees who have heard about instances where offshoring work to low-cost countries has triggered layoffs. So it is not surprising for them to believe IA will do the same for their jobs. In fact, IA programs – unlike offshore workers – typically automate the repetitive parts of a job, leaving more complex tasks untouched and freeing up time for more high-value activities. For those impacted, education and mentoring on new opportunities and moving into new roles is essential. So, yes – **some work activities are displaced, but new ones, more fulfilling and value-adding, arise**. What are the new ones? Think of these activities that everyone knows are crucial, but that actually none has the time to perform – for example, spending one hour per week with each team member to coach them.

Resistance to change not only comes from employees, but **it also comes from companies' managers**. And the challenges are somewhat different:

- Some managers are **afraid of losing power** and status. "How many people do you manage?" The answer to this question is such a source of pride for many managers. Indeed, it seems to be part of human nature to feel powerful when we have many people reporting to us. If teams shrink thanks to the use of IA, some managers think that makes them less important, less useful to their organization.

- Others think being a "good manager" means maintaining their teams and taking care of them. "**I want to care about**

---

141 Richard Wike and Bruce Stokes, 2018. "In Advanced and Emerging Economies Alike, Worries About Job Automation". Pew Research Center. https://www.pewresearch.org/global/2018/09/13/in-advanced-and-emerging-economies-alike-worries-about-job-automation/

my people," a CEO told us. Therefore, the organization was approaching IA with a light touch, testing it, and implementing it on only fractions of what's possible, without a clear plan for large-scale deployment. Since IA's operational and cost benefits translate directly into competitive strengths, this cautious strategy can actually be more threatening to employees in the long run than the automation itself. Here again, education and communication are vital.

- The key to enabling implementation at scale is to **inform, educate, and incentivize staff and management to accept the change**, and bring IA into their work, departments, and divisions. Later, we will identify how to implement change management initiatives and technologies to meet that challenge.

3. Issues related to data

The Data Warehousing Institute estimates that US businesses lose a cumulative 600 billion dollars a year[142] due to problems with data quality. Managing data gets more difficult every day as the frequency and volume of incoming data continues to increase. Most organizations have disconnected and under-utilized data. As presented in Part Two of the book, **data is the fuel of any IA system**. Each of the capabilities of IA requires optimal data feed. We have seen IA projects fail just because the data was wrongly managed or inaccurate, which resulted in wrong decisions or in automated activities producing erroneous outcomes. For example, we have

---

142 The Data Warehousing Institute, n.d. "Data quality and the bottom line".
http://download.101com.com/pub/tdwi/Files/DQReport.pdf

seen a large part of the revenue of a major publisher collapse, as its poorly managed data model was recommending kids' books to business people.

While data management is a top directive for leading enterprises, it presents many challenges today that can impact an IA transformation. In our experience, the most common ones are due to the difficulty of creating value from an overwhelming volume of unstructured data, the lack of consistency in structured data, data quality issues, and challenges created by data silos.

Like the sailor stranded in a lifeboat after his ship sank, there's water everywhere, but not a drop to drink. Gartner research predicts that **the volume of data** in the world will grow 800% over the next five years, and up to 80% of that data will be completely unstructured.[143] Unstructured data consists of information that doesn't reside in a traditional row–column database. Typical examples are legal documents, images, medical records, and other types of media. Cross-industry studies show that, on average, less than 1% of a company's unstructured data is analyzed or used at all. 80% of analysts' time is spent simply discovering and preparing data.[144]

Since **unstructured data** represents 80% of all data, it is clear that the ability to manage it is key to automating large volumes of work activities. An example of such activity would be automatically keying in the information from different suppliers' contracts (e.g., date, name, object) into a procurement management database. While

---

143 Headwaters Group, 2017. "Your Unstructured Data is Sexy, You Just Don't Know It". https://headwaters.group/your-unstructured-data-is-sexy-you-just-dont-know-it-cio-strategy/

144 Leandro DalleMule and Thomas H. Davenport, HBR, 2017. The 2 Types of Data Strategies Every Company Needs. https://hbr.org/2017/05/whats-your-data-strategy

it is technically feasible to extract useful information from such unstructured data (refer to Part Two, "Capability 1: Vision"), **these applications require a large amount of data and time to learn**.

Structured data is definitely easier to manage, but it is not easy to seize the value from it due to **consistency issues**. Let's take the example of customer data. Most organizations capture information about customers and prospects inconsistently across functions. As a result, the customer data is overwhelming and most often disconnected. Marketing collects data from people who attend events or who download content. Sales collect data about customers involved in the sales process. Customer support captures feedback information about calls and chats. Data is everywhere, across teams and platforms; its volume is growing, and it is disconnected and inconsistent, resulting in difficulty in creating value from it.

Like any other asset, data can range in quality. **Outdated, inaccurate, or incomplete data results in unreliable insights**. In fact, poor data can lead to businesses making poor or uneducated decisions that can have severe impacts in the long run. For example, an investment company lost a few million dollars by taking positions in a market that was about to be regulated. After investigation, we identified that the data it was using for its decision process was outdated and incomplete.

If teams have trouble finding useful data, this probably means that information assets are being housed in insulated, disparate systems where access might be restricted. This issue is known as "**data silos**". Data silos often present a significant, overarching problem which can be due to several factors:

- Management hierarchies: In large organizations, people are often separated into many layers of management and specialized teams. In these situations, information tends to remain within small groups. It doesn't flow to employees who need it for their daily work.

- Technological barriers: In cases where different departments operate using different software, applications are often unable to share or cross-reference information.

- Fragmented data ownership: The management of data quality is driven by multiple stakeholders and frequently measured at a department-by-department level, rather than across the business as a whole.

4. Technical challenges

Go is one of the most complex games in the world. There are more possible Go positions than there are atoms in the Universe. Ke Jie, the world's top Go player, lost against AlphaGo (DeepMind's AI program) in 2017. AlphaGo's achievement makes it probably the most intelligent machine existing on Earth. Nevertheless, it is still woefully unable to produce a simple standard monthly finance report as the finance department of any company would do. That task would be too complicated. It involves too many and too diverse a set of activities, including multiple outputs and inputs, and a mountain of unstructured data. In other words, **automating knowledge work is probably one of the most complex use cases in the world!**

In fact, IA still has a number of **technical limitations**. These include capabilities that IA can't master yet, such as contextual understanding, critical thinking, or radical creativity (unscripted and "out of the blue"). Another limitation typically concerns work tasks that include several steps, are infrequent, and have a high number of variants or exceptions. IA is currently more capable of managing high-frequency, high-volume tasks, like diagnosing based on X-rays, where a machine learning algorithm can be trained easily on millions of images. And the result is a system that outperforms an experienced medical doctor. This is an example of what is called "Narrow AI". The system's capability is superior to a human's, but only for one very specific task. However, when novel situations are introduced, or different tasks need to be performed, the system can't handle them. Humans are still the best at these.

Although IA's level of intelligence has progressed a long way with deep learning, **there is still much to be done to become fully efficient**. Even the technologies assumed to be cutting edge in the AI field are not able to be fully autonomous. As pointed out by a recent New York Times article, Facebook AI and Google Duplex are still heavily supported by humans in the background to ensure the high quality of the outcome expected by their intelligent systems.[145] In fact, Yann LeCun, head of Facebook's AI research, said: "We're very far from having machines that can learn the most basic things about the world in the way humans and animals can do (...). In terms of general intelligence, [machines are] not even close to a rat."

Because of these technical limitations, humans will likely be needed to work hand-in-hand with technology, for at least the coming decade. For this reason, a **capable human-machine interface is**

---

145 Brian X. Chen and Cade Metz, 2019. "Google's Duplex Uses AI to Mimic Humans (Sometimes)". New York Times. https://www.nytimes.com/2019/05/22/technology/personaltech/ai-google-duplex.html

critical, avoiding friction and creating seamless hand-offs. In effect, a "people + machine" combination is much more productive and high quality than humans alone, and it is much more effective than machines alone – there is a real synergy in this combination. Refer to "Enabler 4: Symbiosis of people and IA" for more detail on this topic.

5. Cost and efficiency challenges

From a technical point of view, except for the elements presented in the previous section (which still represent more than 50% of work tasks), all work tasks can be automated today. The primarily remaining challenge is cost. And to reduce costs, we need scale.

The cost of an IA implementation is mainly driven by the time and the value of the human resources involved. The major project steps to follow in order to automate a process are:

1. Assessment of automation potential and prioritization (through data analysis, process walk-throughs, observations, and interviews)

2. Redesign of processes (through workshops)

3. Development and configuration of the automation programs.

While the first two steps take on average about two weeks of a business analyst's or translator's time for one use case (e.g., one sub-process), the third step takes about 6 to 12 weeks. Ironically, **IA projects are still extremely manual and human-resource consuming.** Building a robot using RPA or a low-code platform is a manual click-by-click process. Building a chatbot or a machine learning program involves collecting a certain amount of data to train, test, and validate the algorithm. It also sometimes includes manually labeling the data. It is ironic that automating tasks is a very manual process. As a result, while the licenses for the technologies are not expensive, the implementation costs can be quite high due to the cost of human resources.

In addition, **IA transformations are currently very time-consuming**. The roadmap to automate 20% of the workload of a finance function can take easily 3 to 6 months with a team of 4 to 5 developers and 2 to 3 business analysts. However, it is still worth doing because, depending on the size of this finance department, the payback period will usually be between three months and one year. For example, based on an actual IA deployment, after automating 20% of the workload, a 40-person finance department could recoup the cost of its transformation in six months: a return on investment that's hard to ignore.

Monitoring and maintaining automated processes is also a very manual activity. For example, when the process changes (e.g., a new system, new policies, or simply a change to the format of documents), there is a need to rebuild the part of the process that is impacted. This involves redesigning the process and amending the application to take into account what is changing. The cost involved can be high. Maintaining an automated process is estimated to be about 20% of the initial implementation cost per year. Finally, there is the risk that the impacting change is not anticipated, resulting in a failure of the automated process. Management of changes and their impact on the automated process is vital for success.

6. Talent scarcity

The skillsets required for managing IA transformations are diverse. They range from program managers, business analysts, and translators to developers, data scientists, data engineers, and system architects. These **talents can be difficult to recruit because of their scarcity**. This complexity might differ from one location to another. The next subsection on critical success factors shows ways to mitigate this issue.

7. The complexity of the transformation

According to McKinsey, 50% of the component tasks of the jobs in the world can be automated today using current technologies. However, only 5% of entire jobs can be automated fully, and 60% of jobs can be automated at more than 30%.[146] This means that, **in most cases, only individual tasks are automatable**. It is not even processes (defined as a sequence of tasks) that can be automated. Full roles (composed of a portfolio of processes) are even less automatable, at only 5%.

Hence, transforming a company with IA is complex and requires surgical precision. First, a successful transformation involves identifying the tasks that can be automated (comparing benefits against the cost and effort required – is it worth it?). Second, it involves redesigning the processes which these tasks belong to, as you don't want to risk breaking existing processes. It is not only about seamlessly connecting the automated and non-automated tasks but also about reviewing the overall flow of the end-to-end process. Potential constraints (e.g., bottlenecks) and opportunities to combine

---

146 McKinsey Global Institute, 2017. "A future that works: automation, employment and productivity".

concepts (e.g., lean process management) and technologies need to be identified in order to bring further benefits. Third, it involves logically combining the non-automated tasks in order to re-build a new full-time role for a person. Finally, it requires adjusting the employees' skills through training so that they fit with the new role.

Therefore, we believe that at the current state of technology, **automation should be administered to companies like medication**. In essence, you need to explain why and how you need to give the right dose, and you need to check the pulse regularly. Like surgery, it needs to be prepared for; information and education are key, including understanding and anticipation of the consequences, and mitigating potential risks.

In order to address these challenges, in the coming subsections of the book, we describe a list of success factors, as well as four new enablers. While the success factors describe traditional levers to overcome IA challenges, the four new enablers present recent innovations aimed at complementing them.

How to succeed in your IA transformation

IA can deliver dramatic benefits to companies, but at the same time, IA transformations require significant changes in processes, systems, and organizations. Given these changes and, as discussed in the previous subsection, the challenges related to such efforts, any IA initiative has to be adequately prepared for and carefully managed.

In the following pages, we will share the critical success factors in implementing IA. These are based on our experience with hundreds of IA projects over the past ten years. Before that, we will share a few quotes to highlight these critical success factors, and we will describe a recommended IA transformation roadmap.

1. Quotes to guide a successful transformation

To start with, here are a few quotes that we use every day to guide our actions on the ground.

- **"The tone comes from the top"**: As with any transformation that brings structural changes to an organization, top management support is a prerequisite to succeed at any IA transformation.

- **"Think big, start small, and scale fast"**: Initiate the transformation with the definition of a multi-year, company-wide vision, roadmap, and business case. These plans need to be flexible and adaptable. Then, "start small" with the implementation of a pilot, and take the time to learn from this first experience. Finally, implement the broader scope in stages to manage the risks. Gradually increase the speed and scale of the transformation, and as a result, generate high impact.

- **"IA is a business transformation, not a technology project"**: The perspective of business benefits should guide the transformation. This transformation involves not only technology, but more importantly, people – with change management, and retraining – and processes – with redesigns.

- **"IA is a journey, not a destination"**: IA is not a one-off exercise; it is a never-ending transformation journey. It continually brings additional benefits to the organization by applying evolving concepts, methods, and technologies. Hence, building teams with the right skills to guide the company in this transformation is critical.

- **"Infusing IA into the culture of the company"**: Implementing IA with siloed, isolated teams does not work. Automation needs to be infused into the company. Change management, education, empowerment, and incentivization of everyone in the company is vital. Every employee should know what IA is and what its benefits are, and be empowered and incentivized to identify use cases and build automation.

Next, we list the most important factors to help organizations succeed in their transformation. In addition to these success factors, we also present four new enablers that will allow organizations to scale further in their IA transformation.

2. Recommended IA transformation roadmap

In Figure 3.1, we present a recommended IA transformation roadmap. The advantage of this roadmap is that it allows an iterative approach. It starts with management framing the structural, high-level components of the transformation before they get refined and implemented in the following phases of the project. This ensures the consistency of the final outcome with the initial vision while ensuring the deployments are optimally prioritized and monitored. The transformation roadmap is broken down into four main components, which form anchor points for the next subsections of the book:

- **Project launch** includes setting up management's vision and governance, performing a high-level automation assessment in order to build the business case (estimation of the benefits and costs), and the high-level project roadmap. The critical success factors for this phase are mainly explained in the subsection "Management support, vision, governance, and structure". The main new enabler impacting this project phase is high-level automation assessment supported by machine learning, as presented in "Enabler 3: IA generated by IA".

- **Project preparation** includes identifying and prioritizing the IA opportunities, detailing the implementation roadmap, anticipating IT requirements, performing the vendor and partner selection, and implementing a pilot IA program. The critical success factors for this phase are described in the subsection "Preparing the transformation and scaling it". The new enablers impacting this project phase primarily include process discovery, process mining, and data discovery, presented in "Enabler 3: IA generated by IA", as well as the convergence of technologies (subsection "Enabler 2: Convergence of technologies").

- **Project scaling** includes the actual deployment of the IA opportunities. The highest-priority opportunities to be implemented are the ones impacting end-to-end processes, as they deliver higher value for the organization. These implementations, which might be grouped, are performed sequentially, in waves. Each wave is composed of three main activities: process redesign (using lean or zero-based redesign approaches), deployment sprints (leveraging agile methodology), and the migration of the IA program to the production environment (to deliver actual benefits). We recommend leveraging delivery methodologies such as "agile" to bring flexibility and structure and to ensure delivery on time, on budget, and according to high-quality standards.[147]

The center of excellence and the automation operation center need to be built as early as possible during this phase for the organization to learn. Management activities have to be performed continually during this phase. The critical success factors for this phase are described in the subsection "Preparing the transformation and scaling it". The new enablers impacting this project phase are mostly the democratization of IA (Enabler 1) and the convergence of technologies (Enabler 2), as well as the automated generation code and AutoML, presented in "Enabler 3: IA generated by IA".

---

147 Here is a very valuable source of information on using agile in the context of automation transformations: https://www.mckinsey.com/business-functions/operations/our-insights/the-new-frontier-agile-automation-at-scale

- **Change and talent management** is about managing the "people" dimension of the transformation with activities such as communication, education, retraining, and incentivization. The critical success factors for this phase are explained in the subsection "Driving change and talent management". The new enablers impacting this project phase are the democratization of IA (Enabler 1) and the symbiosis of people and technology (Enabler 4).

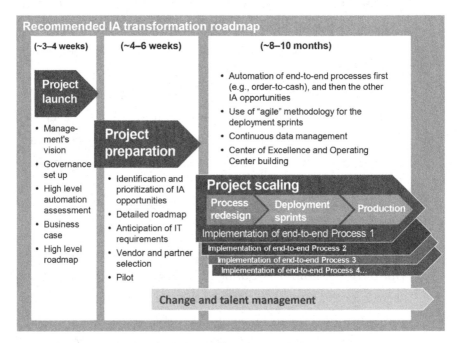

Figure 3.1: A recommended IA transformation roadmap
Source: © Bornet, Barkin & Wirtz

Management support, vision, governance, and structure

In an IA transformation, management's leadership is crucial. It is a foundation for success. Key aspects of management's role should include top management support, the design of an enterprise-level vision, the setup of clear governance, and the building of a center of excellence and an automation operation center.

1. Top management support

Based on our experience, all companies which have succeeded in their IA journeys have started with a strong foundation by building management support and vision. According to a McKinsey survey, companies whose leadership teams are completely aligned on an IA vision and strategy have twice the likelihood of succeeding in their transformation.[148] IA is a strategic and structural transformation for a company. It deals with significant changes in business processes, operating models, and organizational structures. Companies that have undergone this transformation successfully have done so by making substantial investments (both human and financial) to generate significant benefits. In order to make this possible, their **IA initiatives have to be sponsored by the highest level of management in the company** (i.e., its C-levels). Management is supported by a documented **vision** (strategic objectives of the transformation), **business case** (estimating the benefits and costs of the project),

---

148 McKinsey, 2018. "Breaking away: The secrets to scaling analytics". https://www.mckinsey.com/business-functions/mckinsey-analytics/our-insights/breaking-away-the-secrets-to-scaling-analytics?cid=soc-app

and a high-level **roadmap** (key milestones of the implementation for the coming 1 to 3 years). The design of the program is a top-down exercise, while the implementation is a bottom-up one (e.g., it starts with the deployment of a pilot).

2. Enterprise-level vision

According to the same McKinsey survey, successful companies are 3.5 times more likely than their peers to apply IA to three or more functional areas.[149] In these companies, management's expectations are supported by a clearly aligned IA enterprise-wide vision and strategy. An **enterprise-wide scope (as opposed to one or a few departments or divisions) will ensure the highest economies of scale, investment capacities, generated benefits, and scalability**. In summary: "Think big, start small, and scale fast." When set at the enterprise level, the enterprise-wide business case helps to set expectations by estimating the quantitative and qualitative benefits across departments and divisions. It allows management to evaluate and approve the overall required investment in human and financial resources.

3. Clear governance, combining business and IT

In our experience, **effective governance requires three main parties**. First, **an IA leadership committee** that includes top management of the company and people from all key functions taking part in the transformation. It is in charge of overseeing, owning, and sponsoring the achievement of the vision, business case, and roadmap. Second, the project delivery is performed by **an IA center of excellence (CoE)**,

---

149 McKinsey, 2018. "Breaking away: The secrets to scaling analytics", https://www.mckinsey.com/business-functions/mckinsey-analytics/our-insights/breaking-away-the-secrets-to-scaling-analytics?cid=soc-app

under the supervision of the IA leadership committee. Third, the CoE is headed by the **IA CoE leader**, who is responsible for supervising the CoE and monitoring the achievement of the IA leadership committee's vision. The IA CoE leader reports regularly to the AI leadership committee on the status and risks of the transformation. The CoE is composed of both business (the owner of the business processes) and IT (governance of the project) team members at a minimum.

4. An IA center of excellence (CoE) to implement and innovate

The **CoE's role is broader than just implementing the IA programs**; it is also in charge of developing policies, principles, and frameworks to oversee the use of IA in the company. The CoE creates and maintains common assets that can be re-used across initiatives (e.g., tools, templates, standards, programs). In addition, **the CoE is responsible for innovation**. It identifies and tests new concepts and technologies which can deliver additional benefits. It guides the organization through its IA journey.

Based on our experience, establishing an IA CoE has quickly become a leading practice. In addition, in one recent survey of US executives from large companies using IA, approximately 40% said they had already established a CoE. Deutsche Bank, J.P. Morgan Chase, Pfizer, Procter & Gamble, Anthem, and Farmers Insurance are among the non-tech firms that have created centralized IA oversight groups.[150] Sixty percent of top-performing companies have a CoE, according to McKinsey's survey.[151]

---

150 Deloitte, 2018. "State of AI in the Enterprise, 2nd Edition". https://www2.deloitte.com/insights/us/en/focus/cognitive-technologies/state-of-ai-and-intelligent-automation-in-business-survey.html

151 McKinsey, 2018. "Building an effective analytics organization". https://www.mckinsey.com/industries/financial-services/our-insights/building-an-effective-analytics-organization?cid=soc-app

The **talent required within the CoE** is wide and ranges from business and operations excellence to risk and IT departments. According to McKinsey's survey, the CoE of top-performing companies includes a large variety of profiles such as delivery managers, data scientists, data engineers, workflow integrators, system architects, developers, and, most critically, translators and business analysts.[152] A typical structure for a CoE and the roles of key team members are shown in Figure 3.2.

---

152 McKinsey, 2018. "Building an effective analytics organization". https://www.mckinsey.com/industries/financial-services/our-insights/building-an-effective-analytics-organization?cid=soc-app

Intelligent Automation Center of Excellence

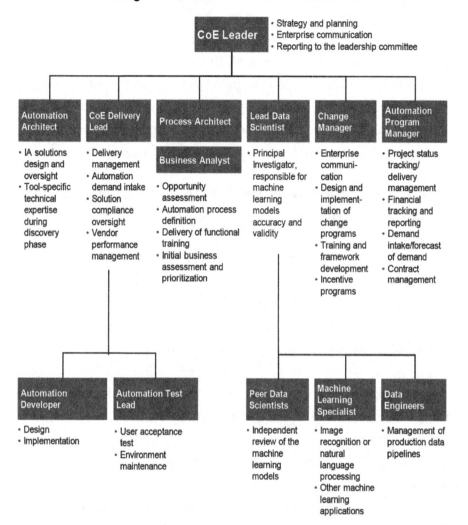

Figure 3.2: Typical IA center of excellence (CoE) structure
Source: adapted from Datarobot[153]

---

153 Andrew Pellegrino, 2019. "The Journey to Intelligent Automation with RPA & DataRobot". https://blog.datarobot.com/journey-to-intelligent-automation-with-rpa-and-datarobot

Technologies and concepts are continually evolving and becoming more sophisticated and affordable. That is, while advancing, these technologies may provide opportunities to deliver enhanced benefits. It is a **strategic role of the CoE** to identify these new opportunities and to guide the company through this never-ending journey. Successful IA journeys are characterized by a CoE that puts in place roadmaps and frameworks from a long-term perspective of being sustainable, flexible, and focused on innovation.

5. An automation operation center (AOC) to maintain automation programs.

When the first IA applications are delivered into the production environment, successful companies often set up an "automation operation center" (AOC). **Distinct from the CoE, it is in charge of maintaining the IA applications and managing the escalation of issues and changes to the application.** Clear boundaries between the CoE and AOC allow each of them to have a sharper focus on their respective roles. On the one hand, the CoE implements the IA transformation, including the deployment of the new IA applications. On the other hand, once these new applications have been delivered, the AOC is in charge of maintaining and evolving them. As such, the IA transformation delivery can't be impacted due to maintenance and evolution efforts. We have often seen the AOC being part of the IT department.

Preparing the transformation and scaling it

The critical success factors that we have identified through our experience preparing and scaling IA transformations are related to the identification and prioritization of IA opportunities, the redesign of processes, vendor and partner selection, the anticipation of IT requirements, and the management of data.

1. Identifying and prioritizing IA opportunities

An effective IA transformation starts with an **IA opportunity assessment**: qualifying processes for automation and prioritizing them. The main prioritization criteria generally used include feasibility (is it technically feasible to automate this task?), complexity (how much effort is necessary to automate this task?), and expected benefits (what are the quantitative and qualitative benefits generated from this automation?) These criteria can be weighted to facilitate the prioritization exercise. This assessment provides the foundation for the creation of the business case and implementation roadmap. Again, the broader the scope (e.g., enterprise-wide instead of a single division), the more synergies the organization can typically benefit from (e.g., through economies of scale and skills leverage).

Identifying a compelling collection of IA opportunities in a company is critical to make sure that the most strategic ones are present and prioritized in the roadmap. Based on our experience, it is wise to start implementing the most impactful opportunities to demonstrate the value of IA to management and employees.

Creating a dynamic is vital. We have seen organizations stopping their IA initiatives after the first IA pilot implementation because they had started with a low-impact IA opportunity.

2. Redesigning processes

The companies we have seen succeed with IA reviewed and optimized their existing processes before automation. They took the time to optimize or redesign their processes, with involvement from process excellence, control, and risk teams, together with business teams. Automating a weak process only results in a weak automation program.

A leading practice is to use techniques like the **zero-based approach or lean methodologies** to adapt processes. While lean methodology targets more incremental process improvements (i.e., process optimization), the zero-based approach focuses on a more radical change of the process (i.e., process redesign). The later helps to design an optimal new process without considering the limitations due to the existing environment. This allows unconstrained creativity, which usually leads to designs producing higher outcomes. But it also takes more time and effort than the lean approach.

It is not practically feasible to redesign all processes in a company, as this would be too time- and resource-consuming. Hence, which processes should be redesigned, and which ones should just be optimized?

Typical prioritization of processes for automation

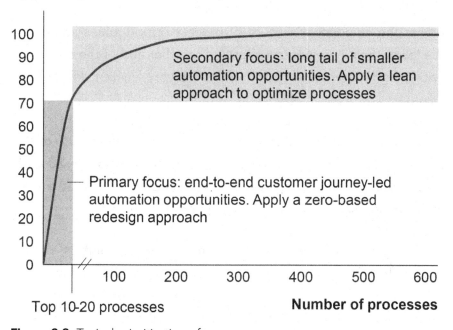

Figure 3.3: Typical prioritization of processes
Source: adapted from McKinsey article "A recipe for banking operations efficiency"[154]

The project activity "Identification and prioritization of IA opportunities", presented in the previous subsection, aims to build a list of the potential IA opportunities in a company and qualify the potential value they will generate for the organization. This list usually includes both high-value opportunities (usually related to end-to-end processes) and lower-value ones (usually associated with isolated tasks). An example of an end-to-end process is an "order-to-cash" process (including tasks from placing the order for a product until the vendor is paid for it), which involves sales, supply chain,

---

154 McKinsey, 2019. "A recipe for banking operations efficiency". https://www.mckinsey.com/industries/financial-services/our-insights/banking-matters/a-recipe-for-banking-operations-efficiency

and finance functions. As shown in Figure 3.3, the amount of smaller opportunities is considerably high, and it presents a long tail. The higher the cumulative amount of process opportunities identified, the lower their incremental value. At the other end of the scale, the end-to-end automation opportunities are very few but deliver high value.

Based on our experience, at most companies, **more than 50% of the potential transformation value comes from the top 10–20 end-to-end processes**. Hence, these processes require specific attention: in-depth redesign and prioritized technological investment.

The long tail of **lower-value automation opportunities** should involve less focus on the redesign. The value will be captured through the systematic use of the **lean methodology** to improve the processes incrementally (e.g., simplify, reduce the number of actions). Today, this project activity can be partially automated using a process discovery tool connected to an automated code generation tool (refer to "Enabler 3: IA generated by IA" in this part of the book).

Process redesign, leveraging a **zero-based redesign approach, will be applied to the end-to-end larger-value processes**. Doing this helps to maximize the streamlining of process activities from upstream to downstream and prevent bottlenecks. Besides, this redesign will provide more benefits (e.g., enhanced experience) if the process has a focus on the client outcome (also called "client journeys").[155] Refer to Part Two, "Combining capabilities to create synergies", for more

---

155 McKinsey, 2017. "The next-generation operating model for the digital world". https://www.mckinsey.com/business-functions/mckinsey-digital/our-insights/the-next-generation-operating-model-for-the-digital-world

detail on how to combine IA technologies to create more value while automating end-to-end processes.

3. Vendor and partner selection

One way that companies can fail in their automation initiatives is by spending too much time on **vendor selection**. We have seen companies spending 3 to 6 months performing a detailed selection. Our view is that they would do better by kicking off their automation journey as soon as possible to start generating benefits earlier than the competition. We recommend spending no more than 1–2 weeks. The solutions offered by the top three vendors by market share of a particular technology usually present rather similar features. For innovative market segments with less than three vendors, the choice is even more straightforward. Besides, the majority of these technologies can now all work together; the problems of integration, as we had with incompatible legacy systems, are issues of the past. IA technologies can be integrated with any other technologies. In addition, virtually all companies with at-scale IA deployments have ended up diversifying their pool of vendors to benefit from the best-of-breed solutions in the market and avoid dependencies. The point is not to lose sight of understanding the vendor landscape. But, still, the priority should be to kick-start the IA journey as soon as possible.

Sixty-two percent of survey respondents at top-performing companies said that they strategically **partner with third parties** to gain access to skill, capacity, and innovation. For example, a large multinational retailer developed a strategic partnership with a start-up incubator that focused on identifying cutting-edge technologies – such as drones – to transform the retail industry.[156] **Leveraging the support from consulting and delivery partners (they can be the same) is critical for gaining the right momentum in the organization with minimum investment.**

4. Anticipating IT requirements

This success factor seems very obvious. But, believe us, more than fifty percent of the projects we have supported have had challenges related to IT components.

The most successful companies anticipate **IT requirements**. They prepare the right infrastructure, ensuring fast and smooth development and migration into production. They keep development, test, and production environments separate, updated, and mirroring each other. They prepare test data ahead of development, with relevant quality and representativeness. Finally, they make sure to acquire an adequate quantity of licenses for IA programs, and to secure the appropriate rights for the robots and other IA applications to access legacy systems.

5. Managing data

As described in the earlier subsection on challenges, data is the fuel for efficient decision-making processes. Poor quality data is one of the critical challenges for IA implementation. Therefore it is crucial to design and implement an organization-wide commitment to treating data as a valuable asset. Here are its key components:

---

156 McKinsey, 2018. "Building an effective analytics organization". https://www.mckinsey.com/industries/financial-services/our-insights/building-an-effective-analytics-organization?cid=soc-app

- **Developing realistic and clear data** focus is key to avoid drowning in data and to create useful insight. It is about concentrating your resources on using the appropriate data. Rather than starting with the data itself, we recommend starting with the list of prioritized IA initiatives and identifying the data needs using them. Collecting and analyzing data should directly serve the objectives of creating insight necessary to implement specific IA opportunities. For example, if the organization is automating a client acquisition process, customer data should be the focus.

- We also recommend **prioritizing and wisely structuring the work on data**. For example, this involves starting by working on datasets that are structured and for which we have evidence of the quality, rather than spreading efforts trying to clean a new set of data.

- Another challenge is about **breaking the data siloes**. Let's keep the same example. If customer data is the focus, the first step will be to identify, list, and qualify the different data sources available. This is usually a very time-consuming exercise. The outcome might not be compelling as, most often, no one in the organization has the complete picture. To succeed in this exercise, we recommend grouping around the same table all departments which are supposed to be dealing with such data. In our example, it could include sales, marketing, after-sales services, and call center operations. This discussion with these departments is an opportunity to understand the sources of data currently available, their characteristics (e.g., structured or unstructured), and their quality.

- To ensure the best outcome from IA transformations, as well as other initiatives, we advise implementing **overarching data principles and policies at the company level**:

  o We recommend developing **policies for data consistency** leveraging, for example, a data dictionary – that is, a living document that ensures the consistency of data across the enterprise. It formally defines all indicators, calculations, and data lineage (the origin of the data and its transformation since then) used across the enterprise. During the conversations necessary to build this dictionary, misunderstandings about terms are identified and corrected. Having a data dictionary ready to use helps to save precious time during future IA initiatives.

  o **Data security and privacy measures** are keys to ensure compliance with data laws and regulations, such as, for example, GDPR.[157] We always recommend asking these questions: Am I entitled to keep this data? Where can I store it? How do I secure access to this sensitive information? Regulations vary widely depending on industry and countries. Working closely with the regulators on these topics is essential. You would not want to jeopardize an IA transformation by not respecting these fundamental points.

  o To ensure the optimal quality of the data used to fuel sensitive IA systems (e.g., those related to compliance), we advise **organizing regular data audits**. Institute a

---

157 Read about the General Data Protection Regulation (GDPR) policy here: https://gdpr-info.eu/

quarterly or biannual data management health audit. Auditing data helps to monitor the security, privacy, bias, lifecycle, quality, and flow of data.

Driving change and talent management

IA is built by people, to be used by people. Hence, people have to be at the center of a successful transformation. Change management and talent management are essential to any IA transformation.

1. Talent management

A critical success factor regarding talent management is to **start building talent as soon as possible**, at the early stages of the transformation. The sooner people are allocated to a project, the more they will know about its background, and the more they will own the outcome of the transformation.

In fact, getting a team trained on an IA technology is not enough to roll out a successful project (we suggest not to believe the vendors who claim it is). Four essential skills are required:

- Detailed knowledge of the business processes in scope

- Knowledge of how to configure an automation program using a certain technology

- Use of the appropriate delivery methods (e.g., Agile)

- Experience of similar projects. Since such projects are so specific by their nature, it is advisable to ensure that at least 30% of the team have already worked on similar projects. Resources can be internal employees or external consultants.

As presented in the subsection on the challenges of implementing IA, finding the right talents can be challenging. As shown in a McKinsey study, **internal recruitment and retraining** are commonly used by companies that are the most digitally mature.[158] Why spend time and resources looking for talents outside of the organization when existing employees can satisfy the need? Indeed, based on our experience, existing employees have a definite advantage in that they already know the specifics of the company. They know the processes and the other teams, and they understand the company culture. This knowledge is priceless and takes a long time to build with talents recruited externally.

In order to identify these internal talents, we have seen successful leaders mobilize employees by creating communities of interest, organizing internal challenges, competitions and games, and holding weekly talks with external experts. This allows them to quickly identify a few employees who are engaged and ready to be reskilled. In our experience, companies can typically find about 60 percent of the required talents internally and retrain them. About 40 percent would necessarily come from external recruitment.

2. Change management

According to a survey by Deloitte, organizations that have succeeded in scaling automation have engaged people and have effectively built buy-in to the change process.[159] These organizations **ensure proper change management and appropriate communication to**

---

158 McKinsey, 2018. "AI adoption advances, but foundational barriers remain", https://www.mckinsey.com/featured-insights/artificial-intelligence/ai-adoption-advances-but-foundational-barriers-remain

159 Deloitte, 2018. Deloitte's third annual RPA Survey, https://www2.deloitte.com/bg/en/pages/technology/articles/deloitte-global-rpa-survey-2018.html

employees. In essence, automation is here to help them focus on more value-added and exciting activities ("taking the robot out of the human"). They evangelize and celebrate IA successes to create a positive dynamic.

In our view, IA transformations are not primarily technology projects. Above all, they are business-focused, and people are at the center of a successful initiative. Here are the actions that were usually taken by leadership at companies where such efforts have been successful:

- **Inspire:** start by explaining to employees the company's vision, the reason why the organization wants to achieve this IA transformation, what these new technologies are, and what the expected benefits are for people and the business. Sharing the example of other organizations that have successfully been through such a transformation helps to reassure and excite employees on these perspectives.

- **Educate**: teach people how to use the new technology in their day-to-day work. Focus on the expected benefits for them; for example, less tedious tasks, access to more insights, the possibility of providing more value, and increasing their own market value in the internal and external labor market. The most successful companies educate to the largest extent possible. The more people are informed about the purpose of the transformation and its expected benefits, the more they will be able to support the change. Besides, the more they know about the technologies used and their capabilities, the more they will be able to identify new IA opportunities to feed into the pipeline continually.

- **Engage**: when people are involved in the transformation, they own the outcome. It is critical to include them in the identification of new automation use cases, the redesign of the processes, and leading the transformation project.

- **Clarify** career paths. The key is to be transparent and honest about the impacts of IA. Technology helps to reduce people's workload. Leaders need to be able to explain what it means for each of their team members. Some employees will still work in the same department, closely with the new technology. Some others might be redeployed to other functions, be trained in new skills, or be made redundant. Managers responsible for these changes need to anticipate the impact on the workforce and the organization in terms of workplace dynamics, culture, employee communication, labor relations, and organization structure. They should review all the options for the evolution of roles: retrain extensively, redeploy with time to adjust, and reduce only as a last option. For example, several roles will evolve to supervising the IA programs, managing the exceptions, and performing quality checks.

- Continuously **coach** people, support them in their professional development, and help them to find their path, update their competencies, and acquire a sustainable, flexible skillset. As humans, **all of us need to be able to project ourselves into our future in order to be confident in it and embrace it**.

New enablers to help organizations thrive with IA

As seen in the previous sections, many critical success factors, in the form of leading practices, can help mitigate the challenges of IA transformations. Nevertheless, a few important challenges like **the complexity, the cost, or the labor-intensive aspect of the IA transformations still remain issues to scaling IA**. New concepts and technologies are emerging from the market to help solve these issues.

In the following sections of the book, we will share five new trends that will help to scale IA. They constitute a response from the market to the current limitations of IA transformations, as presented in the preceding sections. These trends are levers or "enablers", as we call them in this section, that any organization can use to increase the scale of its IA transformations.

Most of these enablers presented in the coming sections already exist in the market. However, they are not yet mature and are still developing. Nevertheless, they offer exciting opportunities for early adopters to gain a competitive edge by experiencing and mastering them before others do.

The four levers are:

- **Enabler 1**. The **democratization of IA** – providing access to IA to a broader group of users.

- **Enabler 2**. The **convergence of technologies** – shifting from isolated technologies providing limited benefits to integrated technologies with substantial synergies.

- **Enabler 3**. **IA generated by IA** – using IA to increase our capacity to invent and deploy IA.

- **Enabler 4**. The **symbiosis of people and technology** – bringing IA closer to people, and people closer to IA, to enhance people's performance while improving technology's intelligence.

- Lastly, in the subsection "**Preparing for the long-term trends**", we provide a perspective on what can be the potential enablers of the future, further expanding the benefits generated by IA.

Enabler 1: Democratization of IA

The democratization of IA is about using technologies that require limited skills to design and build IA applications. With this, most employees in a company can be empowered to create IA programs to help with their day-to-day work activities.

Democratization helps to solve two main challenges:

- **Resources**. Relying on only a handful of skilled people from a center of excellence (CoE) limits the capacity to implement IA at scale. When fewer skills are required to deploy a technology, more people in the organization can participate. Increasing the number of people involved in an IA transformation allows higher speed, scale, and impact.

- **Mindset**. It also allows IA to be embedded into the culture of the organization. As most employees become empowered to build their own IA programs, they become authors of the transformation. This, in turn, drives higher ownership and acceptance of IA.

The democratization of IA leverages two main technologies: low-code and no-code. For enhanced benefits, it is recommended to implement democratization along with some complementary initiatives, namely the creation of appropriate governance and change management programs. In addition, communities and marketplaces are useful platforms that support the spread of IA within the organization and across organizations. Besides, offering the capacity to understand the insight created by IA helps to democratize it by opening its access to more people. We describe these five points in the coming pages.

1. Low-code technologies

Low-code applications provide the opportunity for almost anyone in an organization to automate work activities with only **limited training and skills**. Low-code applications enable business users to easily connect systems, drag and drop actions, build rules, and relate machine learning applications to process-automation programs. These programs are created through a user-friendly interface that uses tools such as graphical functional blocks that connect together to build an entire program.

We discussed these technologies in Part Two of the book, "Capability 2: Execution". Low-code platforms may require technical skills for some activities, such as when creating a specific interface across systems. This differentiates them from no-code platforms, which do not require any additional skill at all, as explained in the next section. More and more technology vendors are simplifying the use of their technologies, allowing more users to deploy them, while at the same time allowing these vendors to sell more software licenses.

An example of this technology, shown in Figure 3.4, is VDS (**Virtual Data Scientist**), created by MIT. This technology generates efficient machine learning models to run predictions through an intuitive user interface available on smartphones or tablets. It empowers users without programming or machine learning expertise (e.g., medical doctors) to build, analyze, and evaluate machine learning models effortlessly.

Figure 3.4: VDS (Virtual Data Scientist) enables doctors with limited data science skills to use machine learning
Source: MIT[160]

For example, suppose **a medical doctor** wants to understand the correlation between the age of the patient and the likelihood of having a blood disease. Using a dataset containing information from intensive care unit patients, the doctor will drag and drop a pattern-checking algorithm (i.e., one that can assess correlation) in the middle of the screen. It appears as an empty box. The doctor moves into this box two other boxes corresponding to the data features "blood disease" and "age". As a result, the interface automatically displays a scatter plot graph of the patients' age distribution.[161]

---

160 Rob Matheson, MIT, 2019. Drag-and-drop data analytics.
http://news.mit.edu/2019/drag-drop-data-analytics-0627

161 Watch the video here: https://youtu.be/En2O3ojmFHA. It shows the medical doctor dragging and dropping algorithms and data features to analyze data correlation.

2. No-code technologies

While low-code technologies allow building IA applications with limited skills, no-code ones **do not require any specific IA skills at all**. Simply put, no-code technologies are business-driven building blocks that leverage reusable low-code components to build IA applications.

In the future, we believe that **a "true" no-code technology also needs to include a "low-effort" or even "no-effort" dimension to increase the accessibility and speed of IA applications**. We explained intelligent chatbots in the "Language capability" in Part Two of the book. These IA applications are not only able to dialogue with people and analyze sentiments, but they can also perform actions (e.g., supporting a user to perform a password change). In the context of "no-code", the idea is to use this technology as a one-stop-shop interface to help workers automate their work activities using only their voice. Such intelligent chatbots can help to build an automation workflow or train a data set using only verbal instructions from a user. An example can be, "robot, could you please help me send the same reminder e-mail I just sent, every month, to the same people, thanks."

No-code technology is still maturing,[162] but in our view, this how IA applications will be developed in the future. See Case Illustration 3.1 for how such a technology could be deployed in the future.

---

162 There are only a few technologies available on the market like Talon, or Dragon by Nuance.

Case Illustration 3.1: Illustration of a potential concept of no-code technology

> ### Description of a potential future no-code application scenario
>
> This hypothetical no-code process automation application combines three technologies that already exist at different levels of maturity. It includes cognitive agents (or intelligent chatbots), process discovery, and the automated generation of code. It would work in 6 steps:
>
> 1. Each employee has a no-code process automation tool on their computer which observes and analyzes the business processes performed on an ongoing basis. This tool can assess automatically which of these processes have the potential to be automated.
>
> 2. The interactions between this program and the employee are managed through a cognitive agent (intelligent chatbot) that is able to dialogue and interact with the employee.
>
> 3. Once a process suitable for automation has been identified, it is compared with the centralized library of existing automation IA applications in the company and on open cross-company platforms. If such a program already exists, the cognitive agent suggests the employee use and, if needed, adapt the existing automated process. The employee is incentivized by rewards (e.g., financial and prizes) for each automated process.
>
> 4. If a process has not been automated before, the tool uses the documentation of the process (as created in step 1) to generate the code and automatically build the IA application.
>
> 5. Once the application is developed, the cognitive agent facilitates a step-by-step review of the new process with the employee in a test environment. As such, it ensures the automated process works according to the employee's expectations.
>
> 6. Once tested and approved, the new automation program is deployed and registered in the library for potential use by other employees.

3. Governance and change management as levers

Based on our experience, to ensure the success of a democratization approach, two initiatives need to be implemented: governance and change management (including incentives).

3.1. Governance

It would be risky and inefficient if any employee in a company could build their own IA tools without much control and coordination. To address this issue, successful organizations have supported their transformation by building structured governance. In these models, the central role is usually played by the center of excellence (CoE), which has an expert role, and which has the exclusive rights to put IA applications into production. The CoE usually leverages a network of champions (business users who have advanced knowledge of the technology) who are the first level of support to other business users, ensuring development is done according to leading practices and making the link with the CoE.

Such governance works in four steps: (1) the business user identifies a need and starts building an IA application, (2) the champion supports the user and reviews the new application to make sure it is aligned with the leading practices, (3) the champion sends the reviewed version of the application to the CoE for final review, approval, and migration into production, (4) the CoE includes this new application into the IA application library so that other business users can also utilize it.

3.2. Change management

In a democratization approach, it is essential to ensure employees are engaged in such a way that they are willing to take time away from their day-to-day work to identify potential IA opportunities and use the technology. Without employee engagement, the IA transformation would miss its objectives of scale. In addition to the usual change management initiatives such as communication and education, incentive programs are crucial. **Incentives encourage employees to find automation opportunities in their realm of responsibility** and translate them into IA applications. Various forms of incentives and even gamification can be used. For example, we have seen companies being successful at organizing "best robot" contests, hackathons, and similar events. For employees who perform well, we have seen organizations offering prizes, new roles, sponsorship of MBA programs, or even access to career fast tracks.

4. Communities and marketplaces help to boost democratization

Built on the principle that together we are stronger, communities and marketplaces are digital platforms that connect programmers, allowing them to share their IA applications and leverage those developed by others. In communities, this sharing is free, while in marketplaces, participants need to pay.

Github, one of the most famous sharing platforms, helps developers share their code and projects with the community for free. It allows leveraging of others' work and hence supports faster implementations. New communities are now emerging such as DAIA (Decentralized AI Alliance) and Kambria. DAIA brings together diverse organizations working on decentralized AI, creating an ecosystem of ecosystems that advances decentralized AI faster with high quality and impact. Rather than just connecting developers as Github does, these new communities connect companies, developers, and projects, allowing them to increase the speed of transformations through online project collaboration. As well as facilitating online project collaboration, Kambria's open innovation platform is built on blockchain technology. It contains protocols uniquely designed with crypto-economics and game theory to incentivize collaboration.

UiPath Go, the **first community** specifically focusing on robotic process automation (RPA), was created in 2017. UiPath Go not only helps developers share best practices, but it also helps organizations to support each other by sharing automation workflows member companies have already built. This includes robots for horizontal and industry-specific processes (e.g., accounts payable, claims and mortgage processing), or RPA integration with cognitive skills such as natural language processing and computer vision. Leveraging reusable components allows companies to scale faster.

5. Explaining the insight created by IA

"I don't trust this system! Why is it recommending this action instead of that decision?" We have heard such words in the mouths of many users of IA applications. Many of the **machine learning algorithms used by IA are considered "black boxes"**, offering no insight into how they reached their outcome. As a result, users lose trust in IA applications; some prefer to ignore them and are back to performing the work manually. There is a need to demonstrate alignment with the business problems to get buy-in from users and other stakeholders. This is true especially in critical domains like healthcare and finance, where accountability and transparency are essential. For example, there is a need to be able to explain why an IA application has led to the decision of diagnosing cancer, or why it has rejected a mortgage.

In order to solve this, some IA applications are now able to produce explainable models while maintaining system performance. Traditional methods generate explainability by generating indicators during the main steps of the decision process followed by the machine. They are supposed to provide the logic explaining how the ultimate indicator has been calculated. But several platforms and methods have recently been built to try to satisfy this need by **using machine learning algorithms** themselves. For example, the LIME[163] method helps to understand the data and the logic that led to a decision. It is about using machine learning to decipher the outcome of machine learning algorithms. IA which is explainable, provable, and transparent will be critical for establishing trust in the technology and boosting its adoption. As an outcome, explainable IA helps to make IA more human.[164]

In our opinion, a solid foundation to ensure that humanity keeps control of IA would start with governments issuing a regulation that makes it mandatory for any organization to be able to explain the outcome of any of its own IA applications, the decisions they make and the resultant actions.

In closing this section, we would like to emphasize the importance of the democratization of IA. We found that organizations that

---

163 Lars Hulstaert, 2018. "Understanding model predictions with LIME". Towards Data Science. https://towardsdatascience.com/understanding-model-predictions-with-lime-a582fdff3a3b

164 Konstantinos Georgatzis and Simon Williams, 2018. "Making AI Human Again: The importance of Explainable AI (XAI) ". Medium. https://medium.com/@QuantumBlack/making-ai-human-again-the-importance-of-explainable-ai-xai-95d347ccbb1c

have used the gamut of democratization tools discussed in this section were able to **boost the speed of their transformation by 20 to 50%, while significantly increasing scope and improving employee experience and engagement**. In fact, Gartner listed democratization as one of the top 10 technology trends in 2020.[165]

---

165 Gartner, 2019. Gartner Top 10 Strategic Technology Trends for 2020. https://www.gartner.com/smarterwithgartner/gartner-top-10-strategic-technology-trends-for-2020/

Enabler 2: Convergence of technologies

As explained in Part Two of the book, IA is defined as a technology that is able to mimic human behavior. To achieve this, it needs to master four main capabilities: vision, execution, language, and thinking & learning. However, as of today, there is no single technology that is able to cover all four capabilities. Therefore, we need to combine technologies to get closer to truly mimicking human behavior.

1. A trend towards more comprehensive technology portfolios

IA technologies are converging. We are confident that it is not a question of whether one technology will dominate the others. Rather, in this age of imperative digital transformation, it is about how technologies will integrate and create synergies, value, and impact.

One sign of such convergence is the **trend of enterprise software vendors** integrating IA capabilities into their products. For example, SAP acquired RPA software company Contextor in late 2018 with the aim of integrating IA into its existing ERP offerings. Now, one of SAP's latest solutions, SAP Leonardo, combines emerging technologies across RPA, machine learning, analytics, big data, internet of things, and blockchain.[166]

166　Read more about SAP Leonardo: https://news.sap.com/2017/07/what-is-sap-leonardo-2/

Microsoft is working on similar integration projects but on an even larger scale with its Microsoft Office user base of 1.2 billion individual users. The technology giant is bringing them a wealth of complementary technologies through its continually growing portfolio of new products, which include cloud, machine learning, a low-code platform, computer vision, and RPA. In May 2020, Microsoft acquired Softomotive, the maker of WinAutomation RPA software. Microsoft then incorporated the software into its Power Automate stack (formerly Microsoft Flow), its automation solution. This integration is likely to allow Microsoft to play a larger role in the IA market.[167]

Similarly, **cloud platform providers** Amazon and Google are competing to make their technology more complete, more integrated, and more accessible to use by non-experts. They are creating one-stop-shop platforms integrating IA technologies such as computer vision, natural language processing, and machine learning. The cloud platform market is expected to quadruple by 2022.[168]

2. APIs are critical for connecting technologies

Using one of the one-stop-shop cloud platforms provided by Amazon or Google allows organizations to seamlessly connect the full gamut of complementary technologies and take full advantage of the possibilities of IA. However, most organizations have several installed platforms, including legacy systems that can't connect with

---

167 Microsoft, 2020. "Microsoft acquires Softomotive". https://flow.microsoft.com/en-us/blog/microsoft-acquires-softomotive-to-expand-low-code-robotic-process-automation-capabilities-in-microsoft-power-automate/

168 Markets and Markets, n.d. "Artificial Intelligence Platform Market by Component (Tools, Services), Deployment Mode (Cloud, On-Premises), Application (Forecasts & Prescriptive Models, Chatbots, Speech Recognition, Text Recognition), End-User, and Region – Global Forecast to 2022". https://www.marketsandmarkets.com/PressReleases/artificial-intelligence-ai-platform.asp

these cloud platforms or other IA applications. In addition, these legacy systems are often not connected and disparate.

To help overcome the challenge of separate systems, Application Programming Interfaces (APIs) are **key enablers for connecting diverse technologies and allowing the seamless, real-time sharing of data between applications**. They are a key component of an IA system. APIs enable data sharing within and across organizations, and between the IA capabilities. For example, they enable the "execution" IA capability to share in real time with the brand manager the outcome of a sentiment analysis assessment from client emails performed by the "language" capability (refer to Part Two of the book).

Sign-up APIs are a well-known example. The traditional approach to registering new users of a mobile application is to require them to (laboriously) enter their details. The next step is to verify their authenticity by sending an SMS code or a verification email. Instead, sign-up APIs are now used to expedite this registration process. Users just need to press the button "sign up with Google" (or any other connected social media site), and the mobile application receives the user's information already verified by Google. As an outcome, APIs improve the quality of the information collected while enhancing the user experience.

API use cases involving two or more companies include the sharing of inventory status between suppliers and retailers for faster ordering, raising invoices, and making payments. Clothing retailers can also obtain the latest weather information from a government agency for a machine learning application that predicts sales.

3. Integration of capabilities into a single technology

Beyond the combination of several technologies, we believe the future trend is about integrating our four IA capabilities from Part Two (i.e., vision, execution, language, and thinking & learning) into a single technology. This will then act as a single interface: a genuine one-stop shop. By avoiding friction and external bridges, a single integrated technology would increase speed, response time, and data quality.

We think cognitive agents, such as Jamie (shown in Figure 3.5), could be a preliminary example of such a technology. Jamie is a cognitive agent created by ANZ Bank, a leading retail bank in New Zealand, to support prospects to open accounts and to help existing clients with their banking transactions. It is able to dialogue with people, to see (e.g., watch clients through their webcams and perform sentiment analysis), and to act (e.g., create a ticket to order a new credit card). And we expect to see Jamie's capabilities expand dramatically in the future.

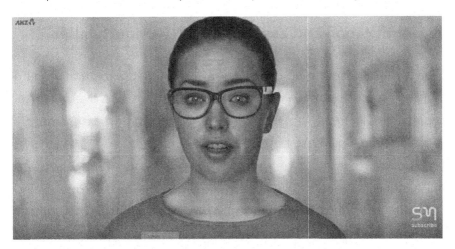

Figure 3.5: Jamie, the cognitive agent
Source: courtesy of ANZ and Soul Machines[169]

169 Soul Machines, 2018. "Jamie's first 100 days". Watch the video here: https://youtu.be/eyoBgNY1KA0

Enabler 3: IA generated by IA

Based on our experience, IA transformations are typically human-workload-intensive, resulting in lengthy and costly projects, hence limiting their scale. But **what if, instead of people, IA (itself) could help organizations implement IA?** New technologies and concepts have recently come to the market to help accelerate and improve the IA implementation process.

As described at the beginning of Part Three, IA implementation projects typically include (1) the identification and assessment of IA opportunities, (2) the design and implementation (including coding) of the IA applications, and (3) the monitoring and maintenance of these applications. For each of these three steps, we will describe the new concepts available and their impacts.

1. Identification and assessment of IA opportunities

Referring to the roadmap of an IA transformation presented in Figure 3.1, the assessment of IA opportunities happens twice over a typical project. The first one, labeled "**high-level automation assessment**", is a quick top-down estimation, based on metrics of the IA benefits for an organization. It helps management build their vision and understand the level of investment required. The second one, called "**identification and prioritization of IA opportunities**", is a more detailed identification and collection of the actual IA opportunities by the business users. It helps build the roadmap of the actual IA implementation. We expect the outcome of both estimations to be as close as possible.

We will first describe the new enabler supporting the high-level assessment. As for the second step (the identification and prioritization of IA opportunities), this can be performed in two dimensions: process or data. In the process dimension, two enablers are available: process discovery and process mining. In the data dimension, the enabler is referred to as data discovery. We will discuss each of these in turn below.

1.1. High-level automation assessment supported by machine learning

As emphasized in the critical success factors related to "Management support, vision, governance, and structure" earlier in this section, a leading practice to secure support from management is to provide a high-level estimation of the benefits expected from the transformation. This is often referred to as a "high-level automation assessment" or a "top-down automation assessment". For example, such an estimation might show that, by leveraging IA, the organization has the potential to increase revenue by 20% while reducing costs by 30% in the coming 18 months.

We have seen many organizations performing this estimation by collecting and summing all automation opportunities across the organization. While this exercise allows you to reach the goal, it is time- and resource-consuming. You can expect this exercise to take 2 to 5 months with significant involvement from project and business teams. As a result, an organization has to spend significant resources upfront. An alternative is to leverage the services of an IA expert for a few weeks, but this is not easy to find and can be costly.

A few consulting or technology companies **recently launched solutions to automate this assessment**.[170] They involve algorithms that have been trained on hundreds of transformations. As input, the model uses drivers like job descriptions, task descriptions, headcount, and organizational charts. The outcome is an estimation of the expected benefits at the organization level, which is then broken down by technology lever (e.g., machine learning, RPA, and computer vision), by function, and by team. For example, a result could be that the team in charge of onboarding in HR can benefit from 35% automation, from a combination of a smart workflow (20%), computer vision (10%), and NLP (5%).

Thanks to this enabler, the outcome is produced in 1 to 2 weeks with minimal human resources involved. It is less detailed and less accurate (expect plus or minus 20% deviation from the prediction) than a comprehensive collection of opportunities. However, in our view, it serves the purpose of convincing top management to allocate the required resources and rally the overall organization to buy into IA.

1.2. Process discovery

After getting the appropriate support funding and kicking off the transformation, it is necessary to build the implementation roadmap. Organizations achieve this by identifying and qualifying automation opportunities. **Process analysis, documentation, and prioritization of opportunities are time-consuming and workload-intensive**. Indeed, these activities require a large number of human resources

---

170 For example, RoboSuite by Reveal Group helps to perform this high-level assessment automatically based on the collection of a few business indicators. https://revealgroup.com/robosuite/robomanager/

to interview, observe, collect, and analyze process data. As a result, this phase often needs 2 to 6 months of work.

It would seem obvious to invite each organization's employees to identify automation opportunities from their day-to-day work. However, in practice, most employees do not have the skills to perform such an assessment, and their analysis can be biased if they are reluctant to change. Process discovery solutions help to automate and accelerate this work. The first process discovery technology was launched in June 2018 by Kryon Systems.[171] Here are the key steps it uses:

1. **Observation**. A program is installed on the user's computer. While users are performing their day-to-day work, it seamlessly records the clicks, the user interface objects, and the process steps, and it takes screenshots. This data is sent to a machine learning server for analysis.

2. **Process assessment**. After a few days of recording, the outcome is a dashboard that presents a list of the processes that were observed. The system ranks them by their potential for being automated. This potential is automatically calculated based on information such as the length of the process, the number of people performing the process, and the number of systems used.

3. **Detailed process analysis**. The dashboard described in the previous step allows clicking on any of these discovered processes and accessing their documentation, which is in the form of flowcharts. Figure 3.6 shows an illustration of such a

---

171 Kryon, 2018. "Kryon Introduces Process Discovery".
https://www.kryonsystems.com/kryon-introduces-process-discovery/

process flowchart. The main process is presented in green in the middle of the page. The variants are shown in pink on the side of the main flow. The indicators presented on the right side show the total duration of the process and the number of times it has been performed, and the dashboard breaks this down by process variants. Each of the process steps (circles on the flowchart) shows a screenshot taken during the observation period. They are useful documents to walk through with users to understand the current process, identify which variants are worth automating, and automate them.

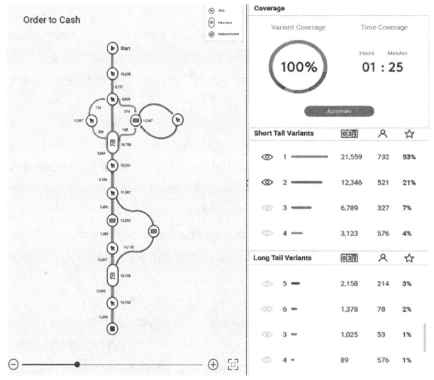

Figure 3.6: Process workflow analysis, including process variants (in pink)
Source: courtesy of Kryon

4. **Self-configuration**: the system generates the code automatically to build the automated workflow. The code generated is not complete and still requires some developer work, but about 60% of it is prebuilt by the technology.

Based on our experience, this type of program helps to make IA implementations 3 to 5 times quicker while approximately doubling the number of use cases discovered.[172]

1.3. Process mining

Launched by startup Celonis in 2016,[173] process mining solutions serve the same objectives as process discovery tools do. **Their difference lies in the way they analyze the process data**. Unlike process discovery solutions, which use computer vision and user-interface object recording, process mining solutions use the logs extracted from systems like ERPs.[174] For both solutions, the outputs are process flowcharts that include the variants of a process.

Process mining solutions are also used to identify non-compliant processes in the context of internal audits, for example. They can evidence that the same process was performed one way 99 times but differently at another time. They also offer the option to identify the user and the time when the non-compliant action was performed.

---

172 Here is an example of such a solution in action: Kryon, 2018. "Kryon Process Discovery". YouTube. Watch a demonstration showing the four steps of a process discovery: https://youtu.be/XF37t_mRbxQ

173 Businesswire, 2016. "Celonis Launches the First Enterprise-Class, Big Data Analytics Process Mining Platform". https://www.businesswire.com/news/home/20161207005173/en/Celonis-Launches-Enterprise-Class-Big-Data-Analytics-Process

174 Here is an example of such a solution in action: SAP Technology, 2016. "Introducing SAP Process Mining by Celonis". YouTube. https://youtu.be/Q0ftAldBeP4

The limit of process mining solutions is that they can only assess and document processes performed on ERPs or other systems generating structured logs. Processes performed on other applications, like spreadsheets, email, or PowerPoint, cannot be recorded.

Process mining and process discovery solutions **can be used in conjunction** to improve the outcome. Process discovery is usually less accurate but offers a more comprehensive view of the overall potential across all processes. In contrast, process mining provides the precise detail of each process execution but only on a few systems.

1.4. Data discovery

While process discovery and process mining solutions are used to perform automation assessments based on business processes, data discovery is used to achieve the same but based on data. This type of solution automates one of the hardest parts of a data scientist's role. It allows them to test millions of questions that the human mind would never even think to test, and it does so in seconds or minutes instead of weeks or months.

Finding relationships between data that can drive business value is resource- and time-consuming. Instead of manually testing a hypothetical outcome against a dataset, data discovery solutions scan massive amounts of data to discover thousands of hidden drivers behind strategic business challenges. These solutions also combine companies' information with external sources (e.g., economy, weather, demographics) to reveal hidden patterns and deeper insights.

For example, a data discovery solution was implemented at a global payment company. In five weeks, it improved fraud detection by 7% with expected cost savings of USD 140M. A similar solution was applied to credit risk scoring for one of the biggest US finance companies. The solution combined the client's data with external data to provide insights that enabled a product to be offered to 31% of the US population, up from only 6% before the data discovery solution was implemented. The project took 12 weeks to implement, and it increased the top line by USD 28M in the first quarter alone.[175]

2. Design and coding of the IA applications

New enablers also leverage IA to help actually design and code IA applications, providing tremendous acceleration of the implementation projects. Two main technologies are available on the market: automated generation of code and AutoML (automation of data scientist tasks).

2.1. Automated generation of code

Technology vendors have started to create applications that can generate the code of RPA robots directly by using the outcome from process discovery and process mining solutions (discussed earlier in the same subsection). What is so exciting about these applications is that **they automatically create and add automation workflows directly into the automation design studio**. Users can then further refine the code. Based on our experience, about 60% of the code for most IA projects can be pre-generated, doubling or tripling the speed of implementation.

---

175 Here is an example of a data discovery platform: https://www.sparkbeyond.com/. Also available in video here: "SparkBeyond at Microsoft Inspire July 2018". YouTube. https://youtu.be/GGvns4CmVoU

Machine learning applications have now started to follow this path, generating their own programming under human supervision. This means they can use machine learning to **generate machine learning code to reduce development time** and improve quality. Released at the end of 2019 by Jacob Jackson and his team, TabNine is an auto-completer that helps to write code faster. It embeds a deep learning model which significantly improves suggestion quality. TabNine has been trained on more than 2 million files from GitHub. It supports most programming languages.[176]

2.2. Automated machine learning (AutoML)

While data discovery platforms help data scientists identify relations between data (what insight can we create?), AutoML solutions support data scientists to build their machine learning applications (how to create the insight?).

In a typical machine learning application, data scientists have a data set consisting of input data points for training. Typically, the raw data is not in a suitable format that could be fed into algorithms. Rather, a data scientist has to apply methods of data pre-processing, feature engineering, and selection that make the data set suitable for machine learning applications. This includes, for example, the detection and handling of skewed data or missing values, or column type detection.

After these pre-processing steps, a data scientist selects the most appropriate algorithms and optimizes their parameters to maximize the predictive performance of the machine learning application. Each of these steps has its challenges and involves significant time and

---

176 Watch the video here: https://youtu.be/kXjVyva0kBY

resources. This involves, for example, testing in parallel the performance of hundreds of different algorithms (e.g., linear regression, decision tree, or naive Bayes) to solve the same prediction, ranking them and finally selecting the one(s) with the most suitable performance. AutoML helps automate these steps.

Figure 3.7 shows an AutoML solution presenting the outcome of a prediction tested simultaneously on several algorithms. The algorithms are ranked using several criteria. In this example, "Vowpal Wabbit Classifier" would provide the best outcome. The **AutoML solution took a few seconds to calculate these predictions with more than a hundred algorithms and finally selected the most suitable algorithm** automatically. It would have taken weeks for a data scientist to do that manually.

Leaderboard			Metric LogLoss	
Model's name	Sample Size	Validation	Cross Validation	Hold Out
⇄ Nystroem Kernel SVM Classifier	64.0% +	0.6277	Run	0.6122
⊂R Gradient Boosted Trees	64.0% +	0.6279	Run	0.6117
🐦 TensorFlow Deep Learning Cla...	64.0% +	0.6352	Run	0.6186
H₂O Deep Neural Network Classifier	32.0% +	0.6717	Run	0.6710
☆ Random Forest Classifer	16.0% +	0.6781	Run	0.6823
XG Boost eXtreme Gradient Boosted	16.0% +	0.7094	Run	0.7180
🐇 Vowpal Wabbit Classifer	16.0% +	0.8113	Run	0.8329

Figure 3.7: The outcome of a prediction tested simultaneously on several algorithms. In this example, Vowpal Wabbit Classifier would provide the best outcome
Source: Courtesy of DataRobot[177]

177 DataRobot, 2019. Benefits to Data Scientists. https://www.datarobot.com/solutions/data-scientists/

3. Monitoring and maintenance of IA applications

When organizations deal with hundreds or thousands of automation programs, managing the changes and failures is challenging. In the context of IA, where we combine different technologies to build end-to-end automation programs, **the failure of any of these components often causes the entire process to fail**. For example, a sudden change of protocol in a data interface could interrupt the data feed of a machine-learning algorithm. The program would not be able to provide the necessary prediction used in a critical automated decision-making process step. As a result of this failed process, the entire end-to-end automated process could be affected, with potentially unpleasant effects on the customer experience. It is therefore crucial to regularly assess the integrity of each component of an IA application, anticipate issues, and find efficient ways to remediate them in the shortest possible time.

According to ChoiceWorx,[178] the seven most common failures of automated processes are the following: credentials expire, the host device changes, the host memory changes, CPU or browser capacity is exceeded, an external application's processing time is too long, the upstream or downstream data flow fails, there are application outages, or the applications change.

One effective way to mitigate the issue of failing IA applications is the use of **an IA application that identifies the potential causes of failures and predicts them**. Such systems are able to proactively

---

178 Choiceworx was the first company to launch, in 2019, a universal intelligent platform for maintenance and monitoring of automation programs: https://choiceworx.com/

adjust the environment (if the change is due to an environment failure) or the automation program (if the program needs to be adjusted). If the change cannot be performed automatically by the system, it alerts a person to address the issue.[179]

---

179 Here is an example of such a platform: https://choiceworx.com/robotinuum/

Enabler 4: Symbiosis of people and IA

"As we humanize machines, we stop mechanizing ourselves."

Kristian Hammond, Professor of Computer Science at Northwestern University

This quote emphasizes that if we don't make machines like us, we have to be like them. In other words, making machines like us does not diminish us, but it augments us.

Human–machine interaction is a cornerstone for unleashing the potential of technology. The past few centuries have brought people and technology ever closer, demonstrating why we refer to their relationship as symbiosis. In this section, we will explore the evolution of the human–technology symbiosis and relate it to the potential future of IA.

In order to further envision what the future of IA technologies may hold, we have analyzed the evolving relationship between humans and technology. The study of human–machine interaction and symbiosis has a long history.

In 1960, J.C.R. Licklider, a famous psychologist and computer scientist, formulated a vision of human–computer symbiosis. It stated that computers and humans would become fluidly interdependent, each providing complementary abilities towards some shared goal that neither could achieve alone. Table 3.1 presents key academic research on this subject and shows our analysis of how this research might be applicable to IA.

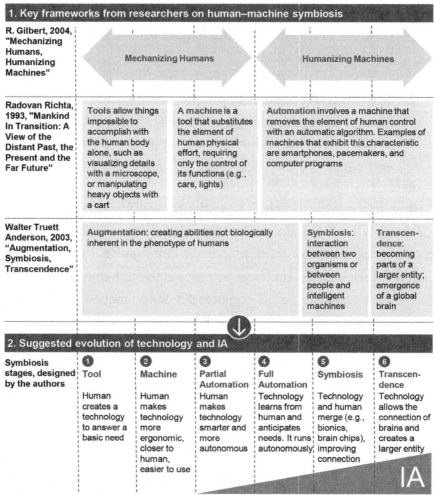

Human–machine symbiosis

1. Key frameworks from researchers on human–machine symbiosis

R. Gilbert, 2004, "Mechanizing Humans, Humanizing Machines"	Mechanizing Humans		Humanizing Machines	
Radovan Richta, 1993, "Mankind In Transition: A View of the Distant Past, the Present and the Far Future"	Tools allow things impossible to accomplish with the human body alone, such as visualizing details with a microscope, or manipulating heavy objects with a cart	A machine is a tool that substitutes the element of human physical effort, requiring only the control of its functions (e.g., cars, lights)	Automation involves a machine that removes the element of human control with an automatic algorithm. Examples of machines that exhibit this characteristic are smartphones, pacemakers, and computer programs	
Walter Truett Anderson, 2003, "Augmentation, Symbiosis, Transcendence"	Augmentation: creating abilities not biologically inherent in the phenotype of humans		Symbiosis: interaction between two organisms or between people and intelligent machines	Transcendence: becoming parts of a larger entity; emergence of a global brain

2. Suggested evolution of technology and IA

Symbiosis stages, designed by the authors	❶ Tool	❷ Machine	❸ Partial Automation	❹ Full Automation	❺ Symbiosis	❻ Transcendence
	Human creates a technology to answer a basic need	Human makes technology more ergonomic, closer to human, easier to use	Human makes technology smarter and more autonomous	Technology learns from human and anticipates needs. It runs autonomously	Technology and human merge (e.g., bionics, brain chips), improving connection	Technology allows the connection of brains and creates a larger entity

Table 3.1: A framework explaining the evolution of human-machine interactions

Source: © Bornet, Barkin & Wirtz

Table 3.2 illustrates the technological evolution of the three key fields of transport, communication, and knowledge work across the six phases we identified in Table 3.1. We believe that the symbiosis of humans and IA occurs in two ways:

1. **The closer people become to IA**, the more they are supported by it. It is about IA augmenting people, helping to solve more complex problems, and create more value (see Phases 1 to 3 in Tables 3.1 and 3.2).

2. **The closer IA becomes to people**, the more it can understand them. It can collect data, and increase the depth and breadth of what it can do for humans (see Phases 4 to 6 in Tables 3.1 and 3.2).

Illustrating these two points, we use the knowledge work application in Table 3.1. It lists some of the IA concepts we have already discussed in this book and also adds four main cutting-edge technologies that will take human–machine symbiosis to higher levels. These four technologies are verbal command enabled technology (VCET), workplace discovery (WD), XR technologies, and the internet of bodies (IoB). We discuss each of them in the following sections.

Symbiosis of people and IA

Suggested evolution of technology and IA   Examples

Phase	Description	Human–techno-logy relation	Transport	Communication	Knowledge work
❶ Tool	Tools allow things impossible to accomplish with the human body alone (e.g., microscope)	Human creates a technology to answer a basic need	Horse	Telegraph	Early computing hardware
❷ Machine	A machine is a tool that substitutes the element of human physical effort, requiring only the control of its functions (e.g., cars, lights)	Human makes technology more ergonomic, closer to human, easier to use	Cars	Wired phone	Office computer, software, enterprise resource planning (ERP), business process management (BPM)
❸ Partial Automa-tion	The partial auto-mation is a machine that removes most of the element of human control	Human makes technology smarter and autonomous	Cars with GPS, collision detection, speed limiter	Smartphone, voice commands	Smart workflows, robotic process automation (RPA)
❹ Full Automa-tion	The full automation is a machine that removes most of the element of human control with an automatic algorithm	Technology learns from human and anticipates needs. It runs autonomously	Driverless car Level 5	Ear phones with voice commands	Machine learning, NLP, computer vision, IA generated by IA

Verbal command enabled technology (VCET) |
| ❺ Symbiosis | Symbiosis: interaction between two organisms or between people and intelligent machines | Technology and human merge (e.g., brain chips), improving connection | Teleportation | Telepathy with technology | Workplace discovery (WD)

XR technologies

Internet of bodies |
| ❻ Trans-cendence | Transcendence: becoming parts of a larger entity; emergence of a global brain | Technology allows the connection of brains and creates a larger entity | Travel using our thoughts | Telepathy with other humans | |

Legend: ▨ The Intelligent Automation era   ▨ Concepts covered in this section of the book

Table 3.2: Technological evolutions explained using the lens of human–machine interaction

Source: © Bornet, Barkin & Wirtz

1. Verbal command enabled technology (VCET): dialogue-enabled interaction

This is about **using verbal commands to ease our interactions with technology**. Commands to trigger an automation program used to be manual (e.g., pressing a button to start the program). A few decades ago, we were able to automate these commands based on events (e.g., send an out-of-office reply automatically when an email is received). A few years ago, commands started to become verbal (e.g., using Alexa to call a phone number). But we are still in the era where we have to remember the right keywords (e.g., use the word "call" or "dial in" to get the program to perform a call). In the coming years, we expect these IA applications will be able to be triggered by full sentences, understand plain language, and be able to propose actions. For example, technology could say: "I heard that you haven't yet received the progress report on this initiative. Should I get you connected via a call with your business partner?"

Dialogue enables a closer connection between users and technologies, allowing better service and higher performance. In the context of IA, cognitive agents (intelligent chatbots) enable technology to dialogue and interact with people, **saving them from having to spend time writing or documenting commands**. The same capability has given rise to a technology movement called "no-code". It allows people to build IA applications using voice commands. For more detail, you can refer to the section "Democratization of IA". We expect that voice assistants will become a more integrated part of our lives and our work.

"What's clear to me today is that in five years the keyboard will be gone as an input device."

Mark Tluszcz, a venture capitalist with a track record for successfully predicting technology trends

2. Workplace discovery: building an in-depth understanding of humans

When technology is closer to people, it can better understand their characteristics and needs, and provide a more efficient and better quality service. **In the context of IA, sensors, cameras, computers and other technologies can collect data**. For example, some organizations have started to use wristbands, cameras, and GPS to collect data about the tasks performed by employees across space and time. Amazon's patent for smart wristbands to be worn by its fulfillment center employees was approved in 2017. According to the patent application, the wristbands use ultrasonic tracking of a worker's hands to "monitor the performance of assigned tasks".[180] The analysis of such information can help to identify areas for improvement. For example, it can determine that a machine should be closer to other machines to decrease the access time and reactivity.

In an office environment, we expect the use of sensors to be more sophisticated. Indeed, office processes tend to involve more verbal interactions, more process exceptions, and more diverse actions in general. This is what researchers from Dartmouth College have already started to address. They have developed a mobile sensing system able to track the performance of office workers.[181] The system has three distinct pieces. (1) A smartphone tracks physical activity, location, phone use, and ambient light. (2) A fitness tracker monitors heart function, sleep, stress, and body measurements (e.g., weight

180 Amazon Technologies, Inc, and Jonathan Evan Cohn, 2017. "Ultrasonic bracelet and receiver for detecting position in 2D plane". United States Patent and Trademark Office. http://pdfaiw.uspto.gov/.aiw?PageNum=0&docid=20170278051&IDKey=0E2634BC1119

181 Kirsten Korosec, 2019. "Researchers developed a sensing system to constantly track the performance of workers". TechCrunch. https://techcrunch.com/2019/06/29/researchers-developed-a-sensing-system-to-constantly-track-the-performance-of-workers/

and calorie consumption). (3) Location beacons placed in the home and office provide information on the time at work and breaks from the desk. The team used the system to track 750 workers for one year. According to the researchers, the aim was to give employees insight into their physical, emotional, and behavioral well-being. The system was also able to tell the difference between high performers and low performers, with 80% accuracy, by establishing correlations between employees' behaviors and their level of performance.

Humanyze, a start-up in this space, created sensor-enabled badges to track the movements and actions of employees and send this data to an analytics platform.[182] This data analysis aims to improve collaboration among employees and is used to answer questions such as: (1) Are people using shared spaces for collaboration, and if yes, there enough shared spaces? (2) How do performing teams work? (e.g., frequency of meetings, use of shared calendars, or other collaboration practices).

We could easily imagine extending such applications to identify and assess opportunities for automation, and even to pre-configure IA applications using the data collected. **Pushing the idea a step further, think of it as building a Google Map of business processes.** Imagine using a process or data discovery tool to collect process information from thousands of companies, then bringing them together, identifying similar patterns, identifying the most optimal ones, and standardizing them to be utilized by any company.

---

182 BBC, 2017. "Wearables at work: Are we trading our souls for a few flashy trinkets?" https://youtu.be/yhU4lm4jXy4

3. XR technologies

Augmented Reality (AR) and Virtual Reality (VR) are commonly referred to as XR technologies. These are emerging as key technologies for improving education, remote work, communication, collaborative work, and also better analysis of data.[183]

Some exciting initiatives in this space include San Francisco startup Meta which is trying to **rid the workplace of computer monitors, trading them in for its AR headsets**.[184] Mimesys, a Belgium-based startup that was acquired by Magic Leap in 2019, presented an innovation at CES 2019 to help collaborate remotely with the use of **holographic telepresence**.[185] It relies on the combination of depth sensors (used on the latest smartphones for 3D face recognition) with augmented and virtual reality. It already successfully implemented such solutions at BNP Paribas and Orange. We recommend watching the demo linked in the footnote.[186] Startup Spatial is pushing this further by enabling people to virtualize the content of computers or phones in space, creating an immersive digital workspace.[187]

Another inspiring example is **Microsoft's hologram** demo[188] presented in July 2019 by Microsoft executive Julia White. She demonstrated the capacity of the technology first to create an incredibly lifelike hologram of herself, and second, to make this hologram speak

---

183 Example of an application with AR Sticky Notes: https://youtu.be/Z8nrEAWlUIw

184 Bloomberg, 2017. "Could This Hologram Headset Replace Your Office?" https://youtu.be/IIbIQ-1Vxi8

185 Pascal Bornet, 2019. "Holographic telepresence is changing the way we communicate remotely in real-time" https://youtu.be/W-nbxsa5FQQ

186 Illustration of Paribas and Orange use cases here: https://youtu.be/13ktlkWppVs

187 Visit Spatial's website here: https://spatial.io/

188 Pascal Bornet, 2019, A hologram of you speaking any language. https://youtu.be/agEStiszjM0

another language in her own voice. This demo combined the two technologies of augmented reality and natural language processing. It opened the door to a whole new generation of communication opportunities. Imagine a world-class professor giving a lecture that anyone could listen to in their preferred language!

4. Internet of bodies

Instead of connecting objects with other objects, as with the internet of things (IoT), the internet of bodies (IoB) connects objects to the human body through devices such as sensors and chipsets that are ingested, implanted, or worn. In other words, **the IoB is the capacity for humans to tighten their connection with technology by embedding technology in their bodies**. The benefits are that technology augments people's capabilities, while people interact faster and more efficiently with the technology surrounding them. The ultimate scenario could be bionic people, which is when machines and humans merge.

Chipsets embedded in employees' bodies are already in use in a few companies, primarily for security authentication purposes. For example, they enable unlocking doors and computers, and operating office machinery. Epicenter, a Swedish co-working office, is offering its members an implantable RFID microchip to replace keys and access badges.[189] In the U.S., for the same use, Three Square Market was the first business to implant RFID microchips in its employees' hands in 2017.[190]

---

189 Mashable Deals, 2017. "Company microchips employees for access to the office". YouTube. https://youtu.be/plvhcVdJvEI

190 CNBC, 2017. "This Wisconsin Company Is The First U.S. Business To Implant Chips In Its Employees". YouTube. https://youtu.be/uAzfUz5Nh-g

In this category of intimate physical augmentation, we distinguish between technology that is **external** (e.g., just worn) and **internal** (e.g., implanted) to our bodies. Examples of external connections include brain–computer interfaces (BCI) using electroencephalography (EEG), often called "brain waves". They are considered external as sensors are usually placed on people's scalps. This technology enables people to communicate with the outside world by **interpreting the EEG signals of their brains**. This technology was initially developed to support disabled people to interact with devices such as wheelchairs, robots, keyboards, and computers. For example, Cornell University researchers designed a program that is able to type words on a computer using a person's brain waves[191], [192]

As an alternative to brain waves, there is also progress being made with harnessing electromyographic (EMG) signals. This is a technique for **recording the electrical activity produced by muscles**. One example is an armband with sensors able to read motor neuron signals coming from our hands or feet. This technology is expected to support amputees to connect with their prosthetics. It is enabled by machine learning, which translates the muscle's electrical activity into intended movements. The armband is then able to transmit this information over Bluetooth to any device, such as prosthetic hands or feet.[193]

191 Xiang Zhang, Lina Yao, Quan Z. Sheng, Salil S. Kanhere, Tao Gu, and Dalin Zhang, 2017. "Converting Your Thoughts to Texts: Enabling Brain Typing via Deep Feature Learning of EEG Signals". https://arxiv.org/abs/1709.08820

192 See the demo in action: Xiang Zhang, 2017. "Online non-invasive brain typing through EEG-based BCI". YouTube. https://youtu.be/Dc0StUPq61k

193 Here is a demo of such technology: Pascal Bornet, 2019. "New generation of prosthetics can read minds... (almost)". YouTube. https://youtu.be/zBkQbZnqwVY

Technologies using internal connections are still less common than external ones, as they are more intrusive. One example is a technology invented by the University of San Francisco. For the first time, neuroscientists were able to generate entire spoken sentences based on an individual's brain activity. The method used for this test with five patients was to implant electrodes within the skull. This technology provides hope to those who have lost their speech due to stroke, throat cancer, ALS, or Parkinson's disease.[194]

Elon Musk's Neuralink project aims to implant 10,000 electrodes, one-tenth the thickness of a hair, into a single human brain, and connect them to a microchip via Bluetooth.[195] The short-term goals are to treat brain diseases. The longer-term ones are to increase the amount of information that could be exchanged bi-directionally between humans and computers.

Pushing this principle of connecting people and technology even further, we can envision a day where this **technology will integrate directly into our thoughts**. For example, you could write and send an email just by thinking of it. This could be an advanced version of the internet of bodies, illustrated in the movie "Upgrade", where a chipset is implanted in the brain of a paralyzed person to help her walk and talk again. Figure 3.8 summarizes the three main levels of a brain–computer interface discussed in this subsection.

---

194 Pascal Bornet, 2019. "Generating speech from brain activity". LinkedIn. https://www.linkedin.com/posts/pascalbornet_speech-brain-innovation-activity-6528513057319157760-KSsR

195 More information on the Neuralink project: https://www.neuralink.com/

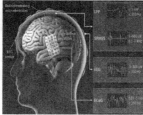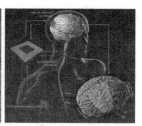

| External sensors | Internal sensors (USF Brain to Speech for disabled) | Augmented intelligence chipsets (movie "Upgrade") |

Figure 3.8: Three levels of a brain-computer interface
Source: © Bornet, Barkin & Wirtz

Preparing for the long-term trends

In the preceding sections, we discussed four key levers that are already emerging and that organizations can already use today to scale their IA transformations. In this section, we will examine the trends expected to affect IA in the long term. When implementing IA, any organization's leadership should keep these in mind to ensure that decisions are aligned with future trends. We believe these trends involve three key technologies, namely reinforcement learning, blockchain, and swarm robotics.

1. Reinforcement learning used in process automation

In the simplest of terms, the process of building a financial report involves collecting specific data from a source system (e.g., income before tax), performing a calculation with other data from other systems (e.g., tax rate), and, based on the results, selecting the appropriate tables to exhibit (e.g., tax credit or tax-deductible). This combination of actions and rules, which leads to an outcome, could be achieved through a machine learning method called reinforcement learning.

Reinforcement learning (RL) is a system that learns by doing. RL refers to goal-oriented algorithms that learn how to attain a complex objective (goal) over many steps. For example, it can learn how to maximize the points won in a game over many moves. Like a child incentivized by praise and punishment, these algorithms are penalized when they make the wrong decisions and rewarded when they make the right ones. See the footnote for a famous illustration of it, using cars racing to cross the finish line of a Formula One circuit. At the start of each generation, 20 cars are spawned. Each car has its own reinforcement learning algorithm, which makes up its "intelligence". If a car hits an obstacle, it dies. Once all cars of a generation have died, a new generation of 20 cars is created, using the algorithms of the two cars which performed best in the previous generation. Generation after generation, these cars learn by themselves how to reach the goal.[196] This particular form of learning was used by DeepMind to build AlphaGo, which defeated the human world champion at Go.

We see more and more use cases of RL in the business world, especially in the fields of industrial automation (e.g., in machine controls)[197] and medicine (e.g., usage of medical equipment, medication dosing, and clinical trials).[198] There are many potential applications for RL that could be implemented now.

With the ability to provide support in identifying the right actions, applied to sequences of tasks, and oriented for decision making, **RL has enormous potential to assist and work with humans in the medium to long term.** Just imagine an RL-enabled robot or virtual assistant working with you, which observes your actions and acts to support you to achieve a goal. All of the necessary components of this technical capability already exist; however, these technologies are very complex, and the amount of time required to train the

---

196 Samuel Arzt, 2016. "Deep Learning Cars". https://youtu.be/Aut32pR5PQA

197 Cyrill Glockner, 2020. "AnyLogic and Project Bonsai help companies teach machines to solve real-world business problems". https://blogs.microsoft.com/ai-for-business/anylogic-project-bonsai/

198 David Sontag, 2017. "Finding optimal treatment policies". https://mlhc17mit.github.io/slides/lecture13.pdf

models is enormous. It will, therefore, still take a few years for RL to become widely used in IA. That is, we are just at the beginning of developing its potential.

2. Blockchain and the company of the future

Blockchain is also referred to as a "distributed ledger technology" (DLT). "Blockchain is a software system that facilitates communication between transacting parties while distributing proofs of transaction agreements to all participants."[199] In other words, blockchain is a decentralized, distributed digital ledger used to record transactions and verify information across many parties.

When a transaction is recorded, it is registered the same way in each ledger of the blockchain. Therefore, the data cannot be changed retroactively without changing all ledgers, which would require a confirmation from the majority of users in the network. This characteristic ensures the integrity and reliability of the transaction information in a blockchain. It prevents fraud and avoids the need for manual verification of transaction authenticity.

Blockchain is not an automation technology, per se. That is, it does not automate tasks, but **it prevents the need for resource-intensive tasks**. In the context of IA, blockchain allows greater productivity, rapidity, and reliability. Blockchain's main applications in a business context are about enabling currency transactions (e.g., Bitcoin) and smart contracts (e.g., Ethereum). The use of blockchain replaces the need for human workers to (1) authenticate parties (e.g., checking and validating the identity, reputation, solvency, rights,

---

199 Thomas Zakrzewski, Distinguished Engineer S&P Global Ratings.

and obligations of an entity or a person), (2) check transactions (e.g., occurrence, completeness, accuracy, valuation, truthfulness), and (3) execute the transaction (blockchain allows instantaneous recording in many systems simultaneously).

Traditionally, these activities of recording, reconciliation, and profile verifications are time- and resource-consuming, error-prone, tedious, and repetitive (e.g., property management, banking). For example, large parts of the banking processes of Anti Money-Laundering (AML) and Know Your Customer (KYC) are expected to disappear when blockchain is used at scale, as they are all about verifying the identity, reputation, and solvency of individuals or companies.

Corporate governance uses a set of rules, policies, and processes involving the agreement of shareholders. Often, this sets in motion a lot of paperwork and bureaucracy. An essential corporate activity is the voting process. Each member of the board of directors votes on key decisions, such as major decisions regarding the company's strategic direction and the dividend distributions. With blockchain, voters have tokens, representing their voting power. Votes are transparently cast and secured on a blockchain network, avoiding any ambiguity of the results. This is critically important because vote results carry immediate legal liability.

Pushing blockchain technology further, **is it possible to imagine a point at which certain operations in an organization can operate autonomously?** Recently, Primavera De Filippi, a legal scholar, internet activist, and artist, presented the concept of Plantoid.[200] It is

---

200 Kat Mustatea, 2018. "Meet Plantoid: Blockchain Art With A Life Of Its Own". Forbes. https://www.forbes.com/sites/katmustatea/2018/01/31/meet-plantoid-blockchain-art-with-a-life-of-its-own

a piece of art in the form of an autonomous metal sculpture of a plant using blockchain. It is built to demonstrate how an organization can operate autonomously using blockchain. No one controls Plantoid; it is self-sufficient and even able to reproduce itself. Here is a summary of the reproduction process:

1. People pay cryptocurrency to the plant sculpture and become the joint owners of it.

2. When the plant has enough money, it opens a call for creating a new plant (the descendant).

3. Some people respond to this call, submitting design proposals for the new plant. The owners vote to select the proposal they prefer.

4. The submitter of the proposal that is chosen receives the funds and builds the descendant.

5. This process can be repeated to infinity.

This example, which uses plant sculptures, shows how autonomous organizations could exist. In the context of a company, the descendants could be investments or profitable projects.

So why are we not using blockchain more extensively? While the benefits of using blockchain are uncontestable, it still has a number of challenges to overcome. For example, it is very slow in performing transactions. It can take from 10 minutes to 4 to 6 hours for a transaction to be confirmed on a blockchain.[201] Ethereum, for

---

201 Abra, n.d. "How long does it take for a native coin (BTC, LTC, BCH, ETH) transaction to be confirmed?" https://support.abra.com/hc/en-us/articles/236149287-How-long-does-it-take-for-a-native-coin-BTC-LTC-BCH-ETH-transaction-to-be-confirmed-

example, can only process about 17 transactions per second at the moment, compared to Facebook, which can handle 175,000 transactions per second.[202] In addition, blockchain is very costly to operate as it consumes a large volume of energy. As of May 2020, a single blockchain transaction can require more than 600 kWh of energy to power it, which is equivalent to the power consumption of an average US household over 20 days.[203]

3. Swarm robotics

In nature, bees, ants, or schools of fish are examples of individuals cooperating to achieve impressive outcomes without the need for planning, control, or even sometimes direct communication between them. Humans, however, have only been able to achieve goals cooperatively through building organizational hierarchies, centralized coordination, and rules. The goal of swarm robotics attempts to draw on the ways such social organisms **use collaborative behaviors to achieve complex tasks** beyond any individual's capability. We are seeing an increasing amount of publications related to swarm robotics and its potential for businesses.[204]

In 2019, Massachusetts Institute of Technology (MIT) released **a new version of M-Blocks**: an intelligent, self-assembling fleet of 16 robotic cubes that can identify themselves, communicate with each other, create structures, climb, flip, jump and roll. M-Blocks can be helpful for inspection tasks (e.g., looking for leaks in an inaccessible

---

202 Pini Raviv, 2018. "How to solve Blockchain's data storage issues once and for all". Bitcoinist. https://bitcoinist.com/solve-blockchains-data-storage-issues/

203 Digiconomist, accessed May 2020. "Bitcoin Energy Consumption Index" https://digiconomist.net/bitcoin-energy-consumption

204 University of Melbourne, 2019. "Your future coworkers could be a swarm of robots". https://www.weforum.org/agenda/2019/03/your-future-coworkers-could-be-swarms-of-robots

pipe). They can also create structures like bridges, ramps, or even staircases for use in disaster response or rescue scenarios. The system could also be useful in other fields like construction, gaming, manufacturing, and healthcare.[205] Similarly, several IA applications hosted in the same or different organizations could interact among themselves, for example, sharing programs and best practices, or transacting. IA applications could work together, accomplishing a common goal without the need for human intervention.

Within a swarm, to communicate together safely, entities need to identify each other. For example, M-Blocks communicate with each other using a QR code. According to Thomas Zakrzewski, Engineer at S&P Global Ratings, it is important to recognize that machines also have identities. Blockchain can ensure the authenticity of applications' identities and allow or deny operations. In essence, **the blockchain is an ideal framework to have applications live and operate within a swarm**. According to him, it is the only framework today that can ensure the execution of an automated workflow by validated digital identities.

A group of agents has been proven to be able to reach an agreement on a goal, including a role and reward for each agent, without the need for a controlling authority.[206] This concept is called a DAO (Decentralized Autonomous Organization). Every company has a large number of processes performed simultaneously, requiring internal and external interactions.

---

205 Rachel Gordon, MIT News, 2019. "Self-transforming robot blocks jump, spin, flip, and identify each other". http://news.mit.edu/2019/self-transforming-robot-blocks-jump-spin-flip-identify-each-other-1030, Watch the video here: https://youtu.be/lwWCLiQPrfA

206 E Castelló Ferrer, 2019, "The Blockchain: a new framework for robotic swarm systems". In: Arai K., Bhatia R., Kapoor S. (eds) Proceedings of the Future Technologies Conference (FTC) 2018. FTC 2018. Advances in Intelligent Systems and Computing, vol 881. Springer, Cham

Supported by blockchain, a group of IA applications could reach an agreement on a common goal, including roles and rewards for each of them. **IA applications act like swarm agents, coordinated and working together to serve the purpose of the company**, sharing the same goal of running and growing the company. By working together, they are more flexible, more resilient, and able to achieve more.

Key takeaways of Part Three

- **Implementing IA is not a magic wand,** and succeeding at an IA transformation is not easy. Despite the widespread global adoption of IA, there remain significant challenges to transforming initial efforts into large-scale, enterprise-wide IA implementations. Success can be easily attained when implementing IA within limited scopes, through proofs-of-concept or pilots. However, scaling up the initiative across an organization introduces another level of complexity.

- In our experience, the **challenges of implementing IA** most often fall into one of a few specific categories: management vision and support, change management, data, technical limitations, costs and efficiency, talent, and the overall complexity of the transformation.

- To solve these challenges, we share **critical success factors** based on our experience of hundreds of IA projects. First, in an IA transformation, **management's leadership** is a foundation for success. Key aspects of management's role should include top management support, the design of an enterprise-level vision, the setup of clear governance, and the building of a center of excellence and an automation operation center. We also describe the **success factors for preparing and scaling the transformation**. They include the identification and prioritization of IA opportunities, the redesign of processes, vendor and partner selection, the anticipation of IT requirements, and the management of data. Finally, IA is built by people, to be used by people. People are at the center of a successful IA transformation. Hence, we explain how **change management and talent management** can be leveraged to reach this objective.

- Despite these success factors, a few important challenges like the complexity, the cost, or the work-intensive aspect of the IA transformations still remain issues to scaling IA. New concepts and technologies are emerging from the market to help solve these issues. We have grouped them into **four enablers** that any organization can use to increase the scale of its IA transformations.

- The **democratization of IA** helps to provide access to technology to more employees. The simpler IA is to understand and to configure, the more people can use it. In addition, employees can actively participate in the transformation, owning part of it. As a result, this helps to engage and motivate them, supporting the change in the organization.

- **Technologies are converging**, shifting from isolated technologies providing limited benefits to integrated technologies generating synergies. IA is a technology that is able to mimic human behavior. To achieve this, it needs to master four main capabilities: vision, execution, language, and thinking & learning. However, as of today, there is no single technology that is able to cover all four capabilities. Therefore, we need to combine technologies to get closer to truly mimicking human behavior. The convergence of technology is increasing the speed, reaction time, and data quality of IA projects, through avoidance of friction and external bridges.

- When **IA helps to generate IA**, transformations are accelerated, more comprehensive, cheaper, and less reliant on the human workforce. IA technology is already able to identify, assess, and prioritize IA opportunities by itself (e.g., using process and data discovery). It can also self-generate configuration code or automate some data science tasks (e.g., AutoML). Other existing technologies can automate the monitoring and maintenance of IA applications to allow more continuity in the services delivered.

- **Symbiosis of people and IA**. The past few centuries have brought people and technology ever closer. Human–machine interaction is a cornerstone for unleashing the potential of IA. In this section, we explore the evolution of the human–technology symbiosis and relate it to the potential future of IA. The closer technology becomes to us, the more it can understand us and increase the depth and breadth of what it can do for us. The key evidence of this trend includes technologies such as verbal command enabled technology (VCET), workplace discovery (WD), XR technologies, and the internet of bodies (IoB).

- While implementing IA, any organization leader should keep in mind the **long-term trends** to ensure that decisions are consistent with future market directions. We believe these trends are mainly influenced by reinforcement learning, swarm robotics and blockchain. With reinforcement learning, IA learns by itself the way to produce a given business outcome. IA applications also act like swarm agents. They are coordinated and work together toward the common goal of growing the company by leveraging blockchain. Such an autonomous system would result in increased flexibility and more resilience.

- These trends will undoubtedly work towards increasing the level of adoption and the scale of IA transformations over the coming years.

PART FOUR:
REINVENTING SOCIETY WITH IA

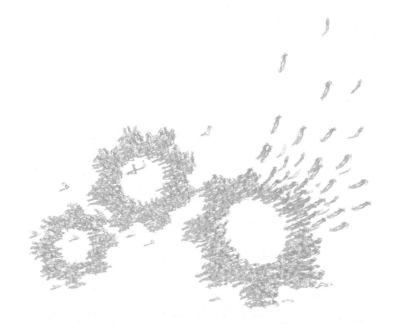

So far, we have explained why, in our view, the world needs IA, and we have explored the components of IA and their promising future. IA is about supporting and augmenting the work currently done by people. Given its recent advances and those expected in the future, is there a risk that employees are not capable of working with IA? As IA performs work on behalf of knowledge workers, is there a risk of making them redundant? Would this be an opportunity to redefine work? What could be the impact on society? What are the imperatives to ensure that our world takes all the positive from IA while mitigating its downsides?

In the pages ahead, we will explore these questions. We will do so with an awareness that no one has a crystal ball to predict the future. The only thing we can do is to identify possible future scenarios based on past and current trends with the objective of getting our world ready for what may happen.

IA is central to the fourth industrial revolution

Since the beginning of work, technology in general, and forms of automation specifically, has brought great improvements to our lives and our jobs. Who would want to be a farmer in the US in the 18th century, working 12 hours per day under a burning sun for a poor salary, completely dependent on environmental conditions you can't control? Who would want to be part of the teams who built the pyramids in Egypt, working for 20 years on a single construction project, carrying rocks every day?

Klaus Schwab, founder and executive chairman of the World Economic Forum, published a book in 2016 titled "The Fourth Industrial Revolution" and coined the term at the Davos meeting that year. He explained how **the first three industrial revolutions transformed our modern society fundamentally**. The first brought the steam engine, the second mass production, and the third digital technology. Each of these revolutions resulted in massive disruptions of our societies. Now, we have entered into the fourth industrial revolution,[207] which is about intelligent and connected technologies, of which IA is a central component.[208]

---

207 Klaus Schwab, 2017. "The Fourth Industrial Revolution".

208 See also how the fourth industrial revolution drives quality and productivity in across virtually all the service sectors: Jochen Wirtz, Paul Patterson, Werner Kunz, Thorsten Gruber, Vinh Nhat Lu, Stefanie Paluch, and Antje Martins, 2018. "Brave New World: Service Robots in the Frontline", Journal of Service Management, Vol. 29, No. 5, 907-931, https://doi.org/10.1108/JOSM-04-2018-0119; Jochen Wirtz and Valarie Zeithaml, 2018., "Cost-Effective Service Excellence", Journal of the Academy of Marketing Science, Vol. 46, No. 1, pp. 59-80. https://link.springer.com/article/10.1007/s11747-017-0560-7; Jochen Wirtz, Kevin Kam Fung So, Makarand Mody, Stephanie Liu, and Helen Chun, 2019. "Platforms in the Peer-to-Peer Sharing Economy", Journal of Service Management, Vol. 30, No. 4, 452-483; https://doi.org/10.1108/JOSM-11-2018-0369.

In this section, we discuss **five critical imperatives to ensure the success of our societies' journey with IA in this fourth industrial revolution**. In our view, they need to get the following right: (1) evolving skills, (2) sharing the wealth, (3) rethinking work, (4) reinventing education, and finally (5) building a potential new society.

We have also identified two extreme scenarios to show the range of outcomes we believe are possible for our society. The optimistic scenario holds that IA will enable the creation of more jobs than we have today (or at least keep this number constant). The pessimistic scenario suggests that IA will massively reduce the number of jobs available.

While the optimistic scenario would mainly involve managing the three first imperatives cited above, dealing with the pessimistic scenario would require a profound transformation of our society. For this scenario, we believe the five imperatives should be met.

The actual outcome will most likely be between optimistic (Scenario 1) and pessimistic (Scenario 2). This is the reason why we believe that, even in the case of Scenario 1, adopting the five imperatives would be beneficial for our world, making it more resilient and human. Above all, in order to mitigate the risks (and we owe this to our children and future generations), we need to be prepared to deal with both scenarios.

Figure 4.1 summarizes these points and provides an overview of this part of the book.

The future with IA: a roadmap for our society

Imperatives	Key components	Scenario 1 (Optimistic) IA would create additional job roles (or keep them stable)	Scenario 2 (Pessimistic) IA would result in a massive displacement of roles
1 Evolving skills	• Education has to be adapted to a world with IA through a transformation at scale • Work in collaboration with technology needs to be incentivized • Redesigning job roles and reskilling of employees is an imperative	Implementation of these 2 imperatives is necessary to ensure a positive impact of IA on society	Implementation of the 5 imperatives is necessary to ensure a positive impact of IA on society
2 Sharing wealth	• Wage inequality increases with technology (including IA) • Universal Basic Income can be a way to solve this		
3 Rethinking work	• Much of today's work sucks • Consider reducing or abolishing work? • Towards more fulfilling and meaningful occupations	Implementation of these 3 additional imperatives is optional, but preferred. Adopting them would help to create a more resilient and human society	
4 Reinventing education	• School comes from "skholē," the Greek word for "leisure" • Education aims at helping people find their purpose in life • Work-obsessed culture is an obstacle to creativity		
5 Building a new society	• A potential society freed from what we call "work" • A new culture focused on humanity and values, and respectful of the environment • To succeed, governments need to plan ahead		

Figure 4.1: The future of work with IA: a roadmap for our society
Source: © Bornet, Barkin & Wirtz

The optimistic scenario

The optimistic scenario is that the fourth industrial revolution will bear significant similarities to the past three industrial revolutions. While technological innovation removes some occupations (e.g., data entry clerk), it creates more new ones (e.g., IT managers, data scientists). Many economists believe in this scenario. According to them, this time is no different from before, and Adam Smith's "invisible hand" theory still applies to the economy.[209]

According to the World Economic Forum, machines and algorithms in the workplace are expected to create 133 million new roles by 2022, while only causing 75 million jobs to be displaced.[210] This means that the potential number of net **new jobs generated by AI could be 58 million over the next few years**. A number of other studies also reach the conclusion that IA will create more jobs than it automates; the most widely cited studies are listed in Table 4.1.

---

209 A. Smith, 1759. "The Theory of Moral Sentiments".

210 World Economic Forum, 2018. "The Future of Jobs 2018".
http://reports.weforum.org/future-of-jobs-2018/

Recent studies on the impact of automation on employment

Sources	Roles displaced (in millions)	Roles created (in millions)	Net roles created / displaced (in millions)	By when	Published date
World Economic Forum	75	133	**58**	2022	2018
Gartner	1.8	2.3	**0.5**	2020	2017
McKinsey	Between 400 and 800	Between 555 and 890	**Between 155 and 90**	2030	2017
Metra Martech	Not detailed	Not detailed	**Between 1 and 2**	2020	2013
The International Federation of Robotics	Not detailed	Not detailed	**Between 1.9 and 3.5**	2021	2013

Table 4.1: List of recent global studies on the impact of automation and artificial intelligence on the future of employment
Source: © Bornet, Barkin & Wirtz

Even if we assume that the net effect is the creation of additional jobs, it is impossible to guess what all these new roles will be. We can make partial predictions – for example, that there will be a need for everything ranging from robot development and maintenance engineers to data ethics managers – but there will be surprises too. Ten years ago, who could have guessed that our global economies would make room for 3 million Uber drivers by 2019?-

The two key assumptions underlying the optimistic scenario are:

- **History will repeat itself**. Previous industrial revolutions have generated significant productivity gains, vastly increased standards of living, and the net addition of new jobs. There is no reason why the current revolution would not have the same impact.

- The **time** between the automation of roles (that become redundant) and the creation of new occupations **is long enough** to allow reskilling the workforce.

The advantage of the optimistic scenario is that changes to our societies are smaller, bringing less potential disruption. We keep the momentum of our economies, with workers shifting to new and more fulfilling jobs created by IA. The drawback is that our society does not have the opportunity to rethink itself and potentially upgrade.

The pessimistic scenario

The pessimistic scenario is that the fourth industrial revolution will not follow the same pattern as the previous ones. Stephen Hawking, Elon Musk, Martin Ford, and several other famous scientists and authors believe in this scenario. They think the nature and the pace of technological innovation have reached a point that has never been seen before in history. **This time might be different.**

They point to examples of exponential technological change as indicators of our untrodden new reality. For instance, more data has been produced in the last two years than has been generated in the entirety of human existence before. Furthermore, Moore's law predicts that computer processing power keeps on doubling every two years.

Our challenge now might be time. The societies of the past had more time to sort things out. For instance, from 1870 to 1970, the number of farmers decreased by 90%. From 1950 to 2010, factory workers decreased by 75%. It required 100 years and 60 years, respectively, for these transitions to happen.

The pace of the transformation has become extremely fast (see the rapid displacement of human labor by machines predicted by 2025 in Figure 4.2). The world may have only 10 to 15 years to adapt to the full impact of the current disruption. Children attending elementary school today will enter the job market in approximately the same timeframe. If we want them to be prepared with employable skills, decisions must be taken now.

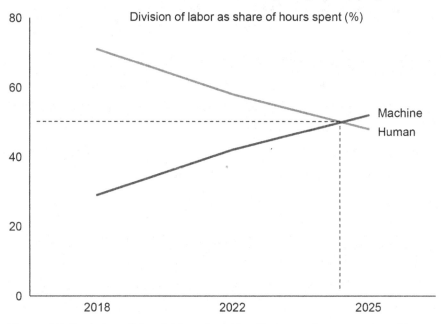

The rate of automation is progressing fast

Figure 4.2: Evolution of the division of workload between human and machine
Source: adapted from Future of Jobs Report 2018, World Economic Forum[211]

Besides, the nature of the current wave of automation is different from the previous industrial revolutions. Whenever a technological disruption happened in the past, people were able to reinvent themselves thanks to their intelligence. That is, we humans have been able to move and adapt from hunting, harvesting, and cultivating to producing manufactured goods in large quantities, and finally to creating value through a vast services economy, all thanks to our intelligence. **This time, it is intelligence itself that is automated by machines.**

---

211 World Economic Forum, 2018. "Future of Jobs Report 2018". https://www.weforum.org/reports/the-future-of-jobs-report-2018

It is much more sophisticated. In these conditions, will we be able to reinvent ourselves again?

The fact that AlphaGo, Google's DeepMind program, decisively beat an 18-time Go world champion supports the argument that this new wave of technology is different from what came before. It is able to learn by itself, adapt, and think (in some ways) better than we can.

Researchers at Yale University and Oxford University performed a survey of 352 AI experts. The outcome is a prediction that **AI will outperform humans** at writing high-school essays (by 2026), driving a truck (by 2027), working in retail (by 2031), and writing a bestselling book (by 2049). These experts believe there is a 50% chance of AI outperforming humans at all tasks in 45 years.[212]

As a result, it is becoming more and more difficult to identify the capabilities that are still particular to people, and that machines can't do. And the critical question becomes, how can we, as people, compete with this revolutionary set of new technological abilities?

Cornell University engineer Hod Lipson pointed out, "For a long time, the common understanding was that technology was destroying jobs but also creating new and better ones. **Now the evidence is that technology is destroying jobs and indeed creating new and better ones but also fewer ones.**"

Let's illustrate this with a well-known phenomenon: the automation of transportation. In 1915, there were 20 million horses employed in the United States. However, the 1920s witnessed a dramatic decline

---

212 Katja Grace, John Salvatier, Allan Dafoe, Baobao Zhang, and Owain Evans, 2018. "When Will AI Exceed Human Performance? Evidence from AI Experts". arXiv.org. https://arxiv.org/abs/1705.08807

in the US horse population. Their numbers fell precipitously to 4.5 million by 1959, due to the invention and widespread adoption of the automobile. By 1968, numbers began to rebound somewhat, to about 7 million, due in part to the growth of horse riding for pleasure. Today, there are more than 9 million horses in the U.S., still mainly used for leisure.

While not a perfect analogy by any stretch, there are some parallels here. Horses suffered a dramatic career decline at the hands of an automated tool that emulated their ability to transport passengers from point A to point B. Their saving grace was employment in a realm they were still uniquely qualified for – and for which there was no alternative. But fewer of them are needed. Are we going to find a similar fate, in which our uniqueness still leaves us employable, but at lower rates? Are we going to have enough time to adapt our skills for this coming revolution?

For these reasons, it appears that this industrial revolution might be different. Lessons drawn from the first three revolutions may not necessarily be applicable to this new era of tumultuous and rapid change. We need to be prepared for such a scenario.

Preparing for both scenarios

We believe that IA will create new job opportunities; we hope the first scenario will be the one in our future. Nevertheless, the pace of innovation and disruption is accelerating drastically. We fear it may be challenging to retrain all of the at-risk workers in time for them to acquire new roles. Failing to do so would leave large swaths of the working population to a fate of underemployment or unemployment for the remainder of their lives. The consequences of such a situation might come in the form of social unrest, revolutions, wars, or other events no one wants for our world.

If the optimistic scenario happens, the impact of the fourth industrial revolution, including from IA, should be constructive for our society. But this is assuming that the first two imperatives presented in the coming subsections ("evolving skills" and "sharing the wealth") are implemented and work.

If the pessimistic scenario happens, it might be tempting to try and decelerate further technological evolution. But it seems unrealistic to constrain an evolutionary process that has been occurring since the beginning of humanity. This wave of technology disruption has started, and we don't seem to have a choice but to embrace it, along with all its consequences. Pushing back may only prove harmful, destructive, and ineffectual. The other option is to accept that this fourth industrial revolution means that most work activities might be taken over by machines and that we will have to reorganize our society accordingly.

Above all, whether the impact of the current industrial revolution follows the optimistic or the pessimistic scenario, the most important thing is that **we need to be ready with a plan for both scenarios** and any combination of them. In fact, we believe the truth will be somewhere in the middle. We should be able to manage the risks involved in both. We need to do that for our children and the coming generations. Imagine telling them in a few decades, "20 years ago, we knew this scenario could happen; but the disastrous results are now taking us by surprise." We owe our children a much more thoughtful and rigorous response and preparation.

Imperative 1: Evolving skills

"The future of work will be a race between education and technology."

Mauricio Macri, President of Argentina
and host of the G20 summit in 2018

For a successful workforce transition to occur during this fourth industrial revolution, companies and government leaders must play a key role and take on associated responsibilities including (1) adapting education as an imperative, (2) transforming the education system at scale, (3) incentivizing the collaboration with technology, and (4) redesigning job roles and reskilling employees.

1. Adapting education as an imperative

Learning about technology certainly helps in today's world. Still, ultimately, in our view, technological expertise is not the most important skill. Indeed, even technical skills are being automated. For example, the startup DataRobot has already automated a large part of the role of data scientists. Surprisingly, it seems that the more technology progresses, the less we need technical skills (refer to Part Three, Democratization of IA).

So what are the skills that we need to teach to ensure that IA has a positive impact? We believe that **adaptability** and **"learning how to learn"** will be the most important skills to acquire in the future.

For example, Finland (often an innovator in education) has reviewed its education system and introduced significant changes we think could become a model worth watching. In the near future, traditional subjects at school will be replaced by the 4 Cs: communication, collaboration, creativity, and critical thinking.[213]

We also believe that we need to transition the workforce **from "knowledge workers" to "insight workers".** Machines can build knowledge (i.e., skills acquired through a learning process). But only humans can generate a real insight (i.e., one that involves gaining an intuitive understanding of something). That is, knowledge workers (who mainly manipulate information) can be replaced by machines. Therefore, we believe that humans should transition to "insight workers", bringing a new set of skills to the table that includes judgment, intuition, and critical thinking.

According to Tony Wagner, Senior Research Fellow at the Learning Policy Institute: "We still talk about a knowledge economy, but the reality is that the world is moving beyond it. What we have now is **an innovation economy**. Knowledge has been commoditized. There is no longer a competitive advantage in simply knowing more than other people because Google knows everything. What the world cares about is not how much you know, but what you can do with it."

Another critical skill that technology will take time to achieve (if it ever can) is **creativity**. Currently, this skill differentiates us from technology and hence makes us complementary partners in the future of work. We strategize, while the machines implement the tactics.

---

213 David J. Hill, 2015. "Finland's Latest Educational Move Will Produce a Generation of Entrepreneurs". SingularityHub. https://singularityhub.com/2015/04/04/finlands-latest-educational-move-will-produce-a-generation-of-entrepreneurs/

In 2016, DeepMind created the program AlphaGo, which won against Lee Sedol, the best Go player in the world. But AlphaGo lost one of its five Go matches against him. The reason for this defeat was that Lee Sedol played a very creative combination called "Amashi" during that game. Through this innovative move, he took AlphaGo by surprise, and it lost the match. Creativity made a difference.

Bernard Golstein, thought leader on the future of education, analyzed the impact of AI on work and education. In his view, the main objective of education in a world influenced by AI is no longer about acquiring specific content ("knowledge") during the so-called formative years. Instead, the "21st Century Compass" (see Figure 4.3) introduced in his 2019 book describes the skills required to navigate the new reality. **Learning how to learn** becomes a central component.[214] According to this framework, we should organize learning programs along five main dimensions:

- Learning to learn: the seldom-taught yet most essential capability when the pace and magnitude of change in the environment around us are increasing so drastically.

- Foundational literacies (numeracy, literacy, and digital literacy): the absolute pre-requisites to access the world.

- Cognitive skills, specifically critical thinking to help us make rational decisions, creative thinking to imagine what does not yet exist, and interdisciplinary thinking because complex problems are not confined to narrow domains.

---

214 Bernard Golstein, 2019. "Duality: Prepare Yourselves and Your Children for the Age of Artificial Intelligence". https://www.amazon.com/DUALITY-Yourselves-Children-Artificial-Intelligence/dp/1071374869

- Socio-emotional skills, particularly resilience to bounce back after inevitable life setbacks, empathy for deep and meaningful human connections, and collaboration because very little is achieved by individuals alone.

- Last but not least, the moral North: that is to say, purpose to define our mission in life and personal ethics to help us decide which roads to travel.

In order to implement this, the traditional role of school must be revisited to equip learners with timeless skills rather than soon-to-be-obsolete content. In parallel, education must be expanded from initial learning to lifelong learning. Lastly, state-of-the-art pedagogy and technology must make their way into the system to make learning more experiential, engaging, personalized, and social.

An example of such a technology is an IA application, built by the company Teradata, that leverages computer vision and deep learning to assess the level of attention and engagement of students. It calculates an "attention score", which is useful for educators to adapt the mix of school subjects or to identify when a break is needed. Its benefits are the capacity to maintain student engagement and optimize learning time.[215]

---

215 P. Bornet, 2020. "Improving learning experience with AI". YouTube. https://youtu.be/rrma9A4LFqU

21st Century Compass

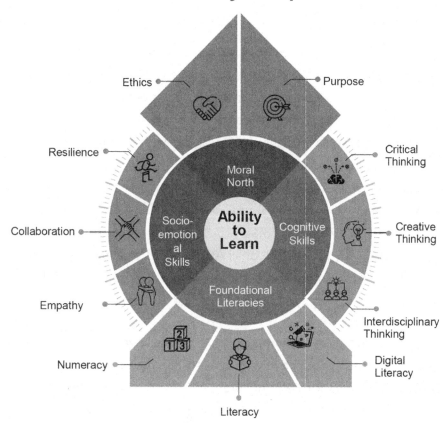

Figure 4.3: The 21st Century Compass: the skills required in a world influenced by AI
Source: courtesy of B. Golstein[216]

2. Transforming the education system at scale

The IA transformation of work will need a significant reshaping of skills required by the future workforce. Our education systems need to support this shift. We can take reference from the past, where

---

216 Bernard Golstein, 2019. "Duality: Prepare Yourselves and Your Children for the Age of Artificial Intelligence".

we have already seen such massive education programs being implemented.

For example, **the "High School Movement" in the US** proved to be one of the best investments the U.S. government ever made. From 1910 to 1940, a grassroots effort led to a "spectacular educational transformation", according to Harvard economists Goldin and Katz.[217] It was a response to a "skills gap" problem with soaring demand for educated workers to staff new white-collar jobs. In order to increase education levels, the government made it mandatory for the entire population to stay at school until the age of 16. The numbers are impressive – in 1910, only 18% of 15- to 18-year-olds were enrolled in a high school, and barely 9% of all American 18-year-olds graduated. By 1940, 73% of American youths were enrolled in high school, and the median American youth had a high school diploma.

This transformation required a large public investment, as these pupils were not productively employed (i.e., there were significant opportunity costs for keeping them in school longer). Besides, the creation of new schools and the hiring of more teachers required significant additional budgets. However, according to Goldin and Katz, **these investments provided people with skills that built the most productive labor force in the world**.

We believe that governments around the world should embark on a similar educational transformation. However, this time it should focus on the new skills needed in the age of IA. Furthermore, it should not only focus on pupils but also on working adults of any age.

---

217 Claudia Goldin and Lawrence F. Katz, 2008. "The Race between Education and Technology".

3. Incentivizing the collaboration with technology

IA is good at repetitive tasks, while humans excel at critical thinking, creative tasks, and solving novel problems. These characteristics make IA and humans complementary. In fact, behavioral economist and data scientist Dr. Colin W. P. Lewis proffered that "Human–computer symbiosis, not artificial intelligence, will spur new jobs."

However, the transition toward promoting this collaboration between IA and humans is difficult. Consider this post on Stack Exchange, a network of communities run by experts and enthusiasts, which went viral (485K views and more than 600 responses).[218] It asked, "Is it unethical for me to not tell my employer that I've automated my job?". After 18 months in a new role, this person wrote a program that automated his work to the point where he is receiving full-time pay for a job that now takes 1 to 2 hours a week to do. Fearful that there may not be another role for him at the company, he decided to hide the automation from his employer. He even tweaked the software to put a human level of errors into the output. Perhaps the question went viral because his dilemma causes all of us to think: "What would I do in his shoes?" and "What would I do if he worked for me?"

If the company had clearly communicated to its employees that not only it allowed, but it also **encouraged employees to automate their work activities**, it would have won on two fronts. First, this would have resulted in a proud and engaged employee. Second, this would have improved the performance of the company. The company could even have used this example to promote and create

---

218 IDrinkandIKnowThings, 2017. "Is it unethical for me to not tell my employer I've automated my job?" The Workplace Stack Exchange. https://workplace.stackexchange.com/questions/93696/is-it-unethical-for-me-to-not-tell-my-employer-i-ve-automated-my-job

a culture of collaboration with technology. For example, why not shift the role of this employee into a coach? He could help other employees automate their laborious tasks. We have seen companies being successful at developing such a culture, with the support of clear communication and incentive programs.

A way of **incentivizing employees to use IA** could be to organize contests with motivating rewards. Employees who have automated the most significant amount of workload could be rewarded with bonuses, fast-track promotions, executive education programs, or even MBAs.

Another way to incentivize employees would be to share some of the saved time with them. For example, companies could empower employees to make four-day workweeks a reality through self-automation.

One innovative way would be the creation of a robot ownership program whereby employees could own the robot they build and rent it to their company for a certain number of years. Of course, the rental fees would have to be set with caution. Nevertheless, such programs could provide employees with a financial incentive for automating significant amounts of work and thereby accelerate the transition from a human to a digital workforce.

4. Redesigning job roles and reskilling employees

Companies need to understand and anticipate the impact of IA on their workforce. They should explore the skills needed by their employees for their IA transformation and develop appropriate training and development plans. Skill adjacency – existing skills that can be applied differently to best complement IA – should be sought out, emphasized, and nurtured. The investments involved might be high, but in our view, they are necessary. For example, as technology reshapes roles, Amazon plans to spend USD 700 million over the next six years to train 100,000 of its workforce in new technology skills.

Sumitomo Mitsui Banking Corporation (SMBC) illustrates how a company can **implement a reskilling program at scale**. A year ago, through enterprise-wide automation implementation, it had eliminated approximately 1.6 million person-hours of work (equivalent to 800 full-time roles).[219] Meanwhile, the headcount had not dropped. Instead, employees' skills were assessed and people were retrained and transferred into a new wholly-owned subsidiary called SMBC Value Creation. It offers IA expertise and methodologies to other banks and financial institutions that seek similar productivity gains.[220]

This exercise, usually under the responsibility of Human Resources (HR) departments, needs to be continuously updated. Indeed, as technologies progress, the human skills required to produce the company's product or service also evolve. As an outcome, job designs evolve, and organizations need to integrate this component into their people strategies. According to a study from Mercer, C-suite executives identified job redesign as the area of talent investment with the highest potential for return on investment.[221]

---

219 Maria Nikolova, 2019. "Limited time as an asset – SMBC forms new business to boost productivity via robotics and AI". FinanceFeeds. https://financefeeds.com/limited-time-asset-smbc-forms-new-business-boost-productivity-via-robotics-ai/

220 SMBC Group, 2019. "Sumitomo Mitsui Financial Group, Inc. to establish a new company designed to support business competitiveness through productivity improvement". https://www.smfg.co.jp/news_e/e110116_01.html

221 Stacy Bronstein, 2019. "With More Business Disruption Expected, Making Organizations "Future-Fit" is Top of Mind, New Study Finds". Mercer. https://www.mercer.com/newsroom/with-more-business-disruption-expected-making-organizations-future-fit-is-top-of-mind-new-study-finds.html

Traditionally, **skill assessments, identification of training needs, and job redesigns** were performed based on employee interviews or observations. These methods were very time-consuming and challenging to scale. Today, the most efficient way is to **leverage IA**, enabling the analysis and assessment of all the employees of a company simultaneously and automatically. The approach and the tools we present in Part One, "Improving the employee experience", can achieve these goals, by automatically identifying the breakdown of the tasks performed by employees, qualifying which of these tasks can be impacted by IA, and suggesting job redesigns and training programs.

Imperative 2: Sharing the wealth

The world's eight richest billionaires control the same amount of wealth as the poorest half of the global population. Billionaire wealth has risen by an annual average of 13 percent since 2010 – six times faster than the wages of ordinary workers, which have risen by a yearly average of just 2 percent.[222] Remarkably, according to the same source, this level of inequality exceeds that experienced in medieval times.

IA enables economies to produce more with fewer resources, and one **danger is that the productivity gains will not be evenly shared**. Rather, skilled people as a group may benefit more than the overall population, and a few innovative companies and talented individuals may be able to capture a disproportionate share of these gains.

Robert Solow, an American economist well known for his theory of economic growth, found in 1957 that **wage inequality increased with technology**, favoring skilled over unskilled labor.[223] Since then, other economists, including Tony Atkinson and Joseph Stiglitz, have emphasized that, as technological advancements progress, economic and social inequalities increase. According to their findings, technological progress leads to an increasing concentration of wealth. Furthermore, the capital invested in every job created in the developed world continues to increase. According to Thomas

---

222 Stacy Bronstein, 2019. "With More Business Disruption Expected, Making Organizations "Future-Fit" is Top of Mind, New Study Finds". Mercer. https://www.mercer.com/newsroom/with-more-business-disruption-expected-making-organizations-future-fit-is-top-of-mind-new-study-finds.html

223 Robert Solow, 1957, "Technical change and the aggregate production function".

Piketty, a leading French economist, returns on capital are higher than income from labor. Inequality will continuously increase in the future.[224] As IA is likely to require fewer but more qualified employees, a grim result of these developments is that the middle class, which is essential for a stable society, seems to be disappearing.

Some economists consider a **Universal Basic Income (UBI)** as a potential means by which sharing the wealth created by rapid productivity gains can be achieved. UBI refers to programs that provide a regular income to the entire population, irrespective of their wealth or employment status. UBI aims to relieve people from the necessity to work to earn a living. As such, the income provided should be sufficient to cover their basic needs. It is then up to the discretion of these individuals whether they want the UBI to be their main source of income or if they want to top it up through paid work.

> **"Everyone has the right to an adequate standard of living."**
>
> Article 25 of the United Nations'
> Universal Declaration of Human Rights

UBI allows individuals to invest in their own human capital through further education. Such investments could create not only economic dividends through increased innovation and productivity, but also social benefits by boosting the creative, social, entertainment, and caring sectors, amongst others.

---

224 Thomas Piketty, 2014, "Capital in the Twenty-First Century".

Maslow's famous hierarchy of needs helps to define and prioritize human needs, as shown in Figure 4.4. Needs must be satisfied one after the other as we climb the pyramid. While work is not part of Maslow's framework, it can help to meet some of the needs articulated in it. Here is how work could help to satisfy the different levels of Maslow's pyramid:

1. Physiological needs: basics of survival such as food and shelter, provided by a salary and stable employment.

2. Security needs: a stable physical and emotional environment, including benefits, a pension, a safe work environment, and fair work practices.

3. Belongingness needs: social acceptance, such as friendships and cooperation on the job.

4. Esteem needs: a positive self-image and respect and recognition, such as job titles, prestigious workspaces, and job assignments.

5. Self-actualization needs: a sense of purpose, and alignment between the company's and the individual's purpose.

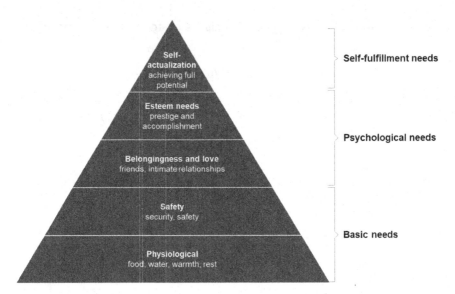

Figure 4.4: The Maslow pyramid
Source: adapted from A. Maslow[225]

The Workforce Purpose Index, published by NYU and Imperative, analyses the work orientations and wellbeing of the U.S. workforce. The outcome of the survey showed that 28% of the 150-million-member US workforce defines the role of work in their lives primarily as a source of personal fulfillment and a way to help others. Another conclusion of this study was that people feeling this personal fulfillment were led by purpose in performing their work.[226] This means **work enables only 28% of the workforce to attain the highest levels of Maslow's pyramid**. This finding could potentially be very different if these people were not obliged to work in order to satisfy their basic needs; rather, they could realize themselves, build and follow their purpose, and further climb the levels of the pyramid.

---

225 Maslow A., 1943. "A Theory of Human Motivation". Psychological Review.
226 NYU and Imperative, 2015. "Workforce Purpose Index".
       https://cdn.imperative.com/media/public/Purpose_Index_2015

UBI addresses the first step of Maslow's pyramid, providing people with the basics for survival. The impact of UBI on work could be to free people's minds, including for thinking about reinventing products, creating new markets, and exploring new ways of delivering value. We believe that the successful companies of the future will be those that begin asking people which problems they are inspired to solve, and which skills they want to develop.

There have been several pilots that contained elements of UBI. None have been conclusive, but collectively, they are beginning to reveal some useful insights. In the most high-profile pilot to date, the Finnish Social Insurance Institution initiated a scheme in 2017 to replace the unemployment benefits of 2,000 randomly selected individuals with an unconditional payment worth around USD 30 per month.[227]

Two years later, the outcome was that the level of employment of the participants, as well as their overall income, was not significantly different from the control group. However, their mental and physical health was significantly better. This is an important finding as it indicates that, on top of sharing the wealth more equally while still incentivizing people to work, UBI can also increase wellbeing.

Another program in Ontario, Canada, reported a similar outcome.[228] Several other pilots are in progress or planned at the time of writing,

227 Kela and the Ministry of Social Affairs and Health, 2019. "Preliminary results of the basic income experiment: self-perceived wellbeing improved, during the first year no effects on employment". https://www.kela.fi/web/en/news-archive/-/asset_publisher/IN08GY2nIrZo/content/preliminary-results-of-the-basic-income-experiment-self-perceived-wellbeing-improved-during-the-first-year-no-effects-on-employment

228 Government of Ontario, 2019. Ontario Basic Income Pilot https://www.ontario.ca/page/ontario-basic-income-pilot

including in Oakland, California, Scotland, Kenya, Uganda, Italy, and the Netherlands.

In order to implement UBI or similar wealth-sharing mechanisms effectively, there is much work to be done. There is a need for more experiments, more data to be collected, and questions to be solved, including how high basic payments should be and how UBI could work across national borders.[229]

To progress, governments must have the courage to fund and implement more and larger pilots. Individuals and organizations can also engage in the conversation around UBI through the growing number of interest groups, online content, and university courses. In this way, we can address those critical questions and move forward to assess, design, and implement the wealth-sharing programs for a future in which the world of work is fundamentally remade.

---

229 Sam Harris, 2018. "The edge of humanity, a conversation with Yuval Noah Harari". https://samharris.org/podcasts/138-edge-humanity/

Imperative 3: Rethinking "work"

In this part, we explain the necessity of evolving "work" as we define it today, and we provide examples of how it has already started to change.

1. Much of today's work sucks

Here are a few sobering realities about work today:

- Globally, according to the International Labour Organization (ILO), stress, excessively long working hours, and consequent diseases contribute to **the deaths of nearly 2.8 million workers every year**, with a cost to society of about $3 trillion per year.[230] These staggering numbers mean that work today kills 40 times more people than wars[231] or twice as many people as road accidents.[232]

- According to a recent Gallup study, **85 percent of employees worldwide do not feel engaged with their work**. The number is higher in some countries than in others. For example, 70 percent of employees in the USA do not feel engaged, but in Japan, it is an astounding 94 percent.[233]

---

230 International Labour Organization, 2019. "Safety and Health at the Heart of the Future of Work". ILO. https://www.ilo.org/wcmsp5/groups/public/---dgreports/---dcomm/documents/publication/wcms_686645.pdf

231 Siri Aas Rustad, 2013. "Conflict Trends". PRIO. www.prio.org/conflicttrends

232 World Health Organization, n.d. "WHO Mortality Database". https://www.who.int/healthinfo/mortality_data/en/

233 Jim Clifton, 2017. "The World's Broken Workplace". Gallup. https://news.gallup.com/opinion/chairman/212045/world-broken-workplace.aspx?g_source=position1&g_medium=related&g_campaign=tiles

- Another Gallup survey found that **two-thirds of workers experience burnout on the job**. The primary drivers of job burnout include unfair treatment at work, tight deadlines, high workload, lack of support from managers, and the added stress from having to respond to emails and texts during off-hours. The potential effects of burnout on health are serious. They include type 2 diabetes, coronary heart disease, gastrointestinal issues, and high cholesterol. The total annual healthcare spending linked to job burnout is estimated to be between $125 billion and $190 billion.[234]

- The book "Bullshit Jobs" by David Graeber, a famous American anthropologist, says that half of the **jobs on earth are like shoveling air**. They are only for people to make money to pay their bills, but not to thrive.

- Finally, Voltaire, a French writer in the 18th century, said, "work saves a man from the three great evils: boredom, vice, and need." We can also take poetic license and repurpose Karl Marx's famous quote on religion by stating, **"work is the opium of the people."** We believe the maturity and advancement that our society has reached over the centuries might give us the right to deserve more than that.

Especially over the past two centuries, it seems **work has been defined in a way that equates people with machines** and aims to make their work standardized, scalable, and repeatable. Why not take the opportunity offered by IA of potentially shrinking the

---

234 Bryan Robinson, 2019. "Two-Thirds Of Workers Experienced Burnout This Year: How To Reverse The Trend In 2020". Forbes. https://www.forbes.com/sites/bryanrobinson/2019/12/08/two-thirds-of-workers-experienced-burnout-this-year-how-to-reverse-the-trend-in-2020/

human workload and use it to elevate society by changing the way we think about work? In addition to focusing it on activities uniquely human in nature (i.e., jobs machines can't do), it could also be about inventing new meaningful occupations that reinforce our humanity, as is outlined in the next sections.

2. Reducing or abolishing work?

The idea of reducing, reinventing, or abolishing work is not new. In his classic 1930 essay "Economic Possibilities for Our Grandchildren", the economist John Maynard Keynes provided a perspective on this type of future. He predicted that the 21st century's workweek would last just 15 hours, and the most important social challenge of the future would be to manage leisure and abundance. "For the first time since his creation, man will be faced with his real, his permanent problem: how to use his freedom from pressing economic cares, how to occupy the leisure, which science and compound interest will have won for him, to live wisely and agreeably and well."

More recently, in August 2019, during his famous debate[235] with Elon Musk, Jack Ma made the point that thanks to the invention of electricity, we've been able to free our time for more leisure. With AI, we will have even more time and be able to enjoy being human. As a consequence, according to Ma, in the near future, **we should not have to work more than three days a week, four hours a day**.

Actually, moving towards shorter workweeks as a consequence of technological evolution has already started to happen. In Japan, the government is urging companies to let their workers have Monday

---

235 New China TV, 2019. "Jack Ma and Elon Musk hold debate in Shanghai". YouTube. https://youtu.be/f3IUEnMaiAU

mornings off.[236] In the UK, Britain's Trades Union Congress (TUC) is pushing for the country to move to a four-day week. More and more enlightened companies want their employees just to work four days a week, to allow healthier and better performance, attracting better talent, and improving gender equality. In 2019, Perpetual Guardian, a company based in New Zealand, tested how its employees would react to a 32-hour workweek. Its 240 staff were required to work 8 hours less per week while maintaining their pay. As an outcome, the workers reported feeling less pressured and more involved with the business. Productivity rose 30–40%, with employees improving their time management, holding shorter meetings, and signaling if they do not want to be disturbed. [237]

We can imagine a society where most of the work is performed by machines, and the wealth created is shared more equally through systems such as a universal basic income (UBI). But if we don't work (full-time), what do we do with the free time we gain?

3. Towards more fulfilling and meaningful activities

We can think of no better activity than to spend more time with our families, our kids, our friends, and our loved ones. As mentioned by Kai-Fu Lee, a leading computer scientist, businessman, and writer, **love** is the main element that differentiates us from technology and makes us human. This is the reason why we are on earth.[238]

---

236 The Guardian, 2018. "Japan urges overworked employees to take Monday mornings off" https://www.theguardian.com/world/2018/aug/03/japan-overworked-employees-monday-mornings-off

237 Reuters, 2019. "Do more with less: New Zealand firm's four-day week". https://www.reuters.com/article/us-worklifebalance-newzealand/do-more-with-less-new-zealand-firms-four-day-week-idUSKBN1XF1TM

238 Kai-Fu Lee, 2018. "AI Superpowers: China, Silicon Valley and the New World Order".

In addition to having more time for our families, we could spend our days performing the activities we choose to do, the ones that energize us, that give us a sense of purpose in life. We could perform them without the pressure of an expected outcome – for example, performing arts, sports, games, research, and even work (for those who choose to do it).

We could also focus our time and actions on improving society. For example, we could spend more time caring for others, our neighbors, and the weakest in our society. We could also collaborate on caring for the planet – identifying pollution sources, reducing and abolishing them, and monitoring them over time. We could work together to solve climate change. Many of us are currently highly engaged in solving environmental issues – and would most certainly like to dedicate more time to the mission if afforded the time to do so.

One more option is that **we may become occupied with fulfilling activities that we've not yet dreamt up**. Drawing a parallel with history, during the first industrial revolution, thanks to automation, the amount of time dedicated to leisure dramatically increased. This was when the world witnessed the creation of cinemas, a boom in music and theater, and other new forms of art and entertainment. In the future, we will likely have the opportunity to become creative with more advanced technologies, opening the door to new ways of entertainment, and new opportunities to learn.

Because so many offices and workplaces will no longer be used by employees, space could become available to build public facilities that are well-equipped with combinations of libraries, leisure centers, artists' studios, social and care spaces, equipment for programming, research labs, studios for making videos and music, and more.

The absence of "work", as we define it today, does not mean the end of our economic world or the end of capitalism. Machines could be able to create more output while we would have more time for leisure and to consume. As a result, economic growth and progress could continue flourishing. In a 1926 interview published in World's Work magazine, Henry Ford said: "leisure is an indispensable ingredient in a growing consumer market because working people need to have enough free time to find uses for consumer products, including automobiles."

Getting to this new definition of work would require significant changes to our societies. The most fundamental one is education.

Imperative 4: Reinventing education

The word *school* **comes from "skholē", the Greek word for "leisure"** or "rest". The origin and implications of the word were focused on thoughtful reflection, discussion, and tentatively providing answers to "how should we best enjoy our life?" Education originally aimed to guide people to find their purpose in life. Today, the intent of most schooling has taken on a more career-oriented bent, as many go to learn the skills to enable them to earn a salary. Sadly, this continued evolution toward trade-oriented education is what we expect will continue in the future of education. There seems to be a need to review the purpose of education.

Why are we teaching? The answer is to prepare the next generation for work. So, why are we working? Besides the obvious answer of it being a means of survival, the philosophical answer is that work seems to be deeply embedded in our culture. That said, work, as a dominant occupation within everyone's life, is actually quite a new concept. Indeed, during antiquity, work was delegated to servants, serfs, and slaves, so that other social classes could take advantage of life. Work is a recent invention. From this, it seems humans are not intrinsically made to work (at least not the cubicle version of it). Still, society, and our culture, conditions us to define ourselves by the jobs we do. And, let's face it, an aspiration to the 9-to-5 rat race does not seem to be part of human nature. Kids aged 5 to 10 often ask their parents, "why do I need to work?".

Many of us come to a point where **we confuse our personality and our social status with our work**. Indeed, when we meet someone new, our first question is often "What do you do?" The answers will usually trigger associations in the mind of the person asking. This dynamic certainly comes from our childhood, when adults always asked us, "What do you want to be when you grow up?" or "You need to get good grades if you want to have a proper career." But, going back to the fundamental values of humanity, what we could ask our kids is, "What do you like doing?", "What energizes you?", "Can I help you find a purpose in life?", or "Have you helped your friend to overcome that challenge?"

This work-obsessed culture can become an obstacle to adapting our skills for the changing nature of work. We hear some people say, "My work is at risk of being taken over by a machine," and adding, "I don't think I can differentiate my skills far enough from what technology can do. For example, I'm not a creative person."

Unfortunately, 75% of people today think they are not living up to their creative potential.[239] Perhaps it is because our established educational norms and constructs have been designed for a different purpose. As pointed out by Sir Ken Robinson, a leader in the development of education and creativity, our educational systems don't enable students to develop their natural creative powers. Instead, "they promote uniformity and standardization." According to him, we must rejuvenate and harness the creativity that came so naturally to us in our younger years. He says that rather than leaving

---

239 Rupal Parekh, 2012. "Global Study: 75% Of People Think They're Not Living Up to Creative Potential". AdAge. http://adage.com/article/news/study-75-living-creative-potential/234302/

that creativity on the playground, we should nurture it, direct it, and bring it to work with us.

In the classroom, we perform math or physics exercises, repeating them until we have learned the skill. Creativity is deprioritized in favor of prescribed classroom outcomes and only let loose at playtime. Rather than encouraging creativity and imagination, it appears that schools teach students to perform repetitive, rule-driven exercises – precisely the activities at which machines excel. This educational philosophy has even become part of our culture.

We strongly believe **all of us have the capacity to be highly creative**. The proof for that is found on the playground. In essence, watching children at play makes it apparent that they all have a capacity for imagination and creativity. The reason why we typically lose this capacity as adults could lie in the current education system.

Imperative 5: Building a new society

"There seems a general rule that the more obviously one's work benefits other people, the less one is likely to be paid for it."

David Graeber, American anthropologist, and bestselling author

Paid labor does not always map to social good. While raising children and caring for others seem to be some of the most essential social occupations, today, this type of work is compensated poorly or not at all. Could we consider a society where people spend more time caring for their families and others? Our pride could come from our relationships and our children's fulfillment rather than from our careers.

The idea of a society freed from what we call "work" today may not be prevalent, but it isn't new. Graeber, Hester, Srnicek, Hunnicutt, Fleming, and others are part of a group called the "post-workists". They believe that **society will be forced to change** due to two factors that could be combined: (1) automation of people's work by machines and (2) the human impact on the environment.

As a result, **society would need to redefine work**. Life would involve less work, and be calmer, more equal, more communal, more thoughtful, more politically engaged, more fulfilled. In short, it could become transformational for much of our human experience.

The transformation of work, culture, education, and the sustainability of living standards are all in play as IA impacts every element of our global economy. Change at such a large and comprehensive scale is the sort of challenge that governments and educational institutions are best equipped to address.

The role of government is key in potentially managing such transitions. Let us take the example of two wealthy oil countries: Norway and Saudi Arabia. They started with the same asset consisting of millions of barrels of oil in their soil, but the way they have used this gift has resulted in two very different societies. Even though both have among the highest GDP per capita in the world, their social and environmental indicators are very different. As presented in Table 4.2, the standard of living offered by Norway to its citizens is far superior to that in Saudi Arabia. Accordingly, the action of countries' governments is key to ensure that IA has a positive impact on our world.

Comparison between two countries with similar oil assets

Country	Life expectancy at birth (years)	Mean years of schooling	Gross national income per capita (PPP $)	Homicide rate per 100,000	CO$_2$ tonnes per capita
Norway	82	12.6	68,059	0.5	9
Saudi Arabia	74	9.7	49,338	1.3	17

Table 4.2: Comparison of social and environmental indicators for Norway and Saudi Arabia
Source: data from Country Economy[240]

---

240 Country Economy, comparison of Norway versus Saudi Arabia, accessed May 2020.
https://countryeconomy.com/countries/compare/norway/saudi-arabia

Which countries today are the readiest for automation? The Automation Readiness Index (ARI), created by the Intelligence Unit at The Economist, assesses how well 25 countries are prepared for the challenges and opportunities of IA. The top countries on the list are South Korea, Singapore, Germany, Japan, and Canada.[241]

The ARI assessment goes beyond skills and training. It considers other factors, such as a country's innovation environment and its labor market policies. Most of the assessment criteria are linked to government initiatives.

As has been done in so many ways in our past, our institutions need to help re-align priorities, cultural norms, and behaviors. By helping to change our work-focused culture to **a culture focused on humanity and values**, our institutions will need to help society transition to a new reality in which each individual does not have to be an economic contributor. The ways in which we measure our worth must change.

We believe those **governments that plan ahead and do so pragmatically will be best positioned to adapt and thrive**. Those that take a wait-and-see approach, or count on private enterprise alone, will most likely be setting the stage for unrest at an unprecedented scale. We are cautious optimists. But we suggest action. And fast.

---

241 The Economist Intelligence Unit, n.d. "Who is Ready for the Coming Wave of Automation?". The Economist. http://www.automationreadiness.eiu.com

Key takeaways of Part Four

- Over the last three centuries, our world has been through three industrial revolutions. We are now entering into **the fourth industrial revolution**, which is triggered by intelligent and connected technologies, and IA is a crucial component of it.

- This new revolution is not without risks. In our view, to ensure that our world will benefit from IA, our societies' roadmap should include five imperatives: (1) evolving skills, (2) sharing the wealth, (3) rethinking work, (4) reinventing education, and finally (5) building a potential new society.

- We have also identified **two extreme scenarios** to show the range of outcomes we believe are possible for our society. Similarly to the first three industrial revolutions, the optimistic scenario holds that IA will enable the creation of more jobs than we have today (or at least keep this number constant). Conversely, the pessimistic scenario suggests that, due to the fast pace and other specifics of the fourth industrial revolution, IA will massively reduce the number of jobs available.

- While the optimistic scenario would mainly involve managing the three first imperatives cited above, dealing with the pessimistic scenario would require all five imperatives to be met. The actual scenario will most likely be between optimistic and pessimistic. Above all, in order to mitigate the risks (and we owe this to our children and future generations), **we need to be prepared to deal with both scenarios**.

- First, education needs to be adapted to fit the skills expected in the future. It has to focus on people's competitive edge; that is, on tasks machines will never be able to do (well). We need to transition the workforce from "knowledge workers" to "insight workers". In our view, the most crucial of these skills are **creativity, adaptability, and "learning how to learn".**

- The IA transformation of work will need a significant reshaping of skills required by the future workforce. Our education systems need to support this shift. We can take reference from the past, where we have already seen such **massive education programs** being implemented. For example, the "High School Movement" in the US resulted in large-scale high school enrollment of youth, transitioning from 18% of 15- to 18-year-olds in 1910 to 73% in 1940. It has helped to build the most productive workforce in the world.

- Companies and government leaders should implement policies to enable **people to collaborate closely with technology,** taking full advantage of their complementarity of skills. Potential innovative ways of incentivizing employees are vast; for example, the organization of awards, contests, or robot ownership programs where employees could own the robot they have built and rent it to their companies.

- We also recommended that companies support their employees through the shift in skills required. They can do so by preparing **transition plans** which involve skill assessments, identification of training needs, and job redesigns. IA itself can help to achieve this goal.

- According to economists, wage inequality has increased with technology. The second imperative to ensure a positive impact of IA on our world is the **sharing of the wealth created by IA**. Wealth-sharing mechanisms like Universal Basic Income (UBI) aim at providing everyone with a basic income, irrespective of whether they are in paid employment or not. In addition, UBI helps relieve people from the necessity to work to earn their living and let them choose freely what and how they like to contribute to society.

- The third imperative is about **rethinking "work"**. Today's work presents a few sobering realities. According to global studies, due to stress, work kills twice as many people as road traffic. Besides, 85% of workers are not fulfilled by their work. With the support of wealth-sharing mechanisms like UBI, this could be a call to redefine work for the future. The new definition could evolve **towards more purposeful occupations** like taking care of others and our planet, focusing on what energizes us, and creating new forms of leisure.

- The fourth imperative is to reinvent education to support the new definition of work presented above. Schools should evolve away from preparing for career-oriented gainful employment. Going back to its Greek origins, the word *school* means "leisure" or "rest". We could leverage this definition to refocus education on thoughtful reflection; a **discussion that supports people answering the most critical question of their lives: "how should I best enjoy my life?"**

- By using the four first imperatives as a foundation, the fifth imperative is to **consider building a new, more human**

society: a potential society freed from what we call "work" today, embracing a new culture focused on humanity and values and respectful of the environment. To succeed, the role of governments is vital in planning and redefining societies that would be able to integrate this new reality. As has already been done in our past, institutions need to proactively help re-align priorities, cultural norms, and behaviors of societies. Failing to do so would most likely be setting the stage for unrest at an unprecedented scale.

CONCLUSION:

OUR WORLD URGENTLY NEEDS MORE IA!

Machines have taken the lead in automating manufacturing and agricultural production for more than two centuries. In developed countries, rare are factories or farmers who are not supported and augmented by technology in the form of robots or algorithms. We owe this to the compounded benefits of the first three industrial revolutions. As a result, they have significantly increased the level of automation, massively reduced the amount of manual work, and increased production volumes. In addition, they have improved people's standards of living and reduced the number of undernourished people in the world significantly.

Since then, over the last century, a shift in the workforce has happened from the agricultural and manufacturing sectors to services (knowledge work). The human workforce has naturally shifted to occupations that require less manual activities. Nowadays, more than 80% of the workforce are knowledge workers, while in 1840, the same proportion were farmers or factory workers.[242] This means that **today, the majority of the population of workers could benefit from the support of IA**.

The urgency of accelerating the transformation of office work with IA

But despite the great technological capabilities presented in Part One of the book, in the office environment, **knowledge workers are still working in the Stone Age** (or perhaps the Bronze Age). Computers and phones are the equivalents of the plow or the mallet of the pre-industrial revolution agricultural or manufacturing

---

242 World Economic Forum, 2018. "Here's how work has changed in the past 100 years" https://www.weforum.org/agenda/2018/11/the-changing-nature-of-work

companies. They are simple tools. The "automation" of processes is mostly performed by people who are leveraging these tools to manually perform the reports, data entry, or document analyses necessary to run enterprises.

In order to fill in the workforce capacity gap, over the last century, **it has mostly been easier for companies to add human resources than to try to leverage technology**. Also, to maximize profit, organizations have chosen to offshore workload to lower labor cost countries such as India, the Philippines, Poland, and Mexico. Today, more than 30 million people[243] are supporting multinational companies with their back-office functions (e.g., finance, HR, and procurement), their client relationships (e.g., via the web, messaging, or phone), and their IT management (e.g., infrastructure maintenance, and application development).

Nevertheless, **recently, we have seen the limits of such systems when unexpected global disasters, like the COVID-19 crisis, strike the world**. Over 80% of offshore operations were disrupted. The lockdown imposed by governments to stop the spread of the virus forced employees to stay at home. Companies like telecom firm Spark New Zealand and computer maker Acer had to ask their clients not to call, because the continuity of their offshored customer service was broken.[244] This situation has even pushed some offshored organizations to lock down their people in the offices to try to maintain service continuity for a few key clients. Employees were

---

243 Outsource Accelerator, 2020. "Ultimate outsourcing statistics and reports in 2020". https://www.outsourceaccelerator.com/articles/outsourcing-statistics/

244 Economic Times, 2020. "Companies move jobs away from India as coronavirus shakes up back offices". https://economictimes.indiatimes.com/tech/ites/companies-move-jobs-away-from-india-as-coronavirus-shakes-up-back-offices/articleshow/75266407.cms?from=mdr

reported by the media to be living in subhuman conditions for more than 30 days in a row.[245]

More broadly, **the COVID-19 crisis highlighted the gaps in our health and economic systems**. IA has the capacity to help address this by bringing more resilience to our world. For example, companies like Suncorp decided to bring back and automate processes they had previously outsourced to India.[246]

The promise of new advancements in IA

IA has already begun to fundamentally change how we live, learn, and contribute as economic creators of value. As presented in Part One, IA has the power to help solve the majority of the most pressing issues of our world.

Nevertheless, harnessing the benefits of IA is not a silver bullet. Several criteria need to be met to ensure successful implementation. As presented in Part Three of the book, recent innovations in technologies and methods are working towards bringing IA to scale. **What would a new typical IA transformation roadmap look like five years from now**, assuming organizations adopt these enablers? Figure 5.1 presents a tentative answer to this question, comparing the current typical roadmap presented in Part Three of the book with a new hypothetical roadmap five years from now. The main changes compared to a current roadmap are highlighted in Figure 5.1.

---

245 Financial Times, 2020. "Amazon contractors enduring 'subhuman' conditions in Philippines". https://www.ft.com/content/8b7bc787-4f33-4909-85f0-8df36d165b69

246 Ry Crozier, 2020. "Suncorp automates processes it had outsourced to India". https://www.itnews.com.au/news/suncorp-automates-processes-it-had-outsourced-to-india-549311

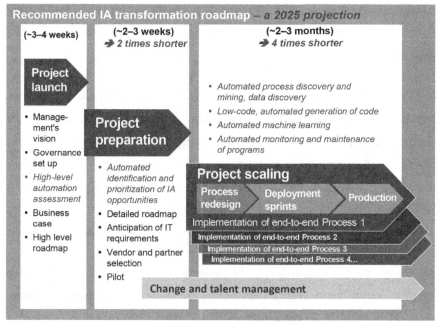

Legend: *project activities in italic could be automated leveraging IA*

Figure 5.1: A typical IA transformation roadmap five years from now, assuming organizations adopt the enablers presented in Part Three of the book
Source: © Bornet, Barkin & Wirtz

As a result of these technological advancements, at some point in time, would IA be able to **run companies autonomously**?

We believe yes, at least partially, and this is coming soon. We see some of these cutting-edge concepts already being launched in the market today. For example, Aera Technology[247] has been building a platform called the "self-driving enterprise", making an analogy to autonomous vehicles. The users of this platform can choose among five levels of autonomy to drive their work and business decisions. Level 1 is entirely manual, while level 3 involves the user taking action

247 Read more about Aera here: www.aeratechnology.com

based on the insight provided by the machine. Level 5 is the fully autonomous stage where technology can act based on its insights, with no human involvement.

Aera's platform ingests most of the data of an enterprise. **It makes real-time recommendations, predicts outcomes, and then acts autonomously based on these insights**. For example, it can automatically order raw materials based on a real-time demand forecast made by the system, integrating market constraints. As presented in Part Three, there is no doubt that blockchain and swarm technologies will provide even more autonomy to such systems in the future.

We are convinced that this type of technology, able to ingest and create instant insight from companies' data, represents a **potential future disruption to business consulting**. Such an application could consist of a software-as-a-service platform that could plug into any company's data. It could identify areas of improvement in real time, and automatically build or execute programs to solve these issues. This could mean the end of the current costly armies of consultants spending months in companies, interviewing, observing, and crunching data.

Such intelligent and autonomous concepts, if applied to the health industry, would allow **comprehensive health monitoring with real-time drug dispensing**. While the pace of innovation is less rapid in this industry due to regulation, we can already witness such innovations. They come in the form of health pods like Bodyo,[248] or wearables like smart contact lenses for diabetic diagnosis.[249] The

---

248 The National, 2019. "Health pods installed in Dubai government offices will collect workers' data". https://www.thenational.ae/uae/health/health-pods-installed-in-dubai-government-offices-will-collect-workers-data-1.732843

249 Science Advances, 2020. "Wireless smart contact lens for diabetic diagnosis and therapy". https://advances.sciencemag.org/content/6/17/eaba3252

most efficient system to monitor our health, according to scientists, would use our body wastes. A smart toilet boasting pressure sensors, machine learning, and cameras has been invented by Stanford University medical school.[250] It will help in the detection of health problems, including diabetes, infections, kidney disease, and cancer. Figure 5.2 shows how this system works. There is no question about it; the coming years will bring exciting advancements powered by IA!

(i) Pressure sensor
(ii) Motion sensor (PIR)
(iii) Urinalysis strip
(iv) Stool camera
(v) Anus camera
(vi) Uroflow camera

Figure 5.2: Stanford's disease-detection "precision health" toilet senses multiple signs of illness through automated analysis
Source: Stanford University medical school[251]

---

250 Stanford University medical school, 2020. "Smart toilet monitors for signs of disease".
     https://med.stanford.edu/news/all-news/2020/04/smart-toilet-monitors-for-signs-of-disease.html

251 Stanford University medical school, 2020. "Smart toilet monitors for signs of disease".
     https://med.stanford.edu/news/all-news/2020/04/smart-toilet-monitors-for-signs-of-disease.html

The need for a people-centric approach

While IA can make a powerful impact, it can have severe downsides if not used appropriately by organizations. The impact of IA goes beyond the context of businesses, as it also **impacts people's lives** and our society as a whole. The five imperatives that we present in Part Four could become the "IA laws" that any organization should respect as they choose to seize the benefits from IA. For example, when using IA, organizations should launch programs to monitor and evolve the skills of all their employees, engage in supporting wealth sharing measures, and manage the impact on the employment of their people.

To be successful in IA transformation, we believe there is a need for **approaches to be more focused on humans**. People are at the center of any successful IA transformation. They need to accept change; they need to implement it, to be the authors of it, to own it. The approach should not just be focused on identifying activities to be automated. There is a risk of an unbalanced outcome, where one dimension is prioritized at the expense of the others. The approach should be holistic. In alignment with the Triple-A artifact that we presented in Part One of the book, it should also include the identification of work activities to be avoided (useless or ineffective) or to be augmented by technology. Based on our research presented in Part One of the book, here is the holistic presentation of the potential impact of IA on work:

How to leverage IA to improve work	Percentage of current work time that could be impacted
Augment **some work activities**: leverage IA to generate more value from work (e.g., generating insights through advanced analytics to help decision making)	32%
Abandon **some work activities**: leverage IA to coach workers in reducing or eliminating non value-added activities (e.g., restricting the volume of meetings and emails)	26%
Automate **some work activities**: leverage IA to automate necessary routine and transactional activities (e.g., automating an expense claim process, or building a weekly report)	42%
Total	100%

Table 5.1: How to leverage IA to improve work (refer to Part One for more detail)
Source: © Bornet, Barkin & Wirtz

The expected outcome is not only an improvement of work productivity but also, and most importantly, an **enhancement of employees' experience**. It is about improving work-life balance, reducing stress, promoting healthy work habits, and coaching the implementation of leading practices in collaboration, management, and inclusiveness.

As presented in Part Four, another imperative is to prevent wealth inequalities from worsening because of IA. **Wealth-sharing mechanisms** like Universal Basic Income (UBI) aim at providing everyone with an equal opportunity to subsist, and even thrive, giving people the freedom to choose their contribution to society. The United Nations countries have committed to reaching a set of 17 sustainable development goals to solve issues that matter the most to our world by 2030. In her 2019 TEDx talk,[252] Hilde Latour explains how UBI is a single solution that could help to achieve all these goals

---

252 Hilde Latour, 2019. TEDx. "Building commons on the blockchain, a new narrative for basic income". https://youtu.be/Lu-Yic59bjl

at once. Indeed, according to her, UBI will not only eliminate poverty, but it will also contribute to other purposes like reducing crime and increasing health. Similarly, in the context of the recent COVID-19 crisis, more than 500 celebrities, politicians, and academics have signed an open letter, calling on governments to enact emergency universal basic income. According to them, as our economic system has been put under unprecedented pressure, UBI is necessary to save lives and restore people's livelihoods.[253]

What to expect next

Spending time with family, creating, socializing, helping each other, protecting our planet... These are activities which only humans are good at, not machines. Machines are good at repeating processes tirelessly and thereby creating value, which we are then able to share equally amongst ourselves. This means we could rely on autonomous technologies to deliver the wealth and food that we need. Meanwhile, we could **fulfill ourselves, focusing on what energizes us**, what makes us human. This could be the foundation of a new society, more equal, fulfilling, and human.

No book of this length could explore all dimensions of such a **renaissance**. For example, there is a need to analyze the mechanisms of transformation more deeply, enabling the safe delivery of such a society. We would also need to work out what the rules and structures could be. **There is much work ahead in planning to accelerate human achievement with IA!**

---

253 Independent, 2020. "Why more than 500 political figures and academics globally have called for universal basic income in the fight against coronavirus". https://www.independent.co.uk/voices/letters/coronavirus-universal-basic-income-ubi-poverty-economy-business-migrants-a9408846.html

We are living in an exciting world, at a fascinating time, when technological progress is exponential and continuously improving our lives. Surprisingly, it might be technology that will make us rediscover what makes us human. The IA revolution that is underway will mainly be about just that. It will be about relearning how to live in harmony with our planet and with other people. **A very bright future, if we give ourselves the chance to seize it!**

ASSET:

IA USE CASES LIBRARY

This library includes **more than 500 use cases**.
At the time of printing this book (October 2020),
it is **the largest list of use cases
currently publicly available**.

A s described in Part Three of the book, a critical success factor in kicking off an IA transformation is to identify, assess, and prioritize the business use cases. As we have supported enterprises in their IA adoption journey over the years, the question we are most frequently asked is, **"Where can I apply these technologies in my business?"**

To attempt to answer that question and to make this book as pragmatic as possible, we have compiled an extensive list of use cases. We define a **use case** as a description of how IA can be applied to existing business activities with the purpose of providing benefits. Use cases present potential areas of application of IA. They are useful tools to spark the imagination and direct the opportunity assessments. We have made them short and clear enough so that they can be adapted to any enterprise context.

All organizations in the world are composed of **functions** (e.g., finance, procurement, human resources). In addition, they all belong to at least one specific **industry** (e.g., banking, public sector). To make this long list of use cases easier to use, we have organized it according to the main business functions and industries present in our economies today.

As a result, what follows is **a compendium of over 500 use cases across industries and business functions**. The inspiration for such a list has been our own varied experiences, supplemented by industry peers and other practitioners' invaluable inputs. In addition, we applied extrapolation, extending the applications of IA from one known area to another similar domain. For example, we have worked on transposing some proven successful use cases from one industry or business function to another.

The purpose of this list of use cases is to stimulate creativity and to demonstrate the vast number of opportunities that exist to apply IA in, literally, all functions and industries.

We have chosen to detail the use cases at a granular level to fit with most organizations' contexts and make these use cases as actionable as possible. Nevertheless, as presented in Part Three of the book, the leading practice is to design and implement IA based on end-to-end processes. To reach this objective, we recommend that you collate together the use cases for the business activities belonging to the same end-to-end process.

For example, the "Purchase to Pay" end-to-end process would include the following groups of use cases:

1. Vendor identification and contracting (in the coming pages, refer to the use cases presented under 2.2 and 2.3 in «IA use cases in the Procurement function»)

2. Purchase order validation and execution (refer to the use cases presented under 2.5 in «IA use cases in the Procurement function»)

3. Product reception and checks (refer to the use cases presented under 4.1 and 4.2 in «IA use cases in the Supply Chain function»)

4. Invoice processing, matching, and payment (refer to the use cases presented under 1.1 in "IA use cases in the Finance function"

The library includes eight functions and five industries. Here is the list:

Business functions use cases

Industry use cases

Business functions use cases

1. IA use cases in the finance function

1.1. Process accounts payable

- Vendor master data set up and maintenance: manage approval workflows for vendor creation, change or deletion, and execute the changes automatically in the systems (E + L)

- Receive, classify, and process vendor official documents like business licenses and identification documents into the vendor system, leveraging intelligent character recognition. Check this information with external sources like government databases or official websites. Send discrepancies for investigation (E + L + V + T&L)

- Process vendor invoices or receipts into accounting systems based on scanned versions of these documents, leveraging intelligent character recognition. Identify exceptions and route the documents into a specific workflow for processing and approval (E + L + V)

Legend of the capabilities: E: Execution, L: Language, V: Vision, T&L: Thinking & Learning. Refer to Part Two of the book for the list of technologies involved in each capability.

– INTELLIGENT AUTOMATION USE CASES LIBRARY –

- Support the workflow processes and approvals for purchase orders and invoices received (E)

- Perform 2- or 3-way match, comparing price, quantity, and products across the purchase order, the goods receipt, and the invoice (E)

- Create and send emails to investigate and resolve gaps with other departments. Manage the back and forth of responses and perform potential actions required to close the gaps, for example, post a balancing journal entry (E + L + T&L)

- Prepare payment lists and process payments and bulk payments through the accounting system or the bank website (E)

1.2. Process accounts receivable

- Set up and maintain client master data: manage approval workflows for client creation, change or deletion, and execute the changes automatically in the systems (E + L)

- Receive, classify, and process client official documents like business licenses and identification documents into the client management system. Check this information with

Legend of the capabilities: *E: Execution, L: Language, V: Vision, T&L: Thinking & Learning.*
Refer to Part Two of the book for the list of technologies involved in each capability.

external sources like government databases or official websites. Send discrepancies for investigation (E + L + V + T&L)

- Format and classify customer invoice input as per end system requirements (E + L)

- Receive client orders from the sales department, check and process them into the accounting system (E + L + V)

- Send payment receipts to clients via email (E + L)

- Allocate cash received into the bank account to the relevant accounts receivable (E + L)

- Generate payment aging reports by extracting data from accounting systems (E + T&L)

- Predict clients likely to pay late or not pay, by using demographic and behavioral information (T&L)

- Identify trends and drivers of unpaid receivables and estimate provisions (T&L)

- Identify, solve and monitor the root cause of payment discrepancies (T&L)

Legend of the capabilities: E: Execution, L: Language, V: Vision, T&L: Thinking & Learning. Refer to Part Two of the book for the list of technologies involved in each capability.

- Track the resolution of payment discrepancies by visualizing the data cascaded from payment discrepancy to dispute case to sales adjustment (T&L)

- Supports approval workflows for credit approvals (E)

- Supporting credit request approvals by collecting client solvency information from internal data sources or the web (E + L)

1.3. Manage accounting journal entries

- Create files and emails to gain approvals for journal entries or to request for information for accrual calculation (E + L)

- Automate the posting of journals to subsystems and general ledgers based on conditions, for example, category, time or amounts (E)

- Create and post standard monthly journal entries using pre-populated templates provided by different business users (E)

- Automate accounting entries submissions and validation within ERP or other systems based on rules;

Legend of the capabilities: *E: Execution, L: Language, V: Vision, T&L: Thinking & Learning.*
Refer to Part Two of the book for the list of technologies involved in each capability.

for example, a specific date and time each month, or the completion of all accounting activities (E + T&L)

- Audit and rationalize the volume of manual journal entries by analyzing the quantity and nature of the journal entries (E + T&L)

1.4. Reconcile accounts and intercompany transactions

- Download, perform and report the reconciliations of the general ledger with the sub-ledgers as per an organization's standard (E)

- Perform intercompany reconciliations on ERP or by extracting the information from systems (E)

- Generate reports categorizing and summarizing discrepancies, and send to relevant controllers for investigations (E + L)

- Identify, solve and monitor the root cause of accounts discrepancies (T&L)

- Create and send emails to investigate and resolve gaps with other finance teams or other departments. Manage the back and forth of responses and perform potential actions required to close the gaps, for example, post a balancing journal entry (E + L + T&L)

- Set up and maintain account master data: manage approval workflows for account creation, change or deletion, and execute the changes automatically in the systems (E + L)

1.5. Reconcile bank transactions and accounts

- Download the statements from each bank account (E)

- Extract Accounts Receivable and Accounts Payable ledgers from the accounting system, and match with bank statements (E)

- Generate reports categorizing and summarizing discrepancies, and send to relevant controllers for investigations (E + L)

- Identify, solve, and monitor the root cause of accounts discrepancies (T&L)

- Create and send emails to investigate and resolve gaps with other finance teams or other departments. Manage the back and forth of responses and perform potential

Legend of the capabilities: *E: Execution, L: Language, V: Vision, T&L: Thinking & Learning. Refer to Part Two of the book for the list of technologies involved in each capability.*

actions required to close the gaps, for example, post a balancing journal entry (E + L)

- Automate the creation of balancing journal entries to solve discrepancies based on rules, for example, discrepancy types or amounts (E)

1.6.   Support regulatory and management reporting

- Extract and cleanse data from structured data sources or unstructured data sources (E + L + V)

- Support workflow of financial data collection from different entities and systems. E.g., send standard data collection form for reporting entities to fill in; manage the reception of completed forms; chase up entities according to a deadline (E + L)

- Support reporting entities to answer frequently asked questions. E.g., questions regarding accounting principles (L)

- Check (basic) reporting packages received from reporting entities for accuracy and completeness (E + L)

- Perform standard, rule-based calculations, and consolidations of the reporting packages (E)

- Prepare management review slide decks by collecting data from multiple finance systems and reports (E + L)

- Support the analysis of financial statements and the generation of insights. Identify drivers and trends, and model the root causes. E.g., price elasticity, volume impacts on margin (T&L)

- Write standard analyses of trends or standard commentaries of graphs (L)

- Compare the reports with online available regulatory data automatically (E + L)

1.7. Manage financial planning and analysis (FP&A)

- Support the workflows for data collection and approvals of budgeting and forecasting (E)

- Pre-populate budgets and forecasts by predicting amounts based on correlations from historical and market data (E + T&L)

- Load pre-populated balances into the planning system (E)

Legend of the capabilities: *E: Execution, L: Language, V: Vision, T&L: Thinking & Learning. Refer to Part Two of the book for the list of technologies involved in each capability.*

- Compare forecasts to actuals and report the variances. Identify, report and monitor the root causes (T&L)

- Perform standard, rule-based calculations, and consolidations of the forecasting packages (E)

- Prepare management review slide decks by collecting data from multiple finance systems and reports (E + L)

- Support the analysis of the financial and business information and the generation of insights. Identify drivers and trends, and model the root causes. E.g., price elasticity, volume impacts on margin (T&L)

- Write standard analyses of trends or standard commentaries of graphs (L)

1.8. Drive operational finance

- Identify levers to improve margin and perform scenario analysis (E + T&L)

- Perform pricing reviews based on customer contracts and pre-approved price lists (E)

- Extract monthly sales data and calculate commissions (E)

- Calculate and process rebates (E)

Legend of the capabilities: E: Execution, L: Language, V: Vision, T&L: Thinking & Learning. Refer to Part Two of the book for the list of technologies involved in each capability.

1.9. Allocate and prioritize capital investment

- Inform investment decisions based on visibility into long-term performance through scenario analyses (E + T&L)

- Leverage granular understanding of "value drivers" to inform business prioritization decisions (E + T&L)

1.10. Visualize and analyze financial data

- Display key business metrics in real time to enable immediate action when required (E + T&L)

- Visualize enterprise-wide aggregated data and make it accessible in the data war room (E + T&L)

1.11. Manage assets

- Identify assets to be tracked, depreciated, and amortized. Calculate and enter depreciation, and send confirmation emails (E + T&L)

- Support workflow for addition or suppression of assets and notify relevant stakeholders with status on a real-time basis (E + L)

- Build asset listing and inventory reports using information from different systems (E)

Legend of the capabilities: *E: Execution, L: Language, V: Vision, T&L: Thinking & Learning. Refer to Part Two of the book for the list of technologies involved in each capability.*

- Leverage blockchain for data consistency and improve open collaboration in asset management (E)

1.12. Optimize working capital

- Use advanced mixed modeling to optimize the spend allocation (T&L)

- Use demand-sensing techniques to drive supply chain efficiency (T&L)

- Leverage external data to optimize credit risk decisions (T&L)

2. IA use cases in the procurement function

2.1. Develop sourcing strategies

- Analyze the organization's spend profile using historical data. For example, analyze demand and inventory trends to develop inventory strategy, or match demand needs to supply capabilities (T&L)

- Develop procurement plans based on demand forecast and inventory levels using historical and actual data, leveraging internal and external data (T&L)

- Categorize the spend categories to help set strategy and monitor performance (T&L)

Legend of the capabilities: E: Execution, L: Language, V: Vision, T&L: Thinking & Learning.
Refer to Part Two of the book for the list of technologies involved in each capability.

- Generate automated reporting and workbooks as key strategy inputs (E)

2.2. Select suppliers

- Build intelligence to select suppliers: automate online market research, leverage existing suppliers' data to inform about their quality and performance, build a supplier rating system (E + T&L + L)

- Understand, research and formulate replies to suppliers' queries regarding terms and conditions and quality standards; provide a status of the procurement process and a status of invoice payments (E + L)

2.3. Manage suppliers

- Set up and maintain vendor master data: manage approval workflows for vendor creation, change or deletion, and execute the changes automatically in the systems (E + L)

- Build, monitor, and manage supplier data using information received from the vendor and external sources. Monitor operational risk management (e.g., financial, legal, reputational). Conduct monitoring and real-time notification of risk events related to vendors (E + L)

Legend of the capabilities: E: Execution, L: Language, V: Vision, T&L: Thinking & Learning. Refer to Part Two of the book for the list of technologies involved in each capability.

- Record receipt of goods and monitor the quality of product delivered (E + L)

- Predict and flag supplier compliance issues (E + L + T&L)

- Analyze risks and performance associated with the pool of suppliers. Identify critical suppliers, and get recommendation on optimally managing the relationship (T&L)

- Generate inbound product quality testing and compliance reporting (E + T&L)

2.4. Manage contracts

- Automate contract creation and updates, and manage searchable contract data in repositories (E + L)

- Monitor contract compliance, including identification of contract obligations and deviations from standard clauses. Identify drivers and opportunities for increased benefits from contracts and improved risk management (L + T&L)

- Create smart contracts using blockchain to enhance remediation of litigation and conflicts (E)

Legend of the capabilities: *E: Execution, L: Language, V: Vision, T&L: Thinking & Learning.*
Refer to Part Two of the book for the list of technologies involved in each capability.

2.5. Order materials and services

- Manage purchase requisitions and purchase order approval workflows. Integrate with buying portal (E)

- Approve the standard purchase requisitions automatically (E + L)

- Verify users' purchase requests and recommend profitable positions in real-time (E +T&L)

- Solicit and track vendor quotes (E + L)

- Generate purchase orders by leveraging the information included in purchase requisitions (E + T&L + L)

- Proactively reconcile purchase order, invoice, and goods receipt (E)

- Identify fraud or potential conflicts of interest in the company based on prediction and historical data analysis (T&L)

- Set up advanced shipping notifications with vendors, for example by using tracking delivery information from their website (E + L)

Legend of the capabilities: *E: Execution, L: Language, V: Vision, T&L: Thinking & Learning. Refer to Part Two of the book for the list of technologies involved in each capability.*

- Support supplier portal updates and integration with internal systems, enabling monitoring of key performance management data (e.g., on-time delivery, quality, cost) (E + L)

2.6. Produce spend analytics & reporting

- Capture and cleanse data to support the generation of reports (E)

- Pre-populate complex periodic reporting requirements (E)

- Collect data from multiple sources and create procurement scorecards to enable analysis and monitor the performance and the risks of the procurement function (E + T&L)

- Archive data for multi-period analysis (E)

3. IA use cases in the human resources (HR) function

3.1. Manage job posting and recruitment

- Match recruitment to company objectives by forecasting and planning the skills and resources needed (E + T&L)

- Identify resource and skills needs based on resource planning prediction (T&L)

Legend of the capabilities: E: Execution, L: Language, V: Vision, T&L: Thinking & Learning.
Refer to Part Two of the book for the list of technologies involved in each capability.

- Post job advertisements simultaneously on diverse platforms (e.g., company websites, social media) (E)

- Source candidates through social media screening (L + T&L + E + V)

- Screen and rank candidates based on their resumes and data collected from professional social media (T&L + E)

- Organize logistics: schedule appointments, request additional documents (E)

- Connect with candidates to perform preliminary tests through questions or games (L + T&L + E)

- Interview candidates and conduct an initial assessment based on word analysis, face screening and sentiment analysis (L + T&L)

3.2. Onboard new joiners

- Process an applicant record received during initial application submission, through to completing the new hire process (E + L)

- Collect, and check the completeness and accuracy of the new joiner's information. Interact with the new

Legend of the capabilities: E: Execution, L: Language, V: Vision, T&L: Thinking & Learning. Refer to Part Two of the book for the list of technologies involved in each capability.

joiner to collect additional information throughout the onboarding process. Generate administrative and legal reminders (E + L)

- Update the new joiner's information simultaneously in several systems like admin, IT and other required departments (E + L)

- Use the new hire profile to trigger an automated activation of user credential creation (i.e., activate a user in the various systems that the new hire accesses from day 1) (E)

- Automatic training setup and basic information flow (E + T&L)

- Feed new hires, transfers, and terminations from the HR system to the procurement system in real time to avoid errors and delays in the provision (or collection) of phones, computers and other tools (E + L)

3.3. Manage human capital

- Inform retentions or promotions by analyzing employees' data: demographics, location, skills, assessments, engagement surveys, and behavioral data (T&L)

Legend of the capabilities: E: Execution, L: Language, V: Vision, T&L: Thinking & Learning. Refer to Part Two of the book for the list of technologies involved in each capability.

- Enable people analytics and performance management (T&L)

- Predict workforce needs based on workload, the nature of projects and the size of clients (T&L + E)

- Identify key risk areas and attributes that can impact a company's short- and long-term HR planning. Perform scenario analyses (T&L)

- Generate insights on diversity, reskilling needs, retirement planning, and behavioral skills, to inform decision-making (T&L)

3.4. Support HR analytics and reporting

- Capture and cleanse data to support the automated generation of reports (E + T&L)

- Pre-populate complex periodic reporting requirements (E + T&L)

- Build reports by consolidating data from diverse sources. Perform analysis based on multiple factors like gender diversity, level of employees, or regional diversity (E + T&L)

Legend of the capabilities: *E: Execution, L: Language, V: Vision, T&L: Thinking & Learning. Refer to Part Two of the book for the list of technologies involved in each capability.*

- Enable predictive analysis of employees' behavior. E.g., early identification of resignation cases, identification of drivers for best performers (T&L)

- Support employee exit behavior analysis and prediction (E + T&L)

3.5. Manage learning and development

- Review employee certification status against requirements (E)

- Notify employees and managers of certification requirements (E + L)

- Predict employees' training needs based on factors like department, job role, quality, and available training courses (E + T&L)

- Improve employee training and learning experience with personalized programs based on interest and knowledge gaps, demographic and behavioral data (T&L)

- Notify employees in case of new relevant knowledge or training content (E + T&L)

- Handle learning queries, reports and registrations via conversational platforms (E + L)

- Determine the return on investment of learning, and review L&D operations based on analytics (E + T&L)

3.6. Manage travel and expenses

- Enter receipts in the expense management system using the scanned versions of these documents (E + L + V)

- Support the workflow of expense approval with rules-based logic (E)

- Auto-approve standard and recurring expenses (E)

- Forecast the travel requirement of company employees and set up a budget accordingly (E + T&L)

3.7. Manage employee queries

- Send HR policy update notification emails to employees (E + L)

- Understand, research, and formulate replies to employees' queries regarding HR policies, HR

Legend of the capabilities: E: Execution, L: Language, V: Vision, T&L: Thinking & Learning. Refer to Part Two of the book for the list of technologies involved in each capability.

processes, or changes in employees' master data, by using intelligent chatbots (E + L)

- Provide other customized services like the generation of employment certificates, or provide the status of leave inventory (E + L)

3.8. Manage employee benefits

- Calculate the benefit applicable per employee via rules using employee level or seniority (E + L)

- Reconcile vendor invoices against employee list and payroll deductions (E + T&L)

- Reply to employee queries about benefit policy (E + L)

3.9. Manage positions

- Compare new hire requisitions against approved position budget and headcount (E)

- Compare salary / hourly wage offer against requisition and approved budget. Identify market standards based on external data analysis (T&L + E)

Legend of the capabilities: *E: Execution, L: Language, V: Vision, T&L: Thinking & Learning.*
Refer to Part Two of the book for the list of technologies involved in each capability.

3.10. Validate time records

- Review employee time records on a daily basis for accuracy and completion (E)

- Notify employee or manager of any missing information to fix defects and maximize payroll accuracy (E)

3.11. Import and validate payroll batches

- Run standard payroll batch extracts and import to payroll in preparation for gross-to-net processing (E)

- Run standard payroll validations with benefits, time worked, and leave (E)

4. IA use cases in the supply chain function

4.1. Manage demand for products and services

- Develop baseline forecasts for products and services using historical data and external factors (E + T&L)

- Build the consensus forecast. Compare consensus plans to the financial budget. Identify gaps and build a bridge report. Provide analytics on differences and communicate with process owners (E + T&L)

Legend of the capabilities: *E: Execution, L: Language, V: Vision, T&L: Thinking & Learning. Refer to Part Two of the book for the list of technologies involved in each capability.*

- Monitor activity against forecast and revise it. Perform an endless loop of forecasting, to provide constantly self-improving output (E + T&L)

- Evaluate and adjust forecasting approach, measure forecast accuracy and identify optimal methods (T&L)

- Identify drivers, correlations, and trends, and conduct automated forecasting including best-fit algorithm selection (T&L + E)

- Monitor the competition and market trends, analyze historical data, and recommend plans to optimize promotions (E + T&L + L)

4.2. Manage materials

- Identify critical materials and supplier capacity. Create an unconstrained and constrained plan (E + T&L)

- Set up and maintain material master data: manage approval workflows for material and material specifications creation, change or deletion, and execute the changes automatically in the systems (E + L)

- Plan inbound material receipts based on production plans and demand forecasts (E + T&L)

Legend of the capabilities: E: Execution, L: Language, V: Vision, T&L: Thinking & Learning.
Refer to Part Two of the book for the list of technologies involved in each capability.

- Perform analyses to prevent over- and under-stocking. Identify drivers. Use the outcome to execute automated actions like sending an order to a vendor (T&L)

- Manage the inbound material flow and material delivery performance (e.g., timing, quality) through the calculation of indicators. Generate reports tracking by materials categories. Calculate adjustments for goods in transit (E + T&L)

- Manage the reception of product: initiate corrective actions in case of mismatch between purchase order and goods received. Process the entries for the reception of product in the manufacturing requirements planning system (E + T&L)

4.3. Operate warehousing

- Estimate and locate physical raw material and finished goods inventory, track product availability using cameras and inventory flows information (E + V)

- Leverage CCTV cameras to identify potential thefts and violations of the safety rules by employees or third-party workforce (T&L + V)

Legend of the capabilities: *E: Execution, L: Language, V: Vision, T&L: Thinking & Learning. Refer to Part Two of the book for the list of technologies involved in each capability.*

4.4. Manage distribution

- Determine and monitor finished goods inventory requirements at the destination, using historical data, and taking into consideration external market data (E + T&L)

- Calculate optimal distribution planning using inventory and transportation constraints. Optimize collaborative replenishment planning, build destination dispatch plan, and monitor capacity utilization (T&L)

- Predict supply and demand events that may impact the customer delivery requirements and recommend actions (E + T&L + L)

- Optimize logistics routes: optimize sequences of dispatch and routes to reduce costs and increase the rapidity of delivery (T&L)

- Monitor and assess distribution performance by collecting data from different sources (e.g., applications, web, emails) to calculate indicators. Assess carrier delivery performance using data from clients, warehouses, and production (quality of products) (E + T&L)

- Process and audit carrier invoices and documents (E + V + L + T&L)

Legend of the capabilities: *E: Execution, L: Language, V: Vision, T&L: Thinking & Learning. Refer to Part Two of the book for the list of technologies involved in each capability.*

- Identify performance trends, perform and analyze benchmark gaps, identify root causes of gaps, and generate reports (E + T&L)

5. IA use cases in the information technology (IT) function

5.1. Manage users

- Understand, research and formulate replies to queries from employees regarding IT policies, IT processes, FAQs and support resolution of incidents using intelligent chatbots (E + T&L + L)

- Execute pre-approved user-requested tasks. For example, installation of new software, password reset or new authorization to access system based on the employee's position (E + T&L + L)

- Perform standard remote user support (e.g., test capacity, usage, memory) to diagnose and solve standard issues (E + T&L)

- Share IT policy with users either on a schedule, or triggered by new amendments of the policy (E)

Legend of the capabilities: E: Execution, L: Language, V: Vision, T&L: Thinking & Learning. Refer to Part Two of the book for the list of technologies involved in each capability.

- Support the management of IT training (emails, scheduling, document sharing). Track IT training completion and scores. Generate reports (E + T&L)

5.2. Manage systems maintenance and incidents

- Generate reports and warnings about daily server and applications performance (E)

- Monitor incidents. Collect incident data from different systems. Analyze incident trends, identify root causes. Build reports for analysis (E + T&L)

- Perform standard incident assessment and rule-based resolution (E)

- Perform predictive maintenance of systems. Identify the root causes and drivers of incidents. Predict the occurrence of incidents based on specific factors, and execute actions (e.g., the automated reboot of a server when the CPU usage is too high)

- Transfer real-time data and help solve issues, rework and missed maintenance, leveraging the IoT connection of hardware devices (E)

Legend of the capabilities: *E: Execution, L: Language, V: Vision, T&L: Thinking & Learning. Refer to Part Two of the book for the list of technologies involved in each capability.*

- Manage assets, optimization, and security by leveraging blockchain (E)

5.3. Manage IT security and data protection

- Track technical threat and vulnerability levels. Register and report security issues (E + T&L)

- Identify data quality issues through anomaly detection. Identify and prioritize the root causes of the most pervasive data quality issues (E + T&L)

- Test, evaluate, and implement information security and privacy and data protection controls (E + T&L)

5.4. Develop and install software

- Test initial application performance. Collect user feedback ratings. Report on the success of testing scenarios. Identify drivers of success to improve software development activities (E + T&L)

- Support the management of files, backups, synchronizations, cleansing of folders. Schedule, trigger and execute batch processing (E + T&L)

- Support workflow for new software access request and approval process (E)

Legend of the capabilities: *E: Execution, L: Language, V: Vision, T&L: Thinking & Learning. Refer to Part Two of the book for the list of technologies involved in each capability.*

- Install pre-approved software on designated servers and user machines (E)

- Track software licenses, identify renewal requirements, launch the approval workflow for license renewal, execute license renewal based on pre-determined rules (E + T&L)

5.5. Manage system and device access

- Set up (or terminate) user profiles (including network, operating systems, applications, databases, and remote access) based on triggers form the HR department (E)

- Perform new device installation (e.g., laptops, smartphones). Back up the data from the old device. Install software and restore backup onto the new device. Test the new setup (E + T&L)

5.6. Manage the IT function

- Collect data to evaluate and report service-level attainment results. Generate and share reports with users to communicate the achievements towards agreed service levels (E + T&L + L)

Legend of the capabilities: E: Execution, L: Language, V: Vision, T&L: Thinking & Learning. Refer to Part Two of the book for the list of technologies involved in each capability.

- Generate standard IT management reports. Distribute selected reports to various stakeholders (E + L)

- Monitor the IT budget. Perform actual versus budget variance analysis and identification of root causes (E + T&L)

5.7. Manage the IT portfolio of systems and services

- Support workflow to collect and analyze user satisfaction and requirements (E)

- Collect and analyze IT services and solutions consumption and usage. Establish and monitor key performance indicators linked to the use of applications (volume of users, frequencies, behaviors) (E + T&L + V)

- Identify improvement opportunities based on customer satisfaction and usage patterns (e.g., need for a new or a different system application). Collect external and internal data on IT services and solutions to address business and user requirements (E + T&L)

- Support the identification of components of incentive programs that improve consumption efficiency (T&L)

Legend of the capabilities: *E: Execution, L: Language, V: Vision, T&L: Thinking & Learning. Refer to Part Two of the book for the list of technologies involved in each capability.*

- Maintain the IT services and solutions catalog. Share with users either on a time-scheduled basis or triggered by new additions to the catalog. Analyze users' behaviors, trigger consumption by providing recommendation based on users' preferences (E + T&L)

6. IA use cases in the customer service function

6.1. Develop the customer service strategy

- Collect information about existing and potential customers from internal (e.g., CRM, emails) and external sources (e.g., social media, websites cookies, databases) (E + L)

- Analyze existing and potential customers based on their demographic, activity, behavioral, and feedback information. Develop customer service segmentation and prioritization (T&L)

- Monitor the effectiveness and efficiency of client segment-specific actions by analyzing their impacts on the clients' purchases, behavior, and feedback. Identify drivers of impact. Perform scenario analysis to optimize the effectiveness and efficiency of the actions (T&L + E + L)

Legend of the capabilities: E: Execution, L: Language, V: Vision, T&L: Thinking & Learning. Refer to Part Two of the book for the list of technologies involved in each capability.

6.2. Measure customer satisfaction

- Solicit and collect customer feedback about request handling, complaints, ad effectiveness, services, and products (through emails, popups or other interactions) (E + L)

- Analyze satisfaction data (identify main items, categorize, and analyze their trends). Support the identification of improvement opportunities. Perform root cause analyses to identify the drivers of satisfaction (T&L)

- Identify and monitor the impact of corrective actions. Perform scenario analysis to optimize client satisfaction (T&L)

- Generate and share customer feedback reports with the product management team (E + L)

6.3. Plan customer service

- Forecast the volume of customer service contacts in order to plan and schedule the customer service workforce. Calculate using historical and actual data, collected internally (e.g., last year's sales) or externally (e.g., weather forecast) (T&L + E + L)

Legend of the capabilities: *E: Execution, L: Language, V: Vision, T&L: Thinking & Learning. Refer to Part Two of the book for the list of technologies involved in each capability.*

- Collect workforce utilization data (e.g., number of interactions on phone or computer), and continuously adjust workforce forecast schedule in real-time (T&L + E)

- Leverage intelligent chatbots to enable 24/7 support, and to guide the client autonomously on more straightforward requests. Combine human and chatbot resources appropriately based on the complexity of requests or products (E + T&L + L)

- Use natural language processing to understand the intent of the customer request. Route customer requests to the available and most relevant customer service representative (e.g., relevance to the product expertise, or the client's personality traits) (T&L + E + L)

6.4. Conduct customer setup and maintenance

- Process customer documents (e.g., identification documents) from pictures or scanned documents into the customer relationship management system. Complete this data with information coming from social media or databases (E + T&L + L + V)

- Crawl the web to fill in missing client contact information (E + L + T&L)

Legend of the capabilities: *E: Execution, L: Language, V: Vision, T&L: Thinking & Learning. Refer to Part Two of the book for the list of technologies involved in each capability.*

- Automate the population of new client data collected during an interaction so that multiple systems are updated from one entry (E)

- Trigger internal notification of new customers to relevant parties, like sales or marketing departments (E)

6.5. Manage customer interactions

- Support the customer representatives in responding to the client's request by prompting answers or suggestions (e.g., promotions) based on the client's intent and understanding. Suggest the next best action to the customer service representative (E + T&L + L)

- Ease the customer service representative's navigation through the applications, opening pages at the appropriate index, and prefilling forms with existing information. After the client interaction, generate the debrief note (summary of the interaction) automatically (E + T&L + L)

- Monitor and evaluate the quality of customer interactions based on outcomes and sentiment analysis. Identify drivers of interaction quality. Support the identification of improvement opportunities (L + T&L)

Legend of the capabilities: E: Execution, L: Language, V: Vision, T&L: Thinking & Learning. Refer to Part Two of the book for the list of technologies involved in each capability.

- Identify and monitor the impact of corrective actions. Perform scenario analysis to optimize service quality (T&L)

- Optimize the outcome of interactions through analyses of voice recordings. Analyze clients' sentiments and the outcomes of interactions to identify drivers of success. For example, identify the keywords or actions from the customer representative that led to the improvement of the client's sentiments during the course of the interaction. Identify the keywords or actions that led to an expected outcome (e.g., a sale). Review the customer representative guidelines and speeches to include these drivers of success (E + T&L + L)

- Perform live sentiment analysis during voice or chat interaction to detect potential issues and remediate them as soon as possible during the interaction. For example, alert managers with real-time warnings if the system detects a potential client upset for more than two minutes (E + T&L + L)

- Analyze customer behavior in real time to identify opportunities for up-selling or cross-selling products or services, and suggest actions to the customer service representative (T&L)

Legend of the capabilities: E: Execution, L: Language, V: Vision, T&L: Thinking & Learning. Refer to Part Two of the book for the list of technologies involved in each capability.

- Automate the follow up with customers to validate resolutions and satisfaction levels (E + L)

7. IA use cases in the marketing function

7.1. Understand and target markets

- Perform market intelligence analysis by collecting and analyzing external data about market demand and offer (e.g., web, press releases). Generate monthly reports to spot changes in the markets (E + L)

- Perform scenario analysis to prioritize market opportunities, based on internal costs, pricing strategy, and expected demand. For example, estimate market share and profitability of a company in a new market, or considering the growth of competition (T&L)

- Collect competitors' market information from internal and external sources. Detect new market entrants, relevant events, campaigns, and competitors' messaging. Generate regular reports, spot changes and set warnings (T&L + E + L)

- Evaluate competitors' products/brands based on predefined criteria. Perform sensitivity analysis to identify

Legend of the capabilities: E: Execution, L: Language, V: Vision, T&L: Thinking & Learning. Refer to Part Two of the book for the list of technologies involved in each capability.

sales growth drivers. Monitor the evolution of market shares and growth drivers over time (T&L + E + L)

- Calculate and refine optimal prices based on costs, demand elasticity, volume, and unit forecast. Perform scenario analysis. Learn and continuously improve its own price-setting ability (T&L + E)

- Track competitors' websites and prices in real time, get notifications when there are changes. Adjust company prices based on predefined rules (T&L + E + V + L)

7.2. Understand and target customers

- Collect information about existing and potential customers from internal (e.g., CRM, emails) and external sources (e.g., social media, databases) (E + L)

- Develop customer segmentation and prioritization by analyzing existing and potential customers based on their demographic, activity, and behavioral data. Support the identification and implementation of specific actions to target each client segment (T&L)

- Monitor the efficiency of client segment-specific actions (e.g., pricing, promotions, product features, distribution channels) by analyzing their impacts on

Legend of the capabilities: *E: Execution, L: Language, V: Vision, T&L: Thinking & Learning. Refer to Part Two of the book for the list of technologies involved in each capability.*

the clients' purchases, behavior, and feedback. Identify drivers of impact. Perform scenario analysis to optimize the efficiency of the actions (T&L + E + L)

- Identify the drivers of customers' loyalty and retention. Perform scenario analysis to increase customers' lifetime value. Monitor and refine actions in time (E + T&L)

- Perform client churn analysis and predictions based on customers' demographics, behavioral data, and competition activity. Identify categories of clients likely to switch to the competition. Design and monitor category-specific actions to prevent these clients from churning (T&L + E + L)

7.3. Optimize the product portfolio

- Evaluate existing products and brands based on sales, profitability, and customer feedback data analysis. Perform root cause analysis to identify drivers of sales growth and client satisfaction (T&L)

- Collect information regarding competitors' products. Identify opportunities for new product ranges. Monitor the market and set alerts for competitors' new moves (E + T&L)

Legend of the capabilities: *E: Execution, L: Language, V: Vision, T&L: Thinking & Learning. Refer to Part Two of the book for the list of technologies involved in each capability.*

- Collect client complaints and after-sales data to support product innovation (E + T&L)

7.4. Manage communication campaigns

- Collect information about competitors' communication campaigns. Analyze competitors' media communication mixes. Estimate competition's budgets, and perform sensitivity analysis with sales growth. Support design of the communication strategy and the company's media plan (E + T&L)

- Monitor promotions performance metrics. Identify the drivers of sales growth, and propose corrective actions to optimize promotion plans (E + T&L)

8. IA use cases in the sales function

8.1. Process sales orders

- Collect current and historical sales order information and promotions. Determine sales trends and patterns. Generate the sales forecast (E + T&L)

- Determine product availability in real time and estimate delivery timing based on inventory levels, production estimates, and available shipping information (E + T&L)

Legend of the capabilities: *E: Execution, L: Language, V: Vision, T&L: Thinking & Learning. Refer to Part Two of the book for the list of technologies involved in each capability.*

- Accept and validate sales orders. Verify completeness of contract-specific documents received. Perform compliance checks with policies. If incomplete, send back for completion (E + T&L)

- Perform automated fulfillment process (including warehousing, picking, packing, shipping the product, and regular communication to the client), process back orders, and handle order inquiries including post-order fulfillment transactions (E + T&L)

- Perform automated sales order tasks on an end-to-end basis, such as recording the outcome of the sales process, and creating their respective invoices (E + T&L)

- Update sales order details, upload contracts, and other supporting documents in systems and send notifications. Collect and maintain customer account information (E)

8.2. Manage customers

- Identify new potential customers. Build profiles of typical customers based on existing clients' demographic and behavioral data. Use these profiles to identify new groups of potential customers in other geographies or other markets (E + T&L)

Legend of the capabilities: E: Execution, L: Language, V: Vision, T&L: Thinking & Learning. Refer to Part Two of the book for the list of technologies involved in each capability.

- INTELLIGENT AUTOMATION USE CASES LIBRARY -

- Automate customer-group research and creation of categories (E)

- Perform automated follow-up actions in case of a client abandoning a cart of products, leaving an onboarding process, or leaving forms incomplete (E)

- Automate contract renewals, generate proposals and trigger client actions (e.g., proposal to be accepted, payment to be made, or contract to be signed) (E + T&L)

- Collect information about potential customers visiting the website (e.g., IP addresses, cookies), and engage in promotion actions to trigger purchase (E + T&L)

- Use website cookies to identify and monitor how users are navigating and interacting with the website. Identify the drivers of customers' experience and purchase. Monitor the adjustment of the website's ergonomics and key messages to fit with the drivers (E + T&L)

- Store customer and sales data on the blockchain to help rapid increase in transparency, trust, and security – eliminating the need for a middleman and directly being in touch with the customers (E)

Legend of the capabilities: E: Execution, L: Language, V: Vision, T&L: Thinking & Learning. *Refer to Part Two of the book for the list of technologies involved in each capability.*

8.3. Up-sell and cross-sell

- Propose customized offerings based on clients' past purchases and habits (E + T&L)

- Identify clients able or willing to buy more based on their demographic and behavioral data. Trigger a call to action by proposing the most appropriate product or service at the right time (E + T&L)

- Automate notification of new products or upgrades to existing customers and getting the response back with feedback direct to the enterprise system (E)

8.4. Manage distribution channels

- Plan and schedule the salesforce. Perform estimates using historical and actual data collected internally (e.g., last year's sales) or externally (e.g., information regarding demand, regulation, or competition moves). Determine optimal sales resource allocation by geography, clients, and products. Perform scenario analysis to identify the most optimal salesforce organization (T&L + E + L)

- Collect sales volumes and salesforce utilization data to adjust workforce forecast schedule and allocation in real-time (T&L + E)

Legend of the capabilities: E: Execution, L: Language, V: Vision, T&L: Thinking & Learning. Refer to Part Two of the book for the list of technologies involved in each capability.

- Leverage intelligent chatbots to enable 24/7 sales support, and to guide the client autonomously using the more straightforward sales processes. Combine human and chatbot resources appropriately based on the complexity of requests or products (E + T&L + L)

- Optimize sales force commissions and incentives based on sales forecasts, costs, margins, and potential for growth. Identify the drivers of sales growth. Perform scenario analysis for incentives and margin optimization (T&L)

- Monitor the performance and effectiveness of sales channels by analyzing internal and external data sources. Perform scenario analysis to drive sales growth and efficiency (E + T&L)

- Calculate and consolidate commission based on contractual rules, latest targets and communications (E + T&L)

- Notify changes in the commission structure to all internal departments (E)

Industry use cases

9. IA use cases in the health and life science industry

9.1. Onboard new patients

- Support the patients' onboarding process through a digitalized intelligent workflow involving task routing, prioritization, monitoring, and escalation of the exceptions (E + T&L)

- Collect available patients' data (e.g., medical history, demographics, data from other hospitals in different locations) from internal and external sources. This includes creating patients' accounts, eligibility verification, processing enrollments, and managing benefits (E + T&L)

- Process patients' scanned documents or pictures (e.g., identification documents, insurance policies) into the patient record system using intelligent character recognition (E + L + T&L + V)

- Manage patients' medical data using blockchain. Share a single, transparent and secured view of each patient's

Legend of the capabilities: E: Execution, L: Language, V: Vision, T&L: Thinking & Learning. Refer to Part Two of the book for the list of technologies involved in each capability.

medical history across health agencies, care providers, patients, doctors and other key actors (E)

9.2. Support appointment scheduling

- Secure patients' authorized connections through voice recognition and other biometrics authentications (L + T&L)

- Support new appointment requests by leveraging an online workflow platform. Direct the appointment request to the appropriate work queue based on its defining attributes, including location, diagnosis, and insurance carrier (E + T&L)

- Prepare the appointment by building out a condensed report, including relevant patient medical history retrieved from different systems, sent to referral management representatives or doctors (E + L + T&L)

- Optimally schedule patient appointments according to diagnosis, location, expected examinations or tests, doctor availability, and other criteria (E + T&L)

- Automate the scheduling or cancellation of appointments and send reminders to patients by email or SMS. Update physicians' calendars in real time (E + T&L)

Legend of the capabilities: E: Execution, L: Language, V: Vision, T&L: Thinking & Learning. Refer to Part Two of the book for the list of technologies involved in each capability.

9.3. Monitor patients' health

- Provide 24/7 remote medical consultation. Leverage virtual nurses (intelligent chatbots) to collect patients' symptoms, offer first diagnoses, recommend actions, and, if necessary, propose an appointment with a doctor (E + L + T&L)

- Collect and regularly update patients' data such as personal data, diagnosis, examination & test results, treatment cycles and hospital appointments, using internal and external sources (E + L + T&L)

- Extract semantic meaning from PDF images of faxed laboratory reports, voice recordings of patient interactions, and free-text EHR (electronic health record) inputs. Enable search queries written in plain text about patients' diagnosis outcomes and treatment cycles (E + L + V + T&L)

- Generate analytics from collected patients' data to offer clinical staff valuable insights supporting more accurate diagnostics and offering tailored treatments to patients (E + L + T&L)

Legend of the capabilities: E: Execution, L: Language, V: Vision, T&L: Thinking & Learning. Refer to Part Two of the book for the list of technologies involved in each capability.

- Create risk scores to provide healthcare providers with insight into which patients might benefit from enhanced services or wellness activities (T&L)

- Use wearable devices (e.g., sensors or smartwatches) to help doctors get patients' real-time data, monitor cases, and suggest care adjustments accordingly (E + T&L)

- Perform remote assistance and facilitate awareness sessions with patients using augmented reality (E + V)

- Monitor patients' health in their hospital rooms in real time. Collect 24/7 patient's visual information, body movement data, and vital data, such as heart rate and blood pressure, using connected devices. Based on the data collected, detect patterns in each patient's health. Predict heart attacks, strokes, sepsis, and other serious complications. Alert nurses in real time in case of emergency. Customize the number of required nurse visits, and free up the time of physicians from data collection and charting (E + L + V + T&L)

- Monitor the use of medication by patients. Confirm and monitor that patients are taking their prescriptions

Legend of the capabilities: E: Execution, L: Language, V: Vision, T&L: Thinking & Learning. Refer to Part Two of the book for the list of technologies involved in each capability.

using visual detection over webcam video recordings of the patients (E + V + T&L)

9.4. Support medical diagnosis

- Support surgeons by enhancing the view of the human organs during critical surgeries using augmented reality (E + V)

- Collect real-time verbal observations and notes dictated by the physician during examinations. Automatically update electronic health records (EHR). Compile charts and summaries about a patient's overall health (E + L)

- Detect in a few seconds the likelihood of a disease through the analysis of tests, X-rays, CT scans, data entry, and other documents. Support cardiologists and radiologists by identifying subtler changes in imaging scans more quickly, potentially leading to earlier and more accurate diagnoses (T&L)

- Design customized treatments. Analyze notes and reports from a patient's file, external research, and clinical expertise to help select the most appropriate, individually tailored treatment path (E + L + T&L)

Legend of the capabilities: E: Execution, L: Language, V: Vision, T&L: Thinking & Learning. Refer to Part Two of the book for the list of technologies involved in each capability.

9.5. Discover drugs

- Design a drug's chemical structure. Analyze the characteristics of billions of molecules, using scientific data available, to optimally combine them and design chemical compounds (E + T&L)

- Collect and summarize data to describe the size and shape of chemical compounds, preferred conditions for maintaining their functionality, and their toxicity, bioactivity, and bioavailability (E + L + T&L)

- Predict a drug's effects and side effects by analyzing and interpreting biomedical data from research experiments (E + T&L)

- Support the identification of suitable candidates for clinical tests by analyzing genetic information (E + V + T&L)

- Support clinical trial approval and documentation processes through the use of intelligent workflow platforms. Digitalize documents by leveraging intelligent character recognition (E + V + L + T&L)

9.6. Adapt staffing levels

- Identify the drivers of fluctuations in the number of patients (e.g., weather, flu epidemics). Predict the potential increase in patient volume and perform scenario analyses to anticipate the required workforce and supplies (T&L)

- Adjust the schedule and the number of staff required according to the prediction of patient traffic. Perform continuous assessments and adjustments to the number of personnel needed. Update staff schedule and send alerts and reminders in real time (E + T&L)

9.7. Support invoicing and claims

- Calculate bill amounts, considering the costs for tests, medicines, wardroom, food, and doctor fees. Generate the bill accordingly and notify patients of their bill amount by email or SMS (E)

- Generate and post claims by retrieving the invoice and treatment information. Check claim eligibility for each patient (E + L)

- Implement discharge instructions. Prepare a draft of discharge guidelines, send reminders to patients about

Legend of the capabilities: *E: Execution, L: Language, V: Vision, T&L: Thinking & Learning. Refer to Part Two of the book for the list of technologies involved in each capability.*

prescription pickups, upcoming doctor's appointments and medical tests (E + L + T&L)

9.8. Improve the patient experience

- Estimate patients' wait time by predicting the volume of patient traffic and by considering actual medical capabilities. Communicate with clients in real time and propose corrective actions to decrease wait time (e.g., transfer patients to another hospital) (E + L + T&L)

- Resolve patients' queries regarding appointments, services, transactions, and other details via a self-service digital platform leveraging intelligent chatbots (E + L)

10. IA use cases in the banking industry

10.1. Onboard clients

- Collect clients' data and documents using a web-based digitalized process workflow. Check data completeness and accuracy in real time (E + T&L)

- Process scans or pictures of clients' documents (e.g., bills, contracts or IDs) into the customer relationship, order fulfillment and risk management systems using intelligent character recognition (E + L + T&L)

- Provide a real-time prediction of the potential for fraud, reputational, money laundering and credit risks (T&L)

- Reconcile clients' data with reference data sources (e.g., the bank's historical data, police or tax databases) to support the client's background check (E + L)

- Support and guide clients in the onboarding process and the selection of products through the use of intelligent chatbots (E + L + T&L)

- Support the overall onboarding process management through a digitalized intelligent workflow involving task routing, prioritization, monitoring, and escalation of the exceptions (E + T&L)

- Perform client profile data enrichment using clients' data available on social media and other public web sources (E + T&L + L)

10.2. Drive customer experience

- Secure clients' authorized connections through voice recognition and other biometric authentications (L + T&L)

- Resolve customer queries regarding services, transactions, and account details via a self-service digital platform leveraging intelligent chatbots (E + L)

Legend of the capabilities: *E: Execution, L: Language, V: Vision, T&L: Thinking & Learning. Refer to Part Two of the book for the list of technologies involved in each capability.*

- Identify variables most accurately predicting customer churn, by leveraging clients' demographic and transactional data. Define churners' profiles, determine the reason driving churn (i.e., root-cause determination) and the potential approach to prevent churn for each of the profiles (i.e., tailored campaigns and offers through the most effective channel) (E + T&L)

- Customize products and services. Use transactional and demographic customer data to define granular customer categories and derive consuming patterns. Customize product offerings and promotions to increase clients' lifetime value (E + T&L)

- Identify "next product to buy" based on customers' demographics data, services and products portfolio, transactional behavior and contact history (E + T&L)

- Increase the volume of new clients, improve users' traffic and client satisfaction levels by building ecosystems with partner companies (e.g., car rental, airlines, hotels). Support the platform with intelligent workflows and enable data sharing (e.g., access to services, sharing of client information) through application programming interfaces (E + T&L)

Legend of the capabilities: E: Execution, L: Language, V: Vision, T&L: Thinking & Learning. Refer to Part Two of the book for the list of technologies involved in each capability.

- Provide additional rewards and offers to customers, based on their behavior and likelihood to stimulate up-sell or cross-sell (E + T&L)

- Locate customers using geographic information systems, and provide them with information on the nearest and most suitable financial access point (e.g., ATM or branch). Match the client to the closest partner store for a promotion or to join the closest event (e.g., new product launch, fundraiser) (E + T&L)

- Provide customized reporting to customers based on their requirements and their habits (E)

10.3. Process mortgages, loans, and credit requests

- Automate the credit sanctioning process using intelligent credit scoring techniques. For example, leverage credit history, social media posts, geolocations, browsing activities, and other data points to discern which data points correlate to the types of borrowers that are most and least likely to pay back their loans or credits (E + L + T&L)

- Support decision-making on overdrafts and impose consequences (e.g., automated charges) (E + T&L)

Legend of the capabilities: E: Execution, L: Language, V: Vision, T&L: Thinking & Learning. Refer to Part Two of the book for the list of technologies involved in each capability.

- Support the collection of information and documents, and the decision-making processes using an intelligent workflow (E + T&L)

- Generate and send letters and documentation of the outcome of the approval process (E + L)

10.4. Manage debt collection

- Monitor the evolution of the debt collection risk by collecting, analyzing, and monitoring economic, social, and contextual data. For example, lack of rain might affect agricultural businesses, or the fall of property prices in a region might affect property agents in reimbursing their debts (E + L + T&L)

- Identify common patterns and early signs of customers at risk of credit default. Engage in early actions to reduce the value at risk (e.g., request additional guarantees, or propose a longer credit period) (E + T&L)

- Perform changes to credit limits and automate credit balance refunds (E + T&L)

Legend of the capabilities: E: Execution, L: Language, V: Vision, T&L: Thinking & Learning. Refer to Part Two of the book for the list of technologies involved in each capability.

10.5. Manage compliance and fraud

- Identify and assess fraud risks (e.g., fraudulent credit card uses, web transactions, bank transfers, or cheques). Analyze historical client transaction, behavioral and demographic data. Identify common patterns of fraud; for example, transactions that deviate with a certain magnitude from the habits of a specific customer. Send an alert to the fraud identification and management team for investigation (E + T&L)

- Apply anti-money laundering risk scoring based on customers' data (e.g., past transactions, social media). Conduct automated data collection and cross-checking with terrorism financing, police and other financial crimes prevention databases (E + L + T&L)

- Monitor fraud and generate alerts. Suspend credit cards or accounts in case of fraud prediction. Manage the communication with clients and insurance firms (E + L)

- Identify unexpected and unusual client transactions locations using geospatial analytics (E + T&L)

- Collect, index, and archive fraud evidence (e.g., forms, police reports, and other documents), and support fraud remediation workflow (E + T&L)

Legend of the capabilities: E: Execution, L: Language, V: Vision, T&L: Thinking & Learning. Refer to Part Two of the book for the list of technologies involved in each capability.

- Manage transactions and contracts with blockchain to help prevent frauds and improve process efficiency (e.g., avoid reconciliations) (E)

10.6. Manage transactions

- Perform routine transactions, reporting, data validation, and other back-office processes to improve efficiency and effectiveness (E + T&L)

- Maintain customer data and transactions on the blockchain to avoid duplicate entries and improve security and credibility (E)

- Reconcile statements, monitor performance and report on compliance (E + T&L)

10.7. Manage branches and ATM fleet

- Optimize branch and ATM footprint strategy using geospatial analytics (e.g., usage data by location) (E + T&L)

- Support network and capital spend planning strategy using historical usage data, information on competition networks, and demand forecast data (E + T&L)

Legend of the capabilities: E: Execution, L: Language, V: Vision, T&L: Thinking & Learning. Refer to Part Two of the book for the list of technologies involved in each capability.

- Reduce required capital expenditure by rationalizing assets and optimizing their utilization. Build and monitor sharing models (E + T&L)

- Identify technical issues and inefficiencies based on usage patterns, lead metrics, traffic analysis, and other parameters. Perform analytics to improve operations (T&L)

- Support the resolution of technical issues. Identify the root causes of issues and suggest real-time remediation actions. Automate some of these actions (e.g., the restart of a server) (E + T&L)

- Prevent outages by implementing predictive maintenance. Apply data-driven insights to help monitor equipment, learn from historical information, anticipate equipment failure, and proactively fix it (E + T&L)

10.8. Support wealth management and investment banking

- Support clients' investment decision-making process by leveraging intelligent chatbots (also called robo-advisors). Suggest the most appropriate products depending on the client's profile and objectives (E + T&L + L)

Legend of the capabilities: E: Execution, L: Language, V: Vision, T&L: Thinking & Learning. Refer to Part Two of the book for the list of technologies involved in each capability.

- Collect real-time data from various financial markets. Analyze the mood or sentiments of different financial markets and predict trends. Answer market research requests (E + L + T&L)

- Conduct portfolio analysis and monitoring. Optimize asset selection and pricing analysis, based on the client's profile and available products, to improve risk management and personalize the portfolio (E + T&L)

- Prepare and file statutory forms and documents (e.g., clients' tax returns) (E)

- Reconcile securities amongst different data sources (E)

- Check daily portfolios and notify the portfolio manager or the client in case of variances from preset recommendations and preferences (E)

- Adjust client portfolios continuously based on reinforcement learning-based trading algorithms (E + T&L)

- Perform data entry and analysis in corporate debt restructuring tools (E + T&L)

Legend of the capabilities: *E: Execution, L: Language, V: Vision, T&L: Thinking & Learning.*
Refer to Part Two of the book for the list of technologies involved in each capability.

- Generate securities and trade reporting and transfer it to authorities (E + L)

11. IA use cases in the public and government sectors

11.1. Manage immigration

- Process visas using online intelligent workflow platform involving rules for instantaneous visa delivery based on specific criteria (E + T&L)

- Develop passport-free immigration checkpoints by identifying citizens using on-the-go biometric markers that include irises and facial features (E + V + T&L)

11.2. Manage tax

- Manage tax declaration through an intelligent online workflow platform, including completeness and accuracy controls, and real-time fraud assessment. Collect and process potential evidence documents using intelligent character recognition (E + V + T&L)

- Automate tax assessments. Analyze and assess predefined risk criteria regarding income tax returns or statements of financial transactions. For example,

Legend of the capabilities: *E: Execution, L: Language, V: Vision, T&L: Thinking & Learning. Refer to Part Two of the book for the list of technologies involved in each capability.*

| *BORNET – BARKIN – WIRTZ*

identify and analyze gaps between employer and employee tax declarations (E + L + T&L)

- Detect tax evasion by matching citizens' financial data with information from social media. Reconcile people's spending patterns to the incomes they declare. Identify those who spend far more than they declare (E + L + T&L)

- Detect unauthorized activities of de-registered firms. Track the financial activity of companies that are supposed to be inactive and alert in case of suspicious transactions (E + L + T&L)

- Support the financial crimes risk management process by acquiring third-party data, monitoring taxpayers' behaviors, employing segmentation, and scoring drivers of risks. Send alerts to the financial crimes risk management team for investigation (E + L + V + T&L)

- Manage tax declarations and transactions with blockchain to help prevent fraud and improve process efficiency (e.g., avoid reconciliations) (E)

Legend of the capabilities: *E: Execution, L: Language, V: Vision, T&L: Thinking & Learning. Refer to Part Two of the book for the list of technologies involved in each capability.*

11.3. Promote safety and security

- Collect and analyze CCTV camera videos to track missing children and known criminals using image and voice recognition capabilities (E + V + T&L)

- Provide an online intelligent workflow platform to support the payment and processing of fixed penalties and firearms licenses (E + V + T&L)

- Predict terrorism. Identify possibly dangerous individuals or groups, taking into account the data concerning previous cases of extremism, crime, or terrorism. Analyze data on potential terrorist behavior, including unusual conversations, texts, interactions and contacts, purchases, or movements in potentially dangerous locations. Track potential recruitment of people through social media platforms. Identify data patterns and apply real-time detection (E + V + L + T&L)

- Perform geospatial analysis of specific aspects of terrorism-related activity, like terrorist training camps or weapons smuggling, by leveraging satellite imagery in conjunction with other spatial data. Develop spatial models of vulnerability to terrorism threats (E + V + T&L)

Legend of the capabilities: *E: Execution, L: Language, V: Vision, T&L: Thinking & Learning. Refer to Part Two of the book for the list of technologies involved in each capability.*

- INTELLIGENT AUTOMATION USE CASES LIBRARY -

- Leverage past crime data (e.g., crime type, location, date, and time) and other external data (e.g., events, weather) to identify patterns and predict crime. Identify hotspots and suggest optimal police patrol presence (E + T&L)

- Monitor multiple locations in real time, analyzing camera and movement detector streams. Recognize violence or criminal activity and distinguish fighting or physical abuse from other people's movements. Send alarms to the police (E + V + T&L)

- Prevent cyber attacks. Monitor and examine users and devices on the network. Analyze operations involving valuable data, reveal patterns and flag suspicious individuals or actions (E + T&L)

- Train police staff to respond in extreme stress situations (e.g., kidnapping, holdups) using virtual reality (E + V)

- Leverage face recognition technology to identify identity fraudsters with multiple driver's licenses (E + V + T&L)

Legend of the capabilities: E: Execution, L: Language, V: Vision, T&L: Thinking & Learning. Refer to Part Two of the book for the list of technologies involved in each capability.

11.4. Manage citizen services

- Recognize traumatic falls or other injuries (e.g., older people and people suffering from severe chronic diseases) through analyzing real-time surveillance cameras. Send a message to alert emergency services (E + V + T&L)

- Link and integrate citizens' data stored in multiple departments and agencies (e.g., tax, immigration, credit, medical, social security, and more). Create a central platform to manage all services and profile changes. Generate insights to provide a higher quality of services and stimulate innovation (E + L + T&L)

- Perform sentiment analysis of social media to understand the level of satisfaction of the citizens regarding public services. Create alerts to identify critical incidents in real time. Generate insights from data collected to support service innovation (E + L + T&L)

- Secure clients' connections to the public service platform through voice recognition and other biometric authentications (L + T&L)

Legend of the capabilities: E: Execution, L: Language, V: Vision, T&L: Thinking & Learning. Refer to Part Two of the book for the list of technologies involved in each capability.

- Resolve citizens' queries regarding services, transactions, permit applications, incident reporting, and case management via a self-service digitalized intelligent workflow. Perform task routing, prioritization, monitoring, and escalation of the exceptions to the proper authorities (E + T&L)

- Handle incoming citizen queries, leveraging intelligent chatbots (L + T&L)

- Customize public services. Use citizens' transactional and demographic data to define granular citizen categories and derive consuming patterns. Customize service portfolio to increase citizens' satisfaction (E + T&L)

- Identify and suggest additional services and resources to citizens who are applying or interacting with services (E + T&L)

- Locate citizens using a geographic information system, and provide them with information on the closest events or activities (E + T&L)

- Support the overall onboarding process management through a digitalized intelligent workflow involving task routing, prioritization, monitoring, and escalation of the exceptions (E + T&L)

- Automate processing of queries, applications, and issuing or renewing of documents that don't require a high level of authorization (E)

- Leverage blockchain to secure citizens' data and transactions, including secured access to public facilities, personal data, votes, or payment transactions (E)

11.5. Education

- Use sensors and vision to analyze the way students interact with the learning materials. Generate insights about students' learning abilities and the areas they need to work on and how (E + L + T&L)

- Gather and analyze data from a wide range of sources (e.g., classwork, classroom participation, behavior, tests, and others). Provide teachers with a detailed and customized understanding of each student's specific strengths and weaknesses. Support teachers to develop personalized learning plans (E + V + L + T&L)

- Leverage mass digitization systems to automatically scan large quantities of books or any bound material which can

---

Legend of the capabilities: E: Execution, L: Language, V: Vision, T&L: Thinking & Learning. *Refer to Part Two of the book for the list of technologies involved in each capability.*

become searchable and available remotely (E + V + L + T&L)

- Manage admissions and enrolments, student finance management and other services via a self-service digitalized intelligent workflow (E)

- Optimally schedule course timetables according to location, teacher availability, and learning objectives. Automate the scheduling or cancellation of lessons and send reminders to students by email or SMS. Update teachers' calendars in real time (E)

- Create "global classrooms" by leveraging mobile applications or augmented reality, bringing education across borders, especially to poor/remote areas (E + V)

11.6. Climate change and ecology

- Sense trash volume with IoT-integrated trash cans. Generate pickup requests. Optimize trash collection routes, taking traffic conditions into account (E + T&L)

- Scan and analyze the garbage on the conveyor belt using cameras. Remove and sort identified waste using a robotic arm (E + V)

- Manage the intermittent supply of renewable energy so that more can be incorporated into the grid. Identify and address problems in the grid, and restore power more quickly when it fails (E + T&L)

- Collect and analyze data from satellites and ocean exploration to enable the monitoring of shipping, ocean mining, fishing, coral bleaching, or marine diseases. Set up alerts (E + V + T&L)

- Predict tropical storms, weather fronts, and atmospheric rivers based on patterns in clouds from satellite images (E + V + T&L)

- Monitor, predict, and manage the weather, climate, and water-related disasters using a combination of satellite data and numerical weather prediction (NWP) (E + V + T&L)

- Detect of forest fires early using a radio-acoustic sounding system (L + T&L)

- Leverage data from sensors to measure pollutants such as soot, nitrogen oxides, ammonia, ozone, or particulate matter. Improve the measurement data by determining and excluding systematic errors from

Legend of the capabilities: E: Execution, L: Language, V: Vision, T&L: Thinking & Learning. Refer to Part Two of the book for the list of technologies involved in each capability.

individual measuring devices and environmental influences (E + T&L)

- Predict the air pollution level using environmental factors such as weather, traffic index, and fire maps (E + V + T&L)

- Track animal poaching by analyzing thermal images in real time (from static cameras or taken by drones) (E + V + T&L)

- Predict future poaching patterns based on past ranger patrols and records of poachers' behavior from crime data (E + T&L)

- Protect biodiversity by identifying species and monitoring them using images from static cameras, drones, or satellites. Set up alerts (E + V + T&L)

11.7. Manage infrastructures

- Identify traffic patterns for cars, pedestrians and bikes by analyzing videos from surveillance cameras or satellites to redesign traffic infrastructures optimally (e.g., identify the need for a new roundabout) (E + V + T&L)

Legend of the capabilities: *E: Execution, L: Language, V: Vision, T&L: Thinking & Learning. Refer to Part Two of the book for the list of technologies involved in each capability.*

- Map accident data to identify road safety issues (T&L)

- Predict road infrastructure maintenance and replacement needs using geological data, construction data, and accident data (E + T&L)

- Support city planning by analyzing traffic flow, traffic signal timings and the condition of roads (T&L)

- Evaluate the cost-effectiveness of highways and other high-cost projects using analytical modeling. Identify budget allocation requirements. Optimize investment mix (E + T&L)

12. IA use cases in the telecommunication industry

12.1. Onboard clients

- Collect clients' data and documents using a web-based digitalized process workflow. Check data completeness and accuracy in real time (E + T&L)

- Process scans or pictures of clients' documents (e.g., bills, contracts or IDs) into the customer relationship, order fulfillment and risk management systems using intelligent character recognition (E + L)

Legend of the capabilities: E: Execution, L: Language, V: Vision, T&L: Thinking & Learning. Refer to Part Two of the book for the list of technologies involved in each capability.

- Reconcile clients' data with reference data sources (e.g., government databases) to support clients' background checks (E + L)

- Support and guide clients in the onboarding process and the selection of products through the use of intelligent chatbots (E + L)

- Support the overall onboarding process management through a digitalized intelligent workflow involving task routing, prioritization, monitoring, and escalation of the exceptions (E)

- Perform client profile data enrichment using clients' data available on social media and other public web sources (E + T&L + L)

12.2. Drive customer experience

- Secure clients' authorized connections through voice recognition and other biometric authentications (E + L)

- Resolve customer queries regarding services, transactions, and account details via a self-service digital platform leveraging intelligent chatbots (L + T&L)

Legend of the capabilities: *E: Execution, L: Language, V: Vision, T&L: Thinking & Learning. Refer to Part Two of the book for the list of technologies involved in each capability.*

- Identify variables most accurately predicting customer churn, by leveraging clients' demographic and transactional data. Define churners' profiles, determine the reason driving churn (i.e., root-cause determination) and the potential approach to prevent churn for each of the profiles (i.e., tailored campaigns and offers through the most effective channel) (E + T&L)

- Customize products and services. Use transactional and demographic customer data to define granular customer categories and derive consumption patterns. Customize product offerings and promotions to increase clients' lifetime value (E + T&L)

- Increase the volume of new clients and improve user traffic and client satisfaction levels by building ecosystems with partner companies (e.g., car rental, airlines, hotels). Support the platform with intelligent workflows and enable data sharing (e.g., access to services, sharing of client information) through application programming interfaces (E + T&L)

- Identify "next product to buy" based on customers' demographics data, services, and products portfolio, transactional behavior and contact history (E + T&L)

Legend of the capabilities: E: Execution, L: Language, V: Vision, T&L: Thinking & Learning. Refer to Part Two of the book for the list of technologies involved in each capability.

- Provide additional rewards and offers to customers, based on their behavior and likelihood to stimulate up-sell or cross-sell (E + T&L)

- Locate customers using geographic information systems, and provide them with information on the nearest and most suitable branch. Match the client to the closest partner store for a promotion or to join the most relevant event (e.g., new product launch) (E + T&L)

- Provide customized reporting to customers based on their requirements and their habits (E)

12.3. Manage risks and compliance

- Identify and assess fraud risks (e.g., fraudulent uses of mobile services, theft of profiles, or web transactions). Analyze historical client transactions, usage, and demographic data. Identify patterns of fraud; for example, a usage that deviates with a certain magnitude from the habits of a specific customer. Send an alert to the fraud identification and management team for investigation (E + T&L)

- Collect, index, and archive fraud evidence (e.g., forms, police reports, and other documents), and support fraud remediation workflow (E + T&L)

Legend of the capabilities: E: Execution, L: Language, V: Vision, T&L: Thinking & Learning. Refer to Part Two of the book for the list of technologies involved in each capability.

- Identify likely non-paying customer categories by analyzing clients' demographic and usage data, and historical non-payment data. Monitor clients' data to identify early signs of a potential payment default. Optimize treatment at acquisition and collection moments. Engage in early actions to reduce the value at risk (e.g., request additional guarantees, or propose a cheaper subscription) (E + T&L)

- Manage transactions and contracts with blockchain to help prevent fraud and improve process efficiency (e.g., avoid reconciliations) (E)

12.4. Manage transactions

- Perform routine transactions, reporting, data validation, and other back-office processes to improve efficiency and effectiveness (E + T&L)

- Maintain customer data/transaction on the blockchain to avoid duplicate entries, improve security and credibility (E)

- Reconcile statements, performance monitoring and compliance reporting (E + T&L)

Legend of the capabilities: E: Execution, L: Language, V: Vision, T&L: Thinking & Learning. Refer to Part Two of the book for the list of technologies involved in each capability.

12.5. Build and maintain network operations

- Advise on network footprint optimization strategy using geospatial analytics (e.g., usage data by location) (E + T&L)

- Support network and capital spend planning strategy using historical usage data, information on competition networks, and demand forecast data (E + T&L)

- Reduce required capital expenditure by rationalizing assets and optimizing their utilization. Build and monitor sharing models (E + T&L)

- Support network material sourcing, building and construction processes with intelligent digital workflow and monitoring dashboard (E + T&L)

- Identify network issues and inefficiencies based on usage patterns, lead metrics, traffic analysis, and network parameters. Perform analytics to improve network operations (T&L)

- Support the resolution of network issues. Identify the root causes of issues and suggest real-time remediation actions. Automate some of these actions (e.g., the restart of a server) (E + T&L)

Legend of the capabilities: E: Execution, L: Language, V: Vision, T&L: Thinking & Learning. Refer to Part Two of the book for the list of technologies involved in each capability.

- Support the optimal dispatch of field forces and scheduling of maintenance work (E + T&L)

- Support field forces resolving technical incidents by identifying potential defects based on image analysis. Allow remote support of field forces using augmented reality and image sharing (T&L + V)

- Prevent outages by implementing predictive maintenance. Use data-driven insights to help monitor equipment, learn from historical information, anticipate equipment failure, and proactively fix it (E + T&L)

- Constantly re-adjust network configuration based on current needs using a reinforcement learning-based algorithm. Self-analyze and self-optimize to provide more consistent service (E + T&L)

13. IA use cases in the insurance industry

13.1. Support underwriting

- Collect the internal and external data required to assess the level of risk (e.g., market information, individuals' medical data) and to calculate the level of internal margin expected by policy (E + L)

Legend of the capabilities: *E: Execution, L: Language, V: Vision, T&L: Thinking & Learning. Refer to Part Two of the book for the list of technologies involved in each capability.*

- Assess the risks by analyzing categorical variables (such as product type or medical information) and continuous variables (such as weight, height, or employment salary). Suggest pricing for accepted insurable risks based on the likelihood, the magnitude of the risk, the expected internal level of margin, and the competition's rates (E + T&L + L)

- Perform sensitivity analysis to identify the variables impacting the revenue generated by policy (E + T&L)

- Enhance technical pricing and loss prediction modeling based on non-linear models and external data (T&L)

13.2. Manage claims

- Digitalize and process uploaded scanned claim documents by leveraging intelligent character recognition (E + L + V + T&L)

- Check uploaded claims in real time for assessing the potential for fraud and eligibility according to predefined criteria (E + T&L)

- Approve claims in real time. Match the claim description, value and complexity to similar ones stored in a database, searching for any identical claims to determine in seconds if the claim is legitimate and should be approved (E + L +T&L)

- Estimate in real time the eligibility, insurance coverage, and client's payout of a claim based on a picture (e.g., a damaged car). Leverage an algorithm trained on a backlog of images of various severities of damage and the payouts associated with them (E + V)

- Support the overall claims management process through a digitalized intelligent workflow involving task routing, prioritization, monitoring, and escalation of the exceptions (E + T&L)

- Route denied claims into a specific workflow, triggering an automated email to the client, explaining reasons and potential remediation actions (E + L + T&L)

- Predict claims severity as early as possible, to enable efficient triage and handling (e.g., total loss, subrogation, or litigation) and prediction of reserves (E + T&L)

Legend of the capabilities: *E: Execution, L: Language, V: Vision, T&L: Thinking & Learning. Refer to Part Two of the book for the list of technologies involved in each capability.*

13.3. Onboard clients

- Collect clients' data and documents using a web-based digitalized process workflow. Check data completeness and accuracy in real time (E + T&L)

- Process scans or pictures of clients' documents (e.g., bills, contracts or IDs) into the customer relationship, order fulfillment and risk management systems using intelligent character recognition (E + L + T&L)

- Support the overall onboarding process management through a digitalized intelligent workflow involving task routing, prioritization, monitoring, and escalation of the exceptions (E + T&L)

- Perform client profile data enrichment using clients' data available on social media and other public web sources (E + T&L + L)

- Support and guide clients in the onboarding process and the selection of services through the use of intelligent workflows (E + L+ T&L)

- Support clients' policy selection process by leveraging intelligent chatbots (also called robo-advisors). Suggest

Legend of the capabilities: E: Execution, L: Language, V: Vision, T&L: Thinking & Learning. Refer to Part Two of the book for the list of technologies involved in each capability.

the most appropriate policies depending on clients' profiles and objectives (E + T&L + L)

13.4. Drive customer experience

- Secure clients' authorized connections through voice recognition and other biometric authentications (L + T&L)

- Resolve customer queries regarding services, transactions, and account details via a self-service digital platform leveraging intelligent chatbots (L + T&L)

- Identify variables most accurately predicting customer churn, by leveraging clients' demographic and transactional data. Define churners' profiles, determine the reason driving churn (i.e., root-cause determination) and the potential approach to prevent churn for each of the profiles (i.e., tailored campaigns and offers through the most effective channel)

- Customize products and services. Use transactional and demographic customer data to define granular customer categories and derive consumption patterns. Customize product offerings and promotions to increase clients' lifetime value (E + T&L)

Legend of the capabilities: *E: Execution, L: Language, V: Vision, T&L: Thinking & Learning. Refer to Part Two of the book for the list of technologies involved in each capability.*

- Identify "next product to buy" based on customer's demographic data, services and products portfolio, transactional behavior and contact history (E + T&L)

- Increase the volume of new clients, improve users' traffic and client satisfaction levels by building ecosystems with partner companies (e.g., car rental, airlines, hotels). Support the platform with intelligent workflows and enable data sharing with partners (e.g., access to services, sharing of client information) through application programming interfaces (E + T&L)

- Provide additional rewards and offers to customers, based on their behavior and likelihood to stimulate up-sell or cross-sell (E + T&L)

- Provide customized reporting to customers based on their requirements and their habits (E)

13.5. Manage compliance and fraud

- Identify fraudulent claims. Identify common patterns of fraud using a dataset, including existing clients and known fraudulent claims. For example, fraudulent claims could be the ones that deviate with a certain magnitude from the habits of a specific customer, doctor

Legend of the capabilities: E: Execution, L: Language, V: Vision, T&L: Thinking & Learning. Refer to Part Two of the book for the list of technologies involved in each capability.

or hospital. Send an alert to the fraud identification and management team for investigation (E + T&L)

- Collect, index, and archive fraud evidence (e.g., forms, police reports, and other documents), and support fraud remediation workflow (E + T&L)

- Manage transactions and contracts with blockchain to help prevent frauds and improve process efficiency (e.g., avoid reconciliations) (E)

- Conduct compliance reporting and scheduling (E)

- Manage and predict deviations (E + T&L)

13.6. Manage transactions

- Perform routine transactions, reporting, data validation, and other back-office processes to improve efficiency and effectiveness (E + T&L)

- Maintain customer data on the blockchain to avoid duplicate entries, improve security and credibility (E)

- Reconcile statements, monitor performance and report on compliance (E + T&L)

Legend of the capabilities: *E: Execution, L: Language, V: Vision, T&L: Thinking & Learning.*
Refer to Part Two of the book for the list of technologies involved in each capability.

APPENDIX:

LIST OF IA EXPERTS WHO TOOK PART IN THE SURVEY

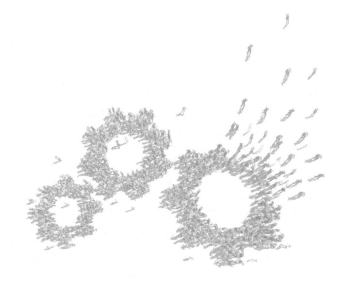

A survey about Intelligent Automation was administered in December 2019 on the web. It collected views on IA: definition, scope, leading practices, expected future, and impact on our society.

We would like to thank all of the passionate and knowledgeable members of the global Intelligent Automation community who contributed to our research. With their input, we are able to present a more informed and validated picture of the state of adoption and readiness.

Those contributors kind enough to share their names are listed below (alphabetical by first name):

Abdul Haseeb	Gabriella D'Elia	Kristopher Carmona	Rohit Arora
Abe Khaleeli	Gareth Blair	Krzysztof Karaszewski	Rohit Basuri
Abhi Saxena	Gaurav Kumar Sumit	Kustaa Kivelä	Ron Lozinsky
Abhilash Reddy	Georgie van der Merwe	Laukeek	Ruth McGuinness
Abhineet	Géri	Leigh Gembus	Ryan Deng
Adam Bujak	Giovanni Guccini	Lena Janack	Sabeha Zedek
Adam Gjorgjievski	Gobish	Lindsey Akers	Sachin Hatikankar
Adam Österman	Gowtham Chilakapati	Lonneke Vink	Saif
Aditya	Gururaja	Lucas Reis	Saikrishna
Adwait Ullal	Gustavo Moura	Maciej Krezolek	Sajeev Nair
Aishwarya Kannan	Guy Nadivi	Maheshwar	Salman
Ajay	Hal Anthony	Majid Moosavinia	Samir Kamal
Allan Surtees	Haran	Manoj Kumar Sharma	Sarah Ghanem
Alois	Harrison Goode	Maor Revah	Satish Jha
Amogh Chandrashekar	Harshal Vaske	Marco	Scott Kennedy
Anand	Hemant Kalra	Mare	Shafiullah
Andrea Danesini	Henri	Mario Olivos	Shaik Limansha Safreen

Andreas Lueth	Hugo Hermsen	Martin Bogan	Shashwat Kumar
Anirban Mazumdar	Ideal Arifi	Maruthi Ayyappan	Shatrugna Ram L A
Aniruddha Chakravarti	Indrajeet Kumar	Matous Maier	Shibin Abraham
Anthony Giardina	Iqbal Bocus	Mauricio Pacheco	Shivaramakrishnan Ramamoorthy
Antoine	Iurii Shubin	Michael Dalton	Siddharth Golecha
Ashish Chaudhary	Jacob Mathew	Michael Engel	Siddheshwar Kore
Ashok Kumar Sahoo	Jacob Mathew	Michele Shiels	Sikandar Girgoukar
Aurel Anthamatten	Jadene Pillay	Mike Smith	Sol
Azlan	Jai Devireddy	MohammadReza	Someshankar
Balaji CS	Jaideep Kala	Molly	Sophie Rawlins
Balaji Sridharan	Jakkam Girish	Mridul Chadha	Sreekiran Challapilla
Bashir Bello	James Lawson	Natacha	Sreenath Gurrapu
Beenish	Jamie Thomas	Neil Munnoch	Sudeepta
Bhavesh Kulkarni	Jan Kozak	Nick Armenta	Sumanth
Binit Amin	Jan Niklas Gajewski	Niki	Surabhi
Brenda	Jatin Gulati	Nitesh Awasthi	Tan Zhang Sheng
Bridget Navoda	Javier Mancilla	Nurul Islam Choudhury	Tanmay Dixit
Chaitanyakumar	Jay Nejal	Omayra Marchany	Tarun Vasudeva
Chris Hartley	JC Abella	Oscar Orozco	Temi Yip

Christopher Parker	Jenny Chong	Paramprit Singh	Thomas Schwarzenböck
Ciara Murphy	Jerald Jackson	Patankar Pramod	Tim Percy
Damo Vasudevan	Jere Laaksonen	Patricio Anguita	Tom Scott
David Francis	Joe Wheatley	Patrick Krippendorf	Toni Tuells
David Napier	Joel Arnold	Patrick Rankin	Tushar Mathur
Davide Rizzo	Jonathan Hobday	Paul Wong	Ujwal Mantri
Debraj Bhattacharyya	Jordan Pierre	Paula M	Vaisakh
Deepak Agarwal	Josmin Jose	Pirro	Vamsi
Deidra Cox	József Papp	Pradeep Kumar	Varun Prabhakar
Dexter	Justin Watson	Prakash Bhatia	Vijesh
Dhaval Shrimankar	Jyoti Sagar	Prasanna	Vikas Kapoor
Dian Kurniawan	Karandeep Kaur	Pratyush Garikapati	Virind Gujral
Disha	Keerthi Kiran Yaga	Preyash	Vis
Doug Gowans	Kelly McLean	Rahul Parmar	Vladimir Voelk
Dwayne Prosko	Keny Lalan	Rajesh	Y Williams
Ed	Keri Smith	Ravikiran SB	Yazid
Eric Bouguen	Kerry Williams	Ray Dudenhoeffer	Younus Baig
Erika Velasco	Khushnuma K	Reny Jacob Reji	Zack Kelemen
Erkan Sirin	Kishore Pardasani	Rima	
Fabian Cesarini	Konstantinos Mantzaris	Robbie de Coster	

APPENDIX:
ARTISTIC INSPIRATION FROM IA

Artistic inspiration 1: Are we going to see this in the museums in the future?
Source: work by the authors

Artistic inspiration 2: The future of work?
Source: work by the authors

Artistic inspiration 3: Differentiating IA from RPA (Robotic Process Automation)
Source: work by the authors

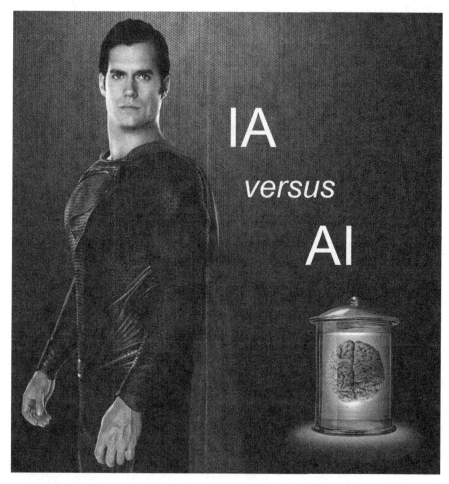

Artistic inspiration 4: Differentiating IA (Intelligent Automation) from AI (Artificial Intelligence)

Source: work by the authors

INDEX

S

T

U

V

W

X

Z

What's next after reading this book?

Congratulations – you have reached the end of the book! Thank you for allowing us to share our experiences and ideas with you. We hope you now feel informed, energized and confident about your own Intelligent Automation journey. While the future is always difficult to predict, we feel confident that the rapidly evolving and advancing set of Hyperautomation tools and methods will play a significant role in positively shaping our work, our lives and our planet. Join us as we strive towards that vision.

Here are a few ways you can stay in touch, and be part of the exciting Intelligent Automation community:

- First, if you liked it, say so – why wait! **Share your views on the book**. We would be honored if you would leave a review on Amazon or your favorite book review site, in order to help us get the message out. Here is the link to the Amazon page for the book:

- **Visit the book's website** to access white papers, online courses, books, and additional tools to support your continuing journey.

  Website: www.hyperautomationbook.com or www.intelligentautomationbook.com

- **Subscribe to our newsletter** to stay informed about the latest news in the field. This can be done through the website.

- **Leave us a message** if you have any questions, require support, or if you are looking for speakers on the topic of IA. Comments can be left on the website ("Contact us") or through our email: intelligentautomationbook@gmail.com.

Together, we can make our world more human with Intelligent Automation!

– The authors

Printed in the United States
by Baker & Taylor Publisher Services